How to Do the History of Homosexuality

David M. Halperin

The University of Chicago Press : : Chicago and London

The University of Chicago Press, Chicago 60637
The University of Chicago Press, Ltd., London
© 2002 by David M. Halperin
All rights reserved. Published 2002
Paperback edition 2004
Printed in the United States of America

11 10 09 08 07 06 05 04   2 3 4 5

ISBN: 0–226-31447–2 (cloth)
ISBN: 0–226-31448–0 (paperback)

Library of Congress Cataloging-in-Publication Data

Halperin, David M., 1952–
   How to do the history of homosexuality / David M. Halperin.
      p. cm.
   Includes bibliographical references and index.
   ISBN 0-226-31447-2 (cloth : alk. paper)
   1. Homosexuality, Male—History. 2. Homosexuality, Male—Historio-
graphy. 3. Homosexuality, Male—Greece—History. I. Title.
HQ76 .H28 2002
306.76'62'09—dc21   2002017357

For Kirk Ormand.   *And for Ann Pellegrini.*

Contents

Acknowledgments

All of the previously published work contained in this volume has been revised since its last appearance in print. Nonetheless, I wish to acknowledge the journals, collections, editors, and presses for which much of this material was originally composed and to thank them for their permission to reproduce some of it here.

"Forgetting Foucault": *Representations* 63 (Summer 1998): 93–120; reprinted in *The Sleep of Reason: Erotic Experience and Sexual Ethics in Ancient Greece and Rome,* ed. Martha Nussbaum and Juha Sihvola (Chicago: University of Chicago Press, 2002), 21–54, and in *Sexualities in History: A Reader,* ed. Kim M. Phillips and Barry Reay (New York: Routledge, 2002), 42–68.

"The First Homosexuality?": the *Bryn Mawr Classical Review* (http://ccat.sas.upenn.edu/bmcr/), 97.12.3 (5 December 1997), *GLQ: A Journal of Lesbian and Gay Studies* 4, no. 4 (1998): 559–78, and in *The Sleep of Reason: Erotic Experience and Sexual Ethics in Ancient Greece and Rome,* ed. Martha Nussbaum and Juha Sihvola (Chicago: University of Chicago Press, 2002), 229–68.

"Historicizing the Subject of Desire": in *Discourses of Sexuality: From Aristotle to AIDS,* ed. Domna C. Stanton (Ann Arbor: University of Michigan Press, 1992), 236–61, and in *Foucault and the Writing of History,* ed. Jan Goldstein (Oxford: Basil Blackwell, 1994), 19–34, 255–61.

"How to Do the History of Male Homosexuality": *GLQ: A Journal of Lesbian and Gay Studies 6*, no. 1 (2000): 87–124.

"Questions of Evidence": in *Queer Representations: Reading Lives, Reading Cultures*, ed. Martin Duberman (New York: New York University Press, 1997), 39–54.

I wish to thank the University of Michigan in Ann Arbor and my colleagues in the Department of English Language and Literature for providing me with the ideal environment in which to reconsider my earlier positions and to rediscover the challenges and pleasures of the history of sexuality. I owe a special gratitude to Martha Vicinus, Steven Mullaney, Linda Gregerson, Valerie Traub, Tobin Siebers, and Lincoln Faller. I have been inspired particularly by my conversations with Valerie Traub. And I am grateful to the administration of the University of Michigan for its generosity and support.

For their help, energy, and good will, I wish to thank Tonya Howe and Matt Johnson. I am especially indebted to Matt Johnson for rehearsing with me in detail the issues addressed in this book and for entering so sympathetically into the process of its composition.

For his confidence, his patience, and his persistence, I owe everything to Doug Mitchell at the University of Chicago Press.

My greatest aspiration for this book is that it to live up to the eloquent, witty, and disturbing image on its cover. For permission to reproduce it, I gratefully acknowledge Peter Lyssiotis, photomonteur extraordinaire.

A very few of my more specific debts are acknowledged in the headnotes to individual essays.

The decade in which the contents of this book were produced was an unexpectedly turbulent one for me. I would like to express my deep appreciation to the friends who helped me get through it: Gayle Boyer, Marie Curnick, Didier Eribon, Suzanne MacAlister, Randy Mackie, Paul Morrison, Martha Nussbaum, Stephen Orgel, Kirk Ormand, Nikos Papastergiadis, Ann Pellegrini, Michael Warner, Marie Ymonet, and my extended family in the Rue des Francs-Bourgeois.

D. M. H.
Roc de la Borie
Théminettes, Lot
July 2001

Introduction: In Defense of Historicism

In the spring of 1989, when I finished work on my book *One Hundred Years of Homosexuality* (a collection of essays about sex and gender in the ancient Greek world), I thought I had said everything I had to say about the history of homosexuality.[1] In fact, I thought I had said everything I had to say, period. My earlier work, on the history of pastoral poetry[2] and on Plato's theory of erotic desire,[3] appeared to me at the time to represent little more than a series of oblique approaches to the subject I had finally found the voice to speak about directly—namely, the erotic play of self and other in love and history. Instead of attempting a major new project of my own, I decided to take advantage of the professional and institutional platform that my most recent book had given me to create opportunities for younger or more active scholars to have their say. I set up a monograph series entitled Ideologies of Desire at Oxford University Press, established a Greek and Latin translation series called The New Classical Canon at Routledge, and co-founded (with Carolyn Dinshaw) *GLQ: A Journal of Lesbian and Gay Studies*. But the history of homosexuality, it turned out, continued to harbor irresistible challenges and provocations.

The present volume assembles, in revised form, a number of my writings from the past decade on the history and theory of sexuality. In particular, it brings together a sequence of essays in which I set out to explore certain historiographical problems raised by the history of homosexuality. Some of those problems were ones that my earlier work had generated but had not adequately addressed or that it had merely touched on; others were problems that had arisen as a result of subsequent developments in the field. In either case, I found myself returning again and again in the course of the 1990s, almost despite myself, to related sets of historiographical issues.

I call those issues *historiographical* rather than *historical* because they have to do with questions of evidence, method, strategy, politics, and identification in the writing of history. The essays collected here cannot claim to be contributions to the history of homosexuality as such. Rather, they are attempts to think through specific theoretical issues connected with writing the history of homosexuality.

That historiographical problematic is what the title of my book is intended to evoke. I mean "how to do the history of homosexuality" to sound interrogative rather than magisterial. This book does not aspire to be an instruction manual so much as a series of reflections on the interpretative quandaries and intellectual pleasures of doing the history of homosexuality. It gathers together the latest fruits of what has been the conceptual adventure of a lifetime: the attempt to think homosexuality historically.

But I don't intend entirely to disclaim the didactic implications of my title. The essays collected here represent my best efforts to clear up a number of difficulties and misunderstandings that I believe have impeded progress in the history of sexuality and have unduly distracted historians. My aim is to be helpful, and my major preoccupation is with the accurate decipherment of historical documents. At the same time, the drive behind much of the writing is, unmistakably, polemical—not in the sense that I wish to crush or silence all opposing points of view, but in the sense that I want to refine and to carry forward a series of contested arguments about the historicity of sexuality that my earlier work on ancient Greece had advanced. In order to make the logical continuities clear, I need to say something here about how I understand the connections between this book and *One Hundred Years of Homosexuality*.

: : :

Everyone who reads an ancient Greek text, and certainly anyone who studies ancient Greek culture, quickly realizes that the ancient Greeks were quite weird, by our standards, when it came to sex. And yet, professional academic training in classical studies typically induces a kind of amnesia about the weirdness of the Greeks. The student of classical antiquity quickly learns to acknowledge, to bracket, and to screen out their erotic peculiarities, the cultural specificities in their experience of *erôs* that fail to correspond to any category or identity in modern bourgeois society. One simply acquires the habit of allowing for their differences, granting them the latitude to be weird, and then one turns one's attention to other topics of greater seriousness or philological urgency.

Like most of my scholarly colleagues in the field of classics, I had become accustomed to noticing, without making anything of, the obvious differences in sexual attitude and behavior between ancient Greek men and the men in my own social world. And, anyway, I didn't have a language for articulating systematically the discontinuities between ancient Greek sexual attitudes or practices and my own. Or, at least, I didn't have such a language until the mid-1980s when it was provided me by the new social history and, specifically, by the work of social constructionist historians of homosexuality, notably George Chauncey.[4] What I, and many others, have learned from this work is that it is not the Greeks who were weird about sex but rather that it is we today, particularly men and women of the professional classes, who have a culturally and historically unique organization of sexual and social life and, therefore, have difficulty understanding the sex/gender systems of other cultures.

One of the most distinctive features of the current regime under which we live is the prominence of heterosexuality and homosexuality as central, organizing categories of thought, behavior, and erotic subjectivity. The rise to dominance of those categories represents a relatively recent and culturally specific development, yet it has left little trace in our consciousness of its novelty. As a result, not only do we have a hard time understanding the logic at work in other historical cultures' organizations of sex and gender, but we have an even harder time understanding our own inability to understand them. We can't figure out what it is about our own experiences of sexuality that are not universal, what it is about sexuality that could be cultural instead of natural, historical instead of biological. All our research into otherness, into cultural alterity, presents to us an endlessly perplexing spectacle of the exotic, which merely reinforces our attachment to our own categories of thought and experience.

The impetus behind *One Hundred Years of Homosexuality* was to ask what the consequences might be of taking the Greeks at their word when they spoke about sex. Suppose that we stopped regarding the Greeks as weird, exotic, and, well, simply Greek. Suppose instead that we took seriously the possibility that human beings in the past might have had radically different experiences of erotic subjectivity. What would happen if we took the Greeks literally, assuming that their expressions of desire were genuine or were true statements about their own experiences? How would such an approach to the Greeks alter our understanding of them and of their culture? But, also, how would it change our understanding of ourselves and of our culture?

How would we experience our own sexuality differently if we experienced it as something historical, as well as something instinctual? How would our sense of what a human being is, of what desire is, of what history is, of who we are, have to change, once we concluded from our study of the Greeks that our erotic lives are modern cultural and psychic productions? It was out of curiosity about where such questions might take us that I made my first tentative forays into the history of sexuality.

: : :

I did not propose to give my inquiries the form of a single, synthetic study. *One Hundred Years of Homosexuality* is a collection of disparate essays; it does not undertake to offer a systematic coverage of the erotics of male culture in the ancient Greek world. At the time I was working on those essays, it seemed like a bad idea to try and produce an overarching, unitary survey of the topic, and I turned down subsequent invitations to do so.

The very nature of the evidence argued against such an undertaking. The surviving ancient documents that bear on homoeroticism are very unevenly distributed in time, place, and genre. Also, K. J. Dover's *Greek Homosexuality* had already provided as systematic a survey of the topic as the nature of the evidence permitted, and, since its scholarship was sound, there seemed little need to replicate it.[5] Finally, what was required, it seemed to me, was not a major new study but a simple conceptual maneuver. The aim of my book, accordingly, was to snip the thread that connected ancient Greek paederasty with modern homosexuality in the minds of modern historians. Once that maneuver had been completed, it would be possible to foreground the historical and ideological uniqueness of homosexuality and heterosexuality as modern concepts as well as modern experiences, and it would be easier to restore to Greek erotic practices their alterity—to resituate them in their original social context and (by refusing to conflate them with modern notions) to bring into clearer focus their indigenous meanings.

That is what some of the later essays in my book tried to do, and that was also the aim of the essays collected in *Before Sexuality,* a book I edited with John J. Winkler and Froma Zeitlin in the same period.[6] I thought that once the conceptual link between paederasty and homosexuality had been severed, and a corresponding gap introduced between modern sexuality and ancient erotic experience, then an abundance of new specialist studies would seize the opportunity to explore diverse aspects of erotic life in antiquity. Instead of another new synthesis, what was needed was just the opposite: a plurality of new and highly particular inquiries into specific texts, materials, topics, and problems, so as to expand our intellectual horizons and contribute to a reexamination of classical antiquity as a whole.

And there have indeed been some distinguished achievements of that kind, most notably Maud Gleason's *Making Men* (1995) and Craig Williams's *Roman Homosexuality* (1999, published in my Oxford series).[7] On the whole, however, classical scholarship on sexual life in ancient Greece in English during the 1990s has been characterized by a series of book-length generalist studies designed to reassert the authority of modern conceptual categories and to restore the hegemony of "sexuality" in studies of classical antiquity.[8]

: : :

My book had a second purpose, at once scholarly and political. It was an attempt to build a bridge between classical scholarship and the emerging field of lesbian and gay studies. Classical scholarship was of course no stranger to lesbian and gay male interests, but such interests had tended to express themselves either privately or covertly. Outside of classics, however, much progress had already been made in lesbian and gay history, historiography, sociology, anthropology, and critical theory. But most of the work in lesbian and gay studies dealt with modern, or at least postclassical, topics. I wished to bring those two areas of intellectual endeavor together, to show classicists how recent work in lesbian and gay studies could be brought to bear on the study of classical antiquity and, conversely, to show practitioners of lesbian and gay studies how the study of antiquity might contribute to contemporary thinking about the history and theory of sexuality.

My larger aim was to help consolidate lesbian and gay studies itself as an interdisciplinary field of scholarship, a goal I pursued in the succeeding years by co-editing *The Lesbian and Gay Studies Reader*.[9] That larger aim explains some of the peculiarities of the earlier book, such as the excessive accumulation of bibliographic citations. I knew that the book's topic and argument would easily find detractors among classicists, and I wished to guard against the book's easy dismissal by fortifying it with as much learning as I could muster. But I also wanted to take stock of the accumulated work in lesbian and gay studies, and gather it together, so that my book could function as evidence, in the teeth of skepticism on the part of outsiders, for the existence of that very field. Simply by listing in one place all the relevant scholarship in lesbian and gay studies that I had uncovered, I hoped to document the sheer size of the field, to display its intellectual breadth and depth, and, by situating my own work in dialogue with the existing scholarship, to extend and consolidate its gains—to make it visible, to make it function as an academic field. And I wanted to show that there was more to gay studies than acts of recovery, stories of "great homosexuals in history," or forms of political affirmation—that the relation of gay scholarship to gay identity was more subtle and complex than is often imagined.

But in the process of assembling this material, I made a couple of big mistakes. First, because a bibliography containing all the works cited in the entire book would have been enormous, unwieldy, and, I thought, pretentious, my bibliography listed only those works cited frequently. Second, and for similar reasons, the index referred readers not to authors cited or mentioned but only to those writers whose work I had substantively discussed.

Let my experience be a lesson to younger academics. Always be sure to include in the index to your book every single author you cite, however fleetingly, for that is the first thing that authors who have written on your topic will look up (*The Chicago Manual of Style* unfortunately prevents me from using a similar tactic to insure the present book against the vanity of rivals). Classicists, of course, if they are good for nothing else, are supposed to be experts at reading footnotes and critical apparatus, but that did not prevent much heavy weather from being made of my alleged omissions of work by feminist scholars, work that I had in fact used and cited, and it led to denunciations of my book by those whose contributions to the field I had set out particularly to honor.[10] The resulting tensions between different progressive currents in classical scholarship, entirely unnecessary, have set back the study of sex and gender in antiquity by many years (as comparison with the greater maturity and sophistication of early modern studies forcefully dramatizes); only now is it starting to catch up.

I have not tried to atone in this book for my purported sins against feminism in *One Hundred Years of Homosexuality,* but I have done my best to clarify, especially in the essay entitled "The First Homosexuality?" (but also in "How to Do the History of Male Homosexuality"), my sense of both how distinct and how interrelated, in theory and practice, are the histories of lesbianism and of male homosexuality.

: : :

One Hundred Years of Homosexuality was very much a book of its moment in time, and its intellectual style reflects the particular trends in scholarly discourse that defined the horizons of critical practice in its day. For example, it attempted to combine the empirical traditions of British and German classical scholarship and ancient social history with the structural traditions of the French *sciences humaines* and with international feminist theory. Further, drawing on developments in cultural anthropology, it aimed to approach the history of sexuality not from the perspective of the history of ideas or *mentalités* but from a culturalist perspective that did not make a strict separation between material reality and social signification but that understood how material conditions give rise to ideological formations as well as how symbolic systems construct material reality. The book also tried to bring the New Historicism[11] to studies of ancient Greece: to approach social action as text, to produce textual readings of cultural forms, and to look at social and symbolic practices together— that is, to treat social practices as part of a signifying system and to treat meanings as elements in social transactions: in short, to inquire into the poetics of culture.

Those were the dominant intellectual influences on my work at the time. I had of course been affected by the work of Michel Foucault, and I had been belatedly impressed by the second volume of his unfinished *History of Sexuality*, which dealt with classical Greece. In fact, to the best of my knowledge, I was the only professional classicist in North America to give *L'usage des plaisirs* a favorable review.[12] That review was incorporated in *One Hundred Years of Homosexuality*, and so was a certain amount of Foucault's conceptual vocabulary, along with some laudatory references to Foucault himself.[13] But I had yet to feel the real force of Foucault's example.

Nonetheless, when the book came to be reviewed, I found myself routinely described as a Foucauldian. That was a surprise on two counts. First, it wasn't true. Second, it wasn't a compliment.

It wasn't true: I can name the most immediate influences on the concrete processes of my writing at the time, and while Foucault was a major influence, he was not the dominant one. More important to me were George Chauncey, the New Historicists, and the French structuralists already mentioned. Foucault did not argue for the social construction of (homo)sexuality; he was not a social historian; and he was not interested in playing the sort of truth games with historical evidence that I was still committed to. My thinking had been formed by gay and Marxist historiographers such as Jeffrey Weeks and Robert Padgug; radical British and North American sociologists such as Stuart Hall, Mary McIntosh,

Kenneth Plummer, Barry D. Adam, John Gagnon, and William Simon; feminist and cultural anthropologists such as Carol Delaney, Don Donham, Gilbert Herdt, David Gilmore, Maurice Godelier, Thomas Gregor, Gayle Rubin, and Sylvia Yanagisako; feminist theorists such as Teresa de Lauretis, Monique Wittig, and Nancy Miller; and the few classicists who showed an interest in various combinations of the aforementioned, such as K. J. Dover, Mark Golden, David Schaps, Susan Cole, Maud Gleason, and most of all my friend Jack Winkler.

It wasn't a compliment: I discovered that "Foucault" had somehow come to signify everything that decent, liberal-minded American classicists liked to define themselves against. "Foucauldian," accordingly, became short-hand for "gay," "male chauvinist," "anti-empirical," "unscholarly," "radical," "untraditional," "opportunistic," "power-hungry," "totalitarian," and, finally, "un-American." It would have been impolitic to come right out and call me those names, of course, so "Foucauldian" covered a multitude of sins. In fact, a surprising number of writings invoked Foucault to disqualify my work or, even better, cited my work as a cautionary example of the terrible things that could happen to you if you allowed yourself to be corrupted by Foucault's influence.[14]

As a result, at the start of the 1990s I suddenly got much more interested in Foucault than I had been when I wrote *One Hundred Years of Homosexuality.* I figured that anyone so brilliant who had become so disreputable must have done something right. And I was moved by an instinct of self-preservation to inquire into the phobic processes by which Foucault himself had become so demonized. Those inquiries eventually took the form of a small book, *Saint Foucault.*[15]

The essays collected in this volume are consequently much more marked by my reading of Foucault than was *One Hundred Years of Homosexuality,* even if they are still not themselves particularly Foucauldian. Two of them, "Forgetting Foucault" and "Historicizing the Subject of Desire," are explicit efforts to recover the radical design of Foucault's own approach to the history of sexuality, to salvage that approach from various misapprehensions and misreadings, and to make it newly available to historians of sexuality as an impetus for innovation and renewal in the field. My belief remains that, far from having exhausted the lessons that Foucault had to teach us, we have yet to come to terms with their startling implications.

In particular, I have wanted to insist on a couple of theoretical points. First, that the distinction between sexual acts and sexual identities, falsely attributed to Foucault, should not be invoked to justify the claim, also false, that before the cultural constitution of homosexuality and heterosexuality in the modern period there were no such things as sexual identities, only sexual acts. Foucault never made that claim, nor did I base *One Hundred Years of Homosexuality* on such a pseudo-Foucauldian distinction between acts and identities. Not only are critiques of Foucault, of Foucauldian histories, or of my book that target such a view mistaken, but the contrary view that they attempt to install in its place, namely, that the sexual identities known to us have always existed in some form or other, is also hasty and ill-judged. If Foucault's work should teach us anything, it is to inquire more closely into the subtle connections between sexual acts and sexual identities in the pre-modern period, to pay more (not less) attention to the changing social and discursive conditions in which the desires of historical subjects are constructed. That, at least, is the argument of "Forgetting Foucault."

In "Historicizing the Subject of Desire," I argue against the recent tendency to reduce the history of sexuality to the history of classifications or representations of sexuality. Such a tendency neatly sidesteps the radical implications of Foucault's attempt to write the history of sexuality from the perspective of the history of discourses. For by doing so, Foucault did not mean to reduce sexuality to discourse, to claim that sexuality was a discourse, or to situate historical change in discourse rather than in sexuality. One effect of (mis)understanding the history of sexuality as a history of the discourses of sexuality has been to preserve the notion of sexuality as a timeless and ahistorical dimension of human experience, while preserving a notion of discourse as a neutral medium of representation. A second effect has been to draw a deceptively simple and very old-fashioned division between representations, conceived as socially specific and historically variable products of human culture, and realities (sexual desire, in this case, or human nature), conceived as something static and unchanging. Foucault, I argue, was up to something much more novel, a radically holistic approach that was designed to avoid such hoary metaphysical binarisms. His aim was to foreground the historicity of desire itself and of human beings as subjects of desire.

If I insist on those points, it is not out of some dogmatic belief in their rightness but because I think they are still useful and promise to make the history of sexuality more exciting, more adventurous, more transformative of our understandings and of ourselves. Contrary to what some have claimed, I do not aspire to found a Foucauldian "school" of classical (or post-classical) studies, even if I were in a position to do such a thing. On the contrary, as the final essay in this volume demonstrates, I think it is time to go well beyond Foucault's particular suggestions and gestures and to devise new and more imaginative ways of realizing the project of historicizing desire.

: : :

Perhaps the overriding purpose of *One Hundred Years of Homosexuality,* at the time the book was written, was to win the once-vehement debate between essentialists and constructionists over the constitution of sexual identity. Against essentialists who claimed that there had been a minority of homosexuals in all times and places, I argued, along with social constructionists, not only that homosexuality was socially and culturally constituted in the modern period but also that the very division between homosexuality and heterosexuality was the product of recent historical developments. My aim was not to champion the cause of a homosexual minority that might be imagined to have existed in every human society, for to do that would be merely to pay heterosexuality the backhanded (and undeserved) compliment of being the normal and natural condition for the majority of human beings in all times and places. My purpose in historicizing homosexuality was *to denaturalize heterosexuality*, to deprive it of its claims to be considered a "traditional value," and ultimately to destroy the self-evidence of the entire system on which the homophobic opposition between homosexuality and heterosexuality depended.

A year after *One Hundred Years of Homosexuality* was originally published, its argument for the social construction of homosexuality was the object of a brilliant critique by Eve Kosofsky Sedgwick in the long introductory chapter to her groundbreaking book, *Epistemology of the Closet.*[16] Sedgwick objected to social constructionist histories of homosexuality (she singled out Michel Foucault's *La volonté de savoir,* the first volume of his *History of Sexuality,* and *One Hundred Years of Homosexuality*) that claimed that at the end of the nineteenth century one model of same-sex sexual relations ("homosexuality") had replaced earlier models ("sodomy," "inversion"), models radically different from "homosexuality as we understand it today."

Sedgwick justly criticized Foucault and myself for drawing too sharp a contrast between earlier sexual categories and a falsely coherent, homogeneous, and unitary notion of "homosexuality as we understand it today," thereby treating the contemporary concept of homosexuality as "a coherent definitional field rather than a space of overlapping, contradictory, and conflictual definitional forces" (45). And she dramatized that conflict by showing that Foucault and I actually had in mind quite different "understandings" of "homosexuality as we understand it today." Sedgwick went on to argue that it is wrong to suppose that earlier sexual categories are simply superseded or replaced by later ones. Rather, she suggested, earlier sexual categories continue to reappear within later ones, producing an ineradicable instability in those later categories.

Sedgwick's aim was "to denarrativize" the narratives written by social constructionist historians and to do so by "focusing on [homosexual definition as] a performative space of contradiction" (48). She went on to produce an original analysis of homo/heterosexual discourse in terms of what she described as a perennial tension among and between four definitional axes, which she identified as minoritizing/universalizing modes of homosexual definition and as gender-transitive versus gender-intransitive or gender-separatist modes of homosexual definition.

The magisterial survey of homosexual/homophobic signification that Sedgwick based on that conceptual move has proven to be uniquely valuable. And yet there is a striking irony—no less striking for its having gone, so far as I know, totally unnoticed—in the portion of her argument in which she makes that crucial move. For what Sedgwick had objected to in the constructionist view was the notion that earlier sexual categories are superseded or replaced—made obsolete—by later ones. At the same time, the announced intention of her critique was to end the essentialist-constructionist debate, "to promote [its] obsolescence" (40), and in this she has been spectacularly successful. As Ross Chambers observes, "Without quite putting an end to the essentialist/constructivist debate, Sedgwick's move has effectively backgrounded it, and allowed an ongoing conversation to bracket it out by, as it were, changing the subject."[17] As a result, the very phrase "social construction" has come to seem a hopelessly out-of-date formula in queer studies, and the mere invocation of it makes a writer appear backward and unsophisticated. I have had almost entirely to avoid it in the essays collected here, in favor of less compromised (if no less contested) terms like "historicism."

Sedgwick, then, deliberately set aside historical questions about the emergence of modern sexual categories and described those questions as effectively superseded by her own approach. In a gesture exactly congruent with the one she criticized, she structured her project in such a way that "the superseded model then drops out of the frame of analysis" (47). But just as the discourses of sodomy or inversion do not disappear with the emergence of the discourses of homosexuality, as Sedgwick rightly argued, so the historical problem of describing the differences between pre-homosexual and homosexual formations will not simply disappear with a heightened awareness (however valuable or necessary) of the crisis of homo- and heterosexual definition in the present.

It has taken me nearly ten years to get my mind around Sedgwick's objection, to absorb it into my own thinking. The final essay in this collection, "How to Do the History of Male Homosexuality," represents my effort to integrate Sedgwick's critique into a reconstituted constructionist approach to the history of homosexuality. Now it is my turn to insist, against Sedgwick, on her very own axiom: despite her dazzling and important demonstration of the futility of playing the truth game called the essentialist-constructionist debate, the terms of that debate have not been superseded for historians by Sedgwick's "focusing on [homo-heterosexual definition] as a performative space of contradiction." Rather than attempt to reassert the terms of the essentialist-constructionist debate in opposition to Sedgwick, however, I try here to reanimate the constructionist historical project in a more self-aware and theoretical spirit, so as bring the Foucauldian historical and narratival critique of homosexual essentialism into greater harmony with the denarrativizing and performative critique advocated by Sedgwick.

For if Sedgwick is right, if earlier historical forms of sexual discourse are not superseded by later ones, if notions of sodomy or inversion continue to appear within the discourses of homosexuality and to assert their definitional authority, there are good historical reasons for that, and those reasons remain to be explored. As I argue in "How to Do the History of Male Homosexuality," the definitional incoherence at the core of the modern notion of homosexuality is a sign of its historical evolution: it results from the way "homosexuality" has effectively incorporated—without homogenizing—earlier models of same-sex sexual relations and of sex and gender deviance, models directly in conflict with the category of "homosexuality" that has nonetheless absorbed them.

In other words, what Sedgwick called "the unrationalized coexistence of different models" of homosexual difference in the discourses of sexuality today (47) is the cumulative effect of a long process of historical overlay and accretion. If, as Sedgwick claimed, our "understanding of homosexual definition . . . is organized around a radical and irreducible incoherence" (85), owing to this unrationalized coexistence of different models, it is because we have preserved and retained different definitions of sex and gender from our pre-modern past, despite the logical contradictions among them. And if that causal explanation is correct, then a genealogy of contemporary homosexual discourse can significantly support and expand Sedgwick's influential discursive critique of the category of homosexuality and can give Sedgwick's critique the historical grounding that, until now, it has signally lacked.

Another way of putting this point is to say that what was wrong with *One Hundred Years of Homosexuality* was not its constructionist theory but its historical practice. Despite the accusations of Foucauldianism leveled against it, the problem with the book, as Sedgwick's critique made clear, was that *it wasn't Foucauldian enough:* it retained too great an investment in conventional social history and made too little use of Foucauldian (or Nietzschean) genealogy. That is the lack that the essays collected here attempt to redeem.

:   :   :

A genealogical approach, one that begins with an analysis of blind spots in our current understanding, or with a problematization of what passes for "given" in contemporary thought, necessarily takes the form of what Foucault called, in a memorable phrase, the "history of the present."[18] Despite its frank ambition to make a political difference, in the ways I have described, *One Hundred Years of Homosexuality* did not consistently aspire to be a history of the present: it often opted for a disciplinary rigor in differentiating between past and present sexual forms, never more so than in its insistence that "homosexuality" was a modern cultural production and that there was no homosexuality, properly speaking, in classical Greece, the ancient Mediterranean world, or indeed in most pre-modern or non-Western societies.

That remains my conviction, and the intervening years, and subsequent accumulation of scholarly research in the history of sexuality, have only deepened it. At the same time, such a formulation seems increasingly unfortunate, and for a number of reasons: (1) it does not acknowledge the complex relations between identity and identification in our attitudes to the past; (2) it has been overtaken by a queer political and intellectual movement opposed to all forms of heteronormativity, and which therefore finds important connections between non-heterosexual formations in both the present and the past; (3) it does not reckon with what, from a non-constructionist perspective, appear as continuities within the history of homosexuality; (4) it misleadingly implies a Eurocentric progress narrative, which aligns modernity, Western culture, metropolitan life, bourgeois social forms, and liberal democracies with "sexuality" (both homo- and hetero-), over against pre-modern, non-Western, non-urban, non-white, non-bourgeois, non-industrialized, non-developed societies, which appear in this light as comparatively backward, not to say primitive, innocent as they are of the "sexuality" which is one of the signatures of Western modernity. Such a progress narrative not only promotes a highly invid-ious opposition between sexually advanced and sexually retrograde cul-tures but also fails to take account of the complexity of contemporary transnational formations of sexuality.[19]

The essays collected in this volume reflect my efforts to rethink the project of a constructionist history of sexuality in the light of those con-siderations. I'll discuss the first three of those considerations together in this section, the fourth in the following one.

When I wrote *One Hundred Years of Homosexuality,* I thought the application of the modern categories of homosexuality and heterosexual-ity to ancient Greek sexual discourses and practices was simply wrong. It was a kind of category mistake—like calling a peasant a proletarian or talking about the "lifestyle" of the Homeric heroes. There was of course a sense in which the modern terms could be applied to the ancients: if they were used descriptively (e.g., to denote same-sex or different-sex sex-ual contacts), no great falsification would result. But if the modern terms were used substantively (to name basic categories of human sexual ori-entation, or "sexuality"), their application to pre-modern societies could only lead to confusion, misunderstanding, and an inability to recover the indigenous terms in which the experiences of past historical cultures had been articulated.

I still believe all this. But there was something priggish about my in-sistence on the alterity of the Greeks, about my effort to get historians of sexuality to adhere unfailingly to neat, categorical, air-tight distinctions between ancient paederasty and modern homosexuality, as if any admis-sion of overlap between the two could *only* be disadvantageous—sloppy, inept, ethnocentric, a wishful fantasy, a cheap thrill. To be sure, I declared at the outset of *One Hundred Years of Homosexuality* that it was not my intention to prevent anyone today from regarding the Greeks as pos-itive gay role models, as sources of gay pride, or as points of reference for an anti-homophobic politics. But at the same time, I really *did* want to interrupt contemporary gay men's straightforward, uncritical identifi-cations with the Greeks, in order to make the Greeks unavailable to us as vehicles of cultural chauvinism. There would be little point in pro-moting a new gay-affirmative practice of classical studies if the result of such gay affirmation was to affirm misogyny, class hierarchy, Eurocen-trism, and racism (not to mention slavery) through an incautious return to Hellenism.

Still, if good politics was a welcome by-product of good history, a sign of its ultimate rightness, it was not the main goal. Like virtue—to which, in my mind, it was closely related—good history was its own reward. There was an intrinsic value in the historian's daily struggle to work against her or his own intuitions, to counter them with a hard-won apprehension of irreducible historical difference. And, in the end, the goal of such a struggle went beyond the rewards of an enlightened historicism: the ultimate purpose was to accede, through a calculated encounter with the otherness of the past, to an altered understanding of the present—a sense of our own non-identity to ourselves—and thus to a new experience of ourselves as sites of potential transformation. Gay history of this sort was a scholarly thought-experiment in which the self, by turning to the past, could come to recognize its own alterity to itself in the present and, ultimately, its undefined possibilities in the future.[20] Such an emancipatory vision of the purpose of history was continuous with the liberatory promise of the lesbian and gay movement as a whole and with its queer trajectory.

So I had good reasons for wishing to find other things for gay men to do with the Greeks besides merely identify with them. What I soon discovered, however, is that identification is not so easily thwarted. And, even more important, it is not dependent on identity. Identification is desire. Just because earlier historical cultures may differ from modern ones in their organization of sex and gender, and just because Greek paederasty differs in a number of crucial respects from contemporary metropolitan gay male identity, it doesn't follow that metropolitan gay men today cannot or should not identify with ancient Greeks. We don't only identify with those who are the same as us, after all: if other people weren't *different* from us, what would be the point of *identifying* with them?[21]

And what's wrong with cheap thrills? It's about time some historian spoke up for them. Historical analysis is no argument against pleasure, least of all against the pleasures of identification, which even the most austere or the most self-aware historical scholar cannot resist for very long. As Jack Winkler once said to me, all Pausanias would have to do is admire the silverware, and we would think Plato's *Symposium* was taking place today in San Francisco. The tendency to refashion past sexual cultures in the image of our own says a lot about our own historical situation, the functioning of contemporary sexual categories, our standard ways of thinking about the past. It is richly informative in its own right. Furthermore, there can be hermeneutic advantages in foregrounding historical correspondences and identities. Identification gets at something, something important: it picks out resemblances, connections, echo effects. Identification is a form of cognition. And the ability to set aside historical differences in order to focus on historical continuities is no less crucial to our personal, political, and cultural projects than is the ethical or ascetic determination to see in the documented experiences of other peoples something else besides self-confirming reflections of ourselves.

If I needed any reminding of that, the new radical movements that appeared almost at the very moment I finished *One Hundred Years of Homosexuality* would have supplied the necessary cues. "We've given so much to [the] world [at large]: democracy, all the arts, the concepts of love, philosophy and the soul, to name just a few gifts from our ancient Greek Dykes, Fags," boasted the leaflet entitled "Queers Read This!" that was apparently dropped by helicopter on the Gay Pride Parade in New York in June of 1990 and that came to be seen as the founding document of Queer Nation, its equivalent of *The Communist Manifesto*.[22] "I belong to a culture that includes Proust, Henry James, Tchaikovsky, Cole Porter, Plato, Socrates, Aristotle, Alexander the Great, Michelangelo, Leonardo da Vinci, Christopher Marlowe, Walt Whitman, Herman Melville, Tennessee Williams, Byron, E. M. Forster, Lorca, Auden, Francis Bacon, James Baldwin, Harry Stack Sullivan, John Maynard Keynes, Dag Hammarskjöld . . ." declares Ned Weeks, the hero and fictional alter ego of militant playwright Larry Kramer in *The Normal Heart* (1985), the most ambitious early literary effort at AIDS activism.[23]

I confess that this sort of gay identification still gives me the creeps. But for all that these declarations savor of a kind of a gay chauvinism, a homosexual essentialism thoroughly disqualified by its implication in the various strategies of elitism and exclusion that identity politics often carries with it, they do not necessarily invalidate the broader queer project of identifying with and reclaiming non-heteronormative figures from the past. Even more promising, however, is the tactic of asserting a continuity with whatever features of ancient, exotic, or culturally distant societies may be at odds with contemporary institutions, practices, and ideologies of homophobia. It is possible, after all, to recruit the queerness of past historical periods not in order to justify one or another partisan model of gay life in the present but rather to acknowledge, promote, and support a heterogeneity of queer identities, past *and* present.[24] There is more than one strategy for entering into a queerer future.

Rather than attempt to block or deny present-day queer identifications with the past, the essays collected here look for ways to take advantage of those identifications, both politically and intellectually—to find in them opportunities for political intervention (in the case of "Historicizing the Subject of Desire") as well as epistemic clues to the multiple temporalities of homosexuality (in the case of "The First Homosexuality?" and "How to

Do the History of Male Homosexuality"). These essays acknowledge that continuities are no less crucial to take into account than historical ruptures and that an adequate history of sexuality needs to make conceptual accommodation for both.

: : :

At the same time, while making allowances for continuities, identifications, and queer correspondences between past and present (as well as for radical differences among multiple experiences in the present), the essays in this volume defend what used to be called a constructionist approach to the history of sexuality. They have been written to uphold my historicist commitments and to immunize them against facile critique on the four grounds previously enumerated. I have tried to explain, as carefully as I can, in as much detail as possible, with the greatest possible nuance, what specifically defines—conceptually and historically—the category and the experience of (homo)sexuality and what sets it off from other documented forms of erotic life.

In that sense, this book makes a qualified but nonetheless passionate case for historicism—that is, for an approach to the history of sexuality that foregrounds historical differences, that attempts to acknowledge the alterity of the past as well as the irreducible cultural and historical specificities of the present.[25] I continue to believe that something very significant happened when sexual object-choice became in the course of the twentieth century, at least in some social worlds, an overriding marker of sexual difference. That is an event whose impact and whose scope we are only now learning how to measure. And I continue to believe that there are concrete scholarly and political benefits to be had from limiting the application of modern sexual categories to the modern period and from attempting to rediscover the indigenous terms, concepts, logics, and practices of different societies—by which I refer to different sectors of our own societies as well as to the different social worlds, past and present, to which our research gives us access. Such a sensitivity to difference need not rule out identification, attention to continuities, or forms of queer multiplicity and solidarity.

Similarly, a sensitivity to difference should not lead to the ghettoization or exotification of the Other, to an othering of the Other as an embodiment of difference itself. Hence, Dipesh Chakrabarty insists that human beings from all historical periods and geographical regions "are always in some sense our contemporaries," arguing that "the writing of history must implicitly assume a plurality of times existing together, a disjuncture of the present with itself."[26] After all, the writing of history, the engagement with the historical past that it represents, is taking place *now*. In terms of his or her location in time, the historian is an irredeemably hybrid animal and should allow no one to forget it.

Such a claim about the simultaneity of temporally disjunct historical experiences, and thus about historical difference within the present itself, was already implicit in Sedgwick's discursive critique of the notion of "homosexuality as we understand it today," which sought to break apart the unity of that supposedly "modern" concept and to promote an atemporal approach to contradictions in sexual discourses. My own response to Sedgwick, here, frankly acknowledges the force of that claim. And the power of that claim can be gauged by the immediate and obvious liabilities that accrue to anyone who tries to challenge it. Who wants to take responsibility for denying the existence today of one or another form of sexual life in the past? And who wants to look a fellow human being in the face and tell that person that his or her sexual practices are out of date, archaic, not really modern? It would seem to be better to insist on the contemporaneity of all historical subjects and to call into question the very distinction between the "modern" and the "pre-modern." Otherwise, historical temporality itself will function as a strategy of exclusion, and as a figure for the assertion of social privilege.

Indeed, too great an emphasis on the historical specificity and time-bound insularity of previous sexual formations, on the obsolescence of Greek paederasty or Renaissance cross-dressing, for example, rapidly produces noxious political effects. It leads to the marginalization of anyone whose sexual or gender practices approximate to those of earlier, pre-modern subjects or do not conform to mainstream notions of "homosexuality as we understand it today."

In a 1978 interview Foucault declared that male homosexuality had no fundamental connection with femininity. Cross-dressing was merely an outmoded strategy of resistance to earlier sexual regimes.[27] Soon, no doubt, it would wither away. Many gay men at the time, still flush from the exhilarating discovery that gay identity could be a masculine identity, similarly regarded drag queens as dinosaurs, the last remnants of a soon-to-be-extinct species. The notion that gay liberation had put an end to earlier (and now disavowed) forms of homosexual existence rooted in past experiences of oppression and homophobia was typical of the period. According to the first (1977) edition of *The Joy of Gay Sex,* written by Charles Silverstein and Edmund White, "one-sided" homosexual relations, though they might still exist, were a vestige from the pre-modern past. Although there was no denying that "in many gay relationships today one partner does the fucking and the other invariably gets fucked," Silverstein and White, enlightened moderns that they were, insisted that such practices were out of date, dying out, and therefore not really gay: "This sort of role-playing, held to as a strict division, seems increasingly on the wane," they said, adding that "most gay men would denounce" such role-playing "as 'old-fashioned' or 'unliberated.' " The representative gay male couple is pictured by Silverstein and White as living in New York and consisting of "a 35-year-old lawyer in love with a 35-year-old doctor; they take turns fucking each other, they share expenses and household duties." [28]

Silverstein and White were registering the existence of a genuinely novel form of social organization, a feature of the way the category of homosexuality was actually being lived—or was being thought to be lived—by some metropolitan gay men in the 1970s. Their testimony reveals the connections between the crypto-normative force of the category of homosexuality itself and the lived ideology of contemporary social and sexual gay male life. But their assertions of the essential modernity of that life, or of that ideology, produces invidious distinctions between the amorous thirty-five-year-old professionals, equally versatile in the bedroom and the kitchen, and those unfortunates whose sexual or domestic lives still bore traces of "one-sidedness."

For example, where did such assertions of homosexual modernity leave the contemporary writer Reinaldo Arenas? Arriving in New York from Cuba in 1980, Arenas was less than enraptured by the "tedious and unrewarding" gay male culture he found there. In fact, he complained vehemently about the very practices that Silverstein and White found so liberated: "The queer gets together with the queer and everybody does everything. One sucks first, and then they reverse roles. How can that bring any satisfaction?" he inquired. [29] Arenas was surely not the only "pre-modern" sexual subject to inhabit the island of Manhattan in 1980. More to the point, a notion of modernity that relegates to pre-modernity all contemporary subjects whose desires do not conform to established definitions of sexual modernity has already confessed its own inability to capture the experience of modernity as such. No wonder Chakrabarty insists that all historical subjects are contemporaries.

Claims about the historical specificity of past sexual practices have a disconcerting tendency to deny the existence of contemporary sexual practices that bear some resemblance to supposedly defunct modes of eroticism. They sometimes have the effect of derealizing such contemporary practices by treating them as residual or archaic. Even worse, claims about the modernity of sexuality insinuate that contemporary societies in which other articulations of sexual desire or other sexual categories prevail are backward, less advanced, pre-modern, or primitive. Constructionist discourse about the modernity of sexuality and the historicity of pre-modern sexual formations often has the effect of aligning marginal or non-standard sexual practices in post-industrial liberal societies with dominant sexual practices in developing nations, thereby perpetuating the hoary colonialist notion that non-European cultures represent the cultural childhood of modern Europe.

No brand of historicism practiced today can afford to remain indifferent to the force of this post-colonial critique. At the same time, there are reasons to resist thinking of all human beings who have ever existed as our contemporaries. Those reasons have to do not only with respect for diversity, with attention to difference, but also with setting limits to the expansiveness of the self, to the imperialism of the hermeneutic ego, and to our pretended powers of understanding. They also have to do with acknowledging the unequal relations of force between the interpreter and the objects of interpretation. Some historical experiences may actually be lost to us. Others are effectively occluded by the very activity of studying them. And in any case the task of understanding our contemporaries is not necessarily more straightforward than that of understanding our predecessors.

One Homeric scholar, speaking of the *Iliad*'s original audience, makes a very stark claim: "We can no more place ourselves actively in that tradition of oral poetry than we can become Greek warriors before Troy."[30] Of course, we can still try to find, or to construct, a temporal continuum in which to forge a relation of simultaneity with the Homeric Greeks, and every scholarly effort to write their history does that to a greater or lesser degree. But every such effort—including every attempt, say, to invoke past or present instances of military elites or tribal warfare in order to make the Homeric heroes our contemporaries, and by means of such a historical ascesis to reanimate the multiple historical worlds we inhabit and to actualize our own potential for becoming Other—every such effort is a necessarily willful act, an act of deliberate cultural appropriation, and it expresses an irreducible epistemic and social privilege. That doesn't mean it's wrong. There are positive uses to be made of inequality and asymmetry, in history as in love. But it does mean that such a move isn't innocent or self-evident: on the contrary, the proceeding needs to be defensible, which means that it needs at least to be available for political and historiographical critique.

And if we hope to recover a sense of what it was actually like to sit in the Theater of Dionysus at Athens sometime around 429 B.C. and watch the first performance of Sophocles' *Oedipus Rex,* our hope is doomed to defeat by a single, simple consideration.[31] For the one thing about the original spectators of the *Oedipus Rex* that we can be sure of is that they did not wonder what it was like to be the original spectators of the *Oedipus Rex*. Our hermeneutic situation as historical interpreters of culture places us in a non-reciprocal relation with the objects of interpretation, and any refusal to cop to that asymmetry out of some misguided democratic impulse is ultimately as risky, and as cruel, as any forcible infliction that, by denying its forcible character, assures its greater efficacy as an infliction. In history as in love, the real harm in power imbalances comes not from the dissymmetry itself but from its sentimentalization or institutionalization, from the denial of the reality of unequal power through its normalizing as the truth of gender, class, race, status, beauty, wealth, romance, professional authority, national identity, historical difference.

: : :

To live in the present is indeed to inhabit simultaneously a multitude of historical worlds. But that does not mean that all those historical worlds are the same. And to agree with Sedgwick that one historical model of sexual relations does not simply supersede or replace another is not to concede that all historical models are always operative at every historical moment, or that there was never a time and place when one particular model achieved hegemony over the others, or that the temporary dominance of one model does not have, if only for a certain time, a decisive impact on the functioning of the others.[32] Even today there remain important differences in global patterns of same-sex sexual practice, and they need to be accounted for, both culturally and historically, not denied.[33] It remains an interesting and enlightening exercise to describe systematically their differences. Without using historicism in order to fashion a pre-modern past defined in part by its correspondence with a disavowed present, or in order to relegate to the realm of the "pre-modern" whatever contemporary forms of erotic life are at odds with modern regimes of sexuality, it should be possible to indicate just how limited in time and space and culture are the notions of homosexuality, heterosexuality, and indeed sexuality. The emergence of those notions, and the social formations to which they refer, have made a historical difference, and to deny this, or to ignore the specific effects of the functioning of those formations, would be to succumb to a new cultural chauvinism, to impose a new and more insidious universalism, to make contemporary life (however we understand what *that* is) the measure of all things.[34]

In fact, it is looking more and more as if the model of (homo)sexuality with which I grew up, and whose genealogy I have tried to map in the essays that follow, never had more than a narrowly circumscribed reach. That model never succeeded for very long in establishing a concept or a practice of sexuality wholly defined by sexual object-choice (same sex or different sex) to the exclusion of considerations of gender identity, gender presentation, gender performance, sexual role, and social difference. It never completely decoupled sexuality from matters of gender conformity or gender deviance, from questions of masculinity and femininity, activity and passivity, dominance and submission, from issues of age, social class, status, wealth, race, ethnicity, or nationality. And canons of homosexuality and heterosexuality in their turn installed their own norms of gender identity and sexual role, while seeming to insist with breathtaking categorical simplicity on the "sameness" or "difference" of the sexes of the sexual partners. It turns out that such notions of sameness or difference contained their own hidden stipulations about the conditions under which members of the same sex could really be considered the "same," or had to be classed, despite the sameness of their sexes, as actually "different."

To say that such a model of (homo)sexuality was limited, or that it was never perfectly embodied by anyone, is not to say that it never existed. Nor is it to claim that such a model of (homo)sexuality did not generate, within its admittedly limited sphere of operation, numbers of significant consequences. The emergence, decline, and concrete social and conceptual effects of the (homo)sexual model continue to solicit the attention of the historian.

To define as accurately and precisely as possible the features of the narrowly circumscribed phenomenon of (homo)sexuality is therefore not to treat (homo)sexuality as the endpoint of historical progress, as the ensign of modernity, as proof of Western cultural superiority. On the contrary, it is from a more exact apprehension of (homo)sexuality's cultural and historical boundedness that we can arrive at a sense of its individual particularity as way of organizing human erotic life and its relation to time itself. Such an understanding of (homo)sexuality ought to allow us at last to see it as the specific social apparatus that it is, something neither good nor bad but, at any rate, something which is not qualified to represent a marker of progress or an advanced stage of development. As Alan Sinfield says, "It would be arrogant to suppose that the ways we have 'developed' in parts of North America and Northern Europe of being lesbian and gay constitute the necessary, proper, or ultimate potential for our sexualities."[35] A historicist approach to (homo)sexuality, far from installing it as the goal to which all human societies strive, ought to have the effect of depriveleging it, enabling it to appear as one of many documented varieties of human social organization, reopening the question of its temporality, and thereby testifying to the heterogeneity of sexual life both past and present.

Nonetheless, a historicist approach to sexuality needs to be argued for as a preference, not insisted on as a truth.

: : :

To write the history of the present is a deliberately paradoxical project. For such a history is necessarily and inevitably framed by contemporary preoccupations and investments. And yet, for that very reason, it looks to the past for something lacking in the present, something that can offer a new leverage against the contemporary problems with which the historian is engaged. Such a history privileges neither the present nor the past, but the unstable relation between the two. Those of us who locate ourselves at their uncertain intersection do so in the hope of finding ourselves changed by the experience.

Whatever change I have undergone during the past ten years is recorded in the essays that follow.

1

Forgetting Foucault

When Jean Baudrillard published his infamous pamphlet *Forget Foucault* in March 1977, "Foucault's intellectual power," as Baudrillard recalled ten years later, "was enormous." After all, the reviews of *La volonté de savoir,* the first volume of Michel Foucault's *History of Sexuality* (published the previous November), had only just started to appear. At that time, according to Baudrillard's belated attempt in *Cool Memories* to redeem his gaffe and to justify himself—by portraying his earlier attack on Foucault as having been inspired, improbably, by sentiments of friendship and generosity—Foucault was being "persecuted," allegedly, by "thousands of disciples and . . . sycophants." In such circumstances, Baudrillard virtuously insisted, "to forget him was to do him a service; to adulate him was to do him a disservice." Just how far Baudrillard was willing to go in order to render this sort of unsolicited service to Foucault emerges from another remark of his in the same passage: "Foucault's death. Loss of confidence in his own genius. . . . Leaving the sexual aspects aside, the loss of the immune system is no more than the biological transcription of the other process."[1] Foucault was already washed up by the time he died, in other words, and AIDS was merely the outward and visible sign of his inward, moral and intellectual, decay. Leaving the sexual aspects aside, of course.

(Baudrillard freely voices elsewhere what he carefully suppresses here about "the sexual aspects" of AIDS: the pandemic, he suggests, might be considered "a form of viral catharsis" and "a remedy against total sexual liberation, which is sometimes more dangerous than an epidemic, because the latter always ends. Thus AIDS could be understood as a counterforce against the total elimination of structure and the total unfolding of sexuality."[2] Some such New Age moralism obviously provides the subtext of Baudrillard's vengeful remarks in *Cool Memories* on the death of Foucault.)

Baudrillard's injunction to forget Foucault, which was premature at the time it was issued, has since become superfluous. Not that Foucault is neglected; not that his work is ignored. (Quite the contrary, in fact.) Rather, Foucault's continuing prestige, and the almost ritualistic invocation of his name by academic practitioners of cultural theory, has had the effect of reducing the operative range of his thought to a small set of received ideas, slogans, and bits of jargon that have now become so commonplace and so familiar as to make a more direct engagement with Foucault's texts entirely dispensable. As a result, we are so far from remembering Foucault that there is little point in entertaining the possibility of forgetting him.

Take, for example, the title of a conference on "Bodies and Pleasures in Pre- and Early Modernity," held from 3 to 5 November 1995 at the University of California at Santa Cruz. "Bodies and pleasures," as that famous phrase occurs in the concluding paragraphs of Foucault's *History of Sexuality,* volume 1, does not in fact describe "Foucault's zero-degree definition of the elements in question in the history of sexuality," as the poster for the conference confidently announces. To be sure, the penultimate sentence of *The History of Sexuality,* volume 1, finds Foucault looking forward to the day, some time in the future, when "a different economy [*une autre économie*] of bodies and pleasures" will have replaced the apparatus of sexuality and when, accordingly, it will become difficult to understand "how the ruses of sexuality . . . were able to subject us to that austere monarchy of sex."[3] An incautious reader might take that phrase, "a different economy of bodies and pleasures," to denote a mere rearrangement of otherwise unchanged and unchanging "bodies and pleasures," a minor modification in the formal design of the sexual "economy" alone, consisting in a revised organization of its perennial "elements" (as the conference poster terms them). And Foucault himself occasionally spoke as if bodies and pleasures constituted the raw material of sexuality.[4] But such an interpretation of Foucault's meaning, reasserting the venerable opposition between material (corporeal) base and ideological (sexual) superstructure, though superficially plausible, is mistaken—and in fact it runs counter to the entire thrust of his larger argument. The change of which Foucault speaks in the next-to-last sentence of *The History of Sexuality,* volume 1, and which he seems fondly to anticipate, involves nothing less than the displacement of the current sexual economy by a different economy altogether, an economy that will feature "bodies and pleasures" instead of, or at least in addition to, such familiar and overworked entities as "sexuality" and "desire."[5]

Foucault makes it very clear that bodies and pleasures, in his conception, are not the eternal building blocks of sexual subjectivity or sexual experience; they are not basic, irreducible, or natural "elements" that different human societies rearrange in different patterns over time—and that our own society has elaborated into the cultural edifice now known as "sexuality." Rather, "bodies" and "pleasures" refer to two entities that have been taken up by the modern apparatus of sexuality, that form part of it and function specifically as its ground, but that modern sexual discourse and practice largely ignore, underplay, or pass quickly over, and that accordingly are relatively undercoded, relatively uninvested by the normalizing apparatus of sexuality, especially in comparison to more thoroughly policed and more easily pathologized items such as "sexual desire." (Or so at least it seemed to Foucault at the time he was writing, in the wake of the sexual liberation movement of the late 1960s and early 1970s, which had exhorted us to liberate our "sexuality" and to unrepress or desublimate our "desire.") For that reason, bodies and pleasures represented to Foucault an opportunity for effecting, as he says earlier in the same passage, "a tactical reversal of the various mechanisms of sexuality," a means of resistance to the apparatus of sexuality.[6] In particular, the strategy that Foucault favors consists in asserting, "against the [various] holds of power, the claims of bodies, pleasures, and knowledges in their multiplicity and their possibility of resistance."[7] The very possibility of pursuing such a body- and pleasure-centered strategy of resistance to the apparatus of sexuality disappears, of course, as soon as bodies and pleasures cease to be understood merely as handy weapons against current technologies of normalization and attain instead to the status of transhistorical components of some natural phenomenon or material substrate underlying "the history of sexuality" itself. Such a notion of "bodies and pleasures," so very familiar and uncontroversial and positivistic has it now become, is indeed nothing if not eminently forgettable.

: : :

In what follows I propose to explore another aspect of the oblivion that has engulfed Foucault's approach to sexuality since his death, one particular "forgetting" that has had important consequences for the practice of both the history of sexuality and lesbian/gay studies. I refer to the reception and deployment of Foucault's distinction between the sodomite and the homosexual—a distinction often taken to be synonymous with the distinction between sexual acts and sexual identities.[8] The passage in *The History of Sexuality*, volume 1, in which Foucault makes this fateful distinction is so well known that it might seem unnecessary to quote it, but what that really means, I am contending, is that the passage is in fact so well forgotten that nothing but direct quotation from it will do. Foucault writes,

> As defined by the ancient civil or canonical codes, sodomy was a category of forbidden acts; their author was nothing more than the juridical subject of them. The nineteenth-century homosexual became a personage—a past, a case history and a childhood, a character, a form of life; also a morphology, with an indiscreet anatomy and possibly a mysterious physiology. Nothing in his total being escapes his sexuality. Everywhere in him it is present: underlying all his actions, because it is their insidious and indefinitely active principle; shamelessly inscribed on his face and on his body, because it is a secret that always gives itself away. It is consubstantial with him, less as a habitual sin than as a singular nature. . . . Homosexuality appeared as one of the forms of sexuality when it was transposed from the practice of sodomy onto a kind of interior androgyny, a hermaphroditism of the soul. The sodomite was a renegade [or "backslider"]; the homosexual is now a species.

> [La sodomie—celle des anciens droits civil ou canonique—était un type d'actes interdits; leur auteur n'en était que le sujet juridique. L'homosexuel du xixe siècle est devenu un personnage: un passé, une histoire et une enfance, un caractère, une forme de vie; une morphologie aussi, avec une anatomie indiscrète et peut-être une physiologie mystérieuse. Rien de ce qu'il est au total n'échappe à sa sexualité. Partout en lui, elle est présente: sous-jacente à toutes ses conduites parce qu'elle en est le principe insidieux et indéfiniment actif; inscrite sans pudeur sur son visage et sur son corps parce qu'elle est un secret qui se trahit toujours. Elle lui est consubstantielle, moins comme un péché d'habitude que comme une nature singulière. . . . L'homosexualité est apparue comme une des figures de la sexualité lorsqu'elle a été rabattue de la pratique de la sodomie sur une sorte d'androgynie

intérieure, un hermaphrodisme de l'âme. Le sodomite était un relaps, l'homosexuel est maintenant une espèce.][9]

Foucault's formulation is routinely taken to authorize the doctrine that before the nineteenth century the categories or classifications typically employed by European cultures to articulate sexual difference did not distinguish among different kinds of sexual actors but only among different kinds of sexual acts. In the pre-modern and early modern periods, so the claim goes, sexual behavior did not represent a sign or marker of a person's sexual identity; it did not indicate or express some more generalized or holistic feature of the person, such as that person's subjectivity, disposition, or character. The pattern is clearest, we are told, in the case of deviant sexual acts. Sodomy, for example, was a sinful act that anyone of sufficient depravity might commit; it was not a symptom of a type of personality. To perform the act of sodomy was not to manifest a deviant sexual identity but merely to be the author of a morally objectionable act.[10] Whence the conclusion that before the modern era sexual deviance could be predicated only of acts, not of persons or identities.

There is a good deal of truth in this received view, and Foucault himself may even have subscribed to a version of it at the time he wrote *The History of Sexuality,* volume 1.[11] Although I am about to argue strenuously against it, I want to be very clear that my aim is to revise it, not to reverse it. I do not want to return us to some unreconstructed or reactionary belief in the universal validity and applicability of modern sexual concepts or to promote an uncritical acceptance of the categories and classifications of sexuality as true descriptors of the basic realities of human erotic life—and, therefore, as unproblematic instruments for the historical analysis of human culture in all times and places. It is certainly not my intention to undermine the principles and practices of the new social history, let alone to recant my previous arguments for the historical and cultural constitution of sexual identity (which have sometimes been misinterpreted as providing support for the view I shall be criticizing here).[12] Least of all do I wish to revive an essentialist faith in the unqualified existence of homosexual and heterosexual persons in Western societies before the modern era. I take it as established that a large-scale transformation of social and personal life took place in Europe as part of the massive cultural reorganization that accompanied the transition from a traditional, hierarchical, status-based society to a modern, individualistic, mass society during the period of industrialization and the rise of a capitalist economy. One symptom of that transformation, as a number of researchers (both before and after Foucault) have pointed out, is that something new happens to the various

relations among sexual roles, sexual object-choices, sexual categories, sexual behaviors, and sexual identities in bourgeois Europe between the end
of the seventeenth century and the beginning of the twentieth.[13] Sex takes
on new social and individual functions, and it assumes a new importance
in defining and normalizing the modern self. The conception of the sexual
instinct as an autonomous human function without an organ appears for
the first time in the nineteenth century, and without it the currently prevailing, heavily psychologized model of sexual subjectivity—which knits up
desire, its objects, sexual behavior, gender identity, reproductive function,
mental health, erotic sensibility, personal style, and degrees of normality
or deviance into an individuating, normativizing feature of the personality called "sexuality" or "sexual orientation"—is inconceivable.[14] Sexuality is indeed, as Foucault claimed, a distinctively modern production.
Nonetheless, the canonical reading of the famous passage in *The History
of Sexuality,* volume 1, and the conclusion conventionally based on it—
namely, that before the modern era sexual deviance could be predicated
only of acts, not of persons or identities—is, I shall contend, as inattentive
to Foucault's text as it is heedless of European history.[15]

Such a misreading of Foucault can be constructed only by setting aside,
and then forgetting, the decisive qualifying phrase with which his famous pronouncement opens: "*As defined by the ancient civil or canonical
codes,*" Foucault begins, "sodomy was a category of forbidden acts."[16]
Foucault, in other words, is making a carefully limited point about the
differing styles of disqualification applied to male love by pre-modern
legal definitions of sodomy and by nineteenth-century psychiatric conceptualizations of homosexuality, respectively. The intended effect of his
rhetorical extravagance in this passage is to highlight what in particular
was new and distinctive about the modern discursive practices that produced the category of "the homosexual." As almost always in *The History of Sexuality,* Foucault is speaking about discursive and institutional
practices, not about what people really did in bed or what they thought
about it. He is not attempting to describe popular attitudes or private
emotions, much less is he presuming to convey what actually went on in
the minds of different historical subjects when they had sex. He is making
a contrast between the way something called "sodomy" was typically
defined by the laws of various European states and municipalities as well
as by Christian penitentials and canon law, on the one hand, and the way
something called "homosexuality" was typically defined by the writings of
nineteenth-century and early-twentieth-century sexologists, on the other.

A glance at the larger context of the much-excerpted passage in *The
History of Sexuality,* volume 1, is sufficient to make Foucault's meaning

clear. Foucault introduces his account of "the nineteenth-century homosexual" in order to illustrate a more general claim, which he advances in the sentence immediately preceding: the "new persecution of the peripheral sexualities" that occurred in the modern era was accomplished in part through "an *incorporation of perversions* and a new *specification of individuals.*"[17] (Earlier efforts to regulate sexual behavior did not feature such tactics, according to Foucault.) The whole discussion of this distinctively modern method of sexual control is embedded, in turn, within a larger argument about a crucial shift in the nature of sexual prohibitions as those prohibitions were constructed in formal discursive practices, a shift that occurred in Europe between the pre-modern period and the nineteenth century. Comparing medieval moral and legal codifications of sexual relations with nineteenth-century medical and forensic ones, Foucault contrasts various pre-modern styles of sexual prohibition, which took the form of specifying rules of conduct, making prescriptions and recommendations, and discriminating between the licit and the illicit, with modern styles of sexual prohibition. These latter-day strategies took the form of establishing norms of self-regulation—not by legislating standards of behavior and punishing deviations from them but rather by constructing new species of individuals, discovering and "implanting" perversions, and, in this way, elaborating more subtle and insidious means of social control. The ultimate purpose of the comparison is to support Foucault's "historico-theoretical" demonstration that power is not only negative but also positive, not only repressive but also productive.

Foucault is analyzing the different modalities of power at work in pre-modern and modern codifications of sexual prohibition, which is to say in two historical instances of sexual discourse attached to institutional practices. He carefully isolates the formal discursive systems that he will proceed to discuss from popular moral attitudes and behaviors about which he will have nothing to say and that he dismisses from consideration with barely a parenthetical glance: "Up to the end of the eighteenth century, three major explicit codes [*codes*]—*apart from regularities of custom and constraints of opinion*—governed sexual practices: canon law [*droit canonique*] , Christian pastoral, and civil law."[18] Foucault goes on to expand this observation in a passage that directly anticipates and lays the groundwork for the famous portrait he will later sketch of the differences between "the sodomy of the old civil and canonical codes" and that novel invention of modern psychiatry, "the nineteenth-century homosexual." Describing the terms in which pre-modern sexual prohibitions defined the scope of their operation and the nature of their target, he writes, "What was taken into account in the civil and religious jurisdictions alike was a general unlawfulness. Doubtless acts 'contrary to nature' were stamped as especially abominable, but they were perceived simply as an extreme form of acts 'against the law'; they, too, were infringements of decrees—decrees which were just as sacred as those of marriage and which had been established in order to rule the order of things and the plan of beings. Prohibitions bearing on sex were basically of a juridical nature [*de nature juridique*]."[19] This passage prepares the reader to gauge the differences between these "juridical" prohibitions against "acts" " 'contrary to nature' " and the nineteenth-century prohibitions against homosexuality, which did not simply criminalize sexual relations between men as illegal but medically disqualified them as pathological and—not content with pathologizing the act—constructed the perpetrator as a deviant form of life, a perverse personality, an anomalous species, thereby producing a new specification of individuals whose true nature would be defined from now on by reference to their abnormal "sexuality." The nineteenth-century disciplining of the subject, though it purported to aim at the eradication of "peripheral sexualities," paradoxically required their consolidation and "implantation" or "incorporation" in individuals, for only by that means could the subject's body itself become so deeply, so minutely invaded and colonized by the agencies of normalization. The discursive construction of the new sexual perversions was therefore a ruse of power, no longer simply prohibiting behavior but now also controlling, regulating, and normalizing embodied subjects. As Foucault sums up his argument, "The implantation of perversions is an instrument-effect: it is through the isolation, intensification, and consolidation of peripheral sexualities that the relations of power to sex and pleasure branched out and multiplied, measured the body and penetrated modes of conduct."[20] Want an example? Take the case of homosexuality. "The sodomy of the old civil and canonical codes was a category of forbidden acts; their author was nothing more than the juridical subject of them. The nineteenth-century homosexual became a personage. . . ." So that's how the overall argument works.

Foucault narrowly frames his comparison between sodomy and homosexuality with the purpose of this larger argument in mind. The point-by-point contrast—between legal discourse (*codes* and *droits*) and psychiatric discourse, between juridical subjects and sexual subjects, between laws and norms, between acts contrary to nature and embodied subjects or species of individuals—is ruthlessly schematic. That schematic reduction is in keeping with the general design of the first volume of Foucault's *History,* which merely outlines, in an admittedly preliminary and tentative fashion, the principles intended to guide the remaining five unfinished studies that Foucault projected for his *History* at the time. His schematic opposition between sodomy and homosexuality is first and foremost a discursive analysis, not a social history, let alone an exhaustive one. *It is not an empirical claim about the historical existence or non-existence of sexually deviant individuals.* It is a claim about the internal logic and systematic functioning of two different discursive styles of sexual disqualification—and, ultimately, it is a heuristic device for foregrounding what is distinctive about modern techniques of social and sexual regulation. As such, it points to a historical development that will need to be properly explored in its own right (as Foucault intended to do in a separate volume), and it dramatizes the larger themes of Foucault's *History:* the historical triumph of normalization over law, the decentralization and dispersion of the mechanisms of regulation, the disciplining of the modern subject, the traversal of sexuality by relations of power, the productivity of power, and the displacement of state coercion by the technical and bureaucratic administration of life ("biopower"). By documenting the existence of both a discursive and a temporal gap between two dissimilar styles of defining, and disqualifying, male same-sex sexual expression, Foucault highlights the historical and political specificity of "sexuality," both as a cultural concept and as a tactical device, and so he contributes to the task of "introducing" the history of sexuality as a possible field of study—and as a radical scholarly and political project. Nothing Foucault says about the differences between those two historically distant, and operationally distinct, discursive strategies for regulating and delegitimating forms of male same-sex sexual contacts prohibits us from inquiring into the connections that pre-modern people may have made between specific sexual acts and the particular ethos, or sexual style, or sexual subjectivity, of those who performed them.

: : :

A more explicit argument to this effect was advanced in the late 1980s by John J. Winkler, in opposition less to Foucault than to what even then were already well-established, conventional, and highly dogmatic misreadings of Foucault. Winkler, a classical scholar, was discussing the ancient Greek and Roman figure of the *kinaidos* or *cinaedus,* a "scare-image" (or phobic construction) of a sexually deviant and gender-deviant male, whose most salient distinguishing feature was a supposedly "feminine" love of being sexually penetrated by other men.[21] "Scholars of recent sex-gender history," Winkler wrote in his 1990 book, *The Constraints of Desire,* "have asserted that pre-modern systems classified not persons but acts and that 'the' homosexual as a person-category is a recent invention." He went on to qualify that assertion as follows: "The *kinaidos,* to be sure, is not a 'homosexual' but neither is he just an ordinary guy who now and then decided to commit a kinaidic act. The conception of a *kinaidos* was of a man socially deviant in his entire being, principally observable in behavior that flagrantly violated or contravened the dominant social definition of masculinity. To this extent, *kinaidos* was a category of person, not just of acts."[22] Ancient Mediterranean societies, of course, did not exactly have "categories of person," types of blank individuals, in the modern sense, as Winkler himself pointed out. The ancient conception of the *kinaidos,* Winkler explained, depended on indigenous notions of gender. It arose in the context of a belief system in which, first of all, the two genders are conceived as opposite ends of a much-traveled continuum and, second, masculinity is thought to be a difficult accomplishment—one that is achieved only by a constant struggle akin to warfare against enemies both internal and external—and thus requires great fortitude in order to maintain. In a situation where it is so hard, both personally and culturally, to be a man, Winkler observed, "the temptation to desert one's side is very great." The *kinaidos* succumbed to that temptation.

The *kinaidos* could be conceived by the ancients in both universalizing and minoritizing terms—as a potential threat to the masculine identity of every male, that is, and as the disfiguring peculiarity of a small class of deviant individuals.[23] Because ancient Mediterranean discourses of sex and gender featured the notion that "the two sexes are not simply opposite but stand at poles of a continuum which can be traversed," as Winkler pointed out, " 'woman' is not only the opposite of a man; she is also a potentially threatening 'internal emigré' of masculine identity."[24] The prospect of losing one's masculine gender status and being reduced to the social ranks of women therefore represented a universal possibility for all men. In such a context, the figure of the *kinaidos* stood as a warning to men of what could happen to them if they gave up the internal struggle to master their desires and surrendered, in womanly fashion, to the lure of pleasure. The clear implication of this warning is that the only thing that prevents men from allowing other men to use them as objects of sexual degradation, the only thing that enables men to resist the temptation to let other men fuck them like whores, is not the nature of their own desires, or their own capacities for sexual enjoyment, but their hard-won masculine ability to withstand the seductive appeal of pleasure-at-any-price. The *kinaidos,* on this view, is not someone who has a different sexual orientation from other men or who belongs to some autonomous sexual species. Rather, he is someone who represents what *every* man would be like if he were so shameless as to sacrifice his dignity and masculine gender status for the sake of gratifying the most odious and disgraceful, though no doubt voluptuous, bodily appetites. Such a worthless character is so radical and so complete a failure as a man that he could be understood, at least by the ancients, as wholly reversing the internal gender hierarchy that structured and defined normative masculinity for men and that maintained it against manifold temptations to effeminacy. The catastrophic failure of male self-fashioning that the *kinaidos* represented was so complete, in other words, that it could not be imagined as merely confined within the sphere of erotic life or restricted to the occasional performance of disreputable sexual acts: it defined and determined a man's social identity in its totality, and it generated a recognizable social type—namely, the "scare-image" and phobic stereotype of the *kinaidos,* which Winkler so eloquently described.

As the mere existence of the stereotype implies, the ancients were quite capable of conceptualizing the figure of the *kinaidos,* when they so desired, not only in anxiously universalizing terms but also in comfortably minoritizing ones. Although some normal men might acknowledge that the scandalous pleasures to which the *kinaidos* succumbed, and which normal men properly avoided, were universally pleasurable in and of themselves,[25] still the very fact that the *kinaidos* did succumb to such pleasures, whereas normal men did not, contributed to defining his difference and marked out the vast distance that separated the *kinaidos* from normal men. Just as some moderns may think that, whereas anyone *can* get addicted to drugs, only people who have something fundamentally wrong with them actually *do,* so some ancients evidently thought that, although the pleasures of sexual penetration in themselves might be universally pleasurable, any male who actually pursued them suffered from a specific constitutional defect— namely, a constitutional lack of the masculine capacity to withstand the appeal of pleasure (especially pleasure deemed exceptionally disgraceful or degrading) as well as a constitutional tendency to adopt a specifically feminine attitude of surrender in relations with other men. Hence, the desire to be sexually penetrated by other men, which was the most dramatic and flagrant sign of the *kinaidos*'s constitutional femininity, could be interpreted by the ancients in sharply minoritizing terms as an indication of a physiological anomaly in the *kinaidos* or as the symptom of a moral or mental "disease."[26] Conceived in these terms, the *kinaidos* did not represent the frightening possibility of a failure of nerve on the part of every man, a collapse in the face of the ongoing struggle that all men necessarily waged to maintain and defend their masculinity; he was simply a peculiar, repugnant, and perplexing freak, driven to abandon his sexual and gender identity in pursuit of a pleasure that no one but a woman could possibly enjoy. (And there were even some abominable practices, like fellatio, which a *kinaidos* might relish but no decent woman would so much as contemplate.)

The details in this minoritizing conception of the *kinaidos* have been filled in with great skill and documented at fascinating length by Maud Gleason, most recently in her 1995 book, *Making Men*. "The essential idea here," writes Gleason, corroborating Winkler's emphasis on the gender deviance of the *kinaidos* and calling attention to what she fittingly terms the ancient "semiotics of gender" that produced the *kinaidos* as a visibly deviant kind of being, "is that there exist [according to the axioms of Greek and Roman social life] masculine and feminine 'types' that do not necessarily correspond to the anatomical sex of the person in question."[27] Gleason approaches the figure of the *kinaidos* from an unexpected and original scholarly angle—namely, from a close study of the neglected scientific writings of the ancient physiognomists, experts in the learned technique of deciphering a person's character from his or her appearance. Gleason's analysis of the ancient corpus of physiognomic texts makes clear that the portrait they construct of the figure of the *kinaidos* agrees with the stereotypical features commonly ascribed by the ancients to the general appearance of gender-deviant or "effeminate" men. Like such men, the *kinaidos* could be identified, or so the Greeks thought, by a variety of physical features: weak eyes, knees that knock together, head tilted to the right, hands limply upturned, and hips that either swing from side to side or are held tightly rigid. Latin physiognomy agrees largely with the Greek tradition in its enumeration of the characteristics of the *cinaedus*: "A tilted head, a mincing gait, an enervated voice, a lack of stability in the shoulders, and a feminine way of moving the body." Gleason adds that a *kinaidos* could also be known by certain specific mannerisms: "He shifts his eyes around in sheep-like fashion when he speaks; he touches his fingers to his nose; he compulsively obliterates all traces of spittle he may find—his own or anyone else's—by rubbing it into the dust with his heel; he frequently stops to admire what he considers his own best feature; he smiles furtively while talking; he holds his arms turned outward; he laughs out loud; and he has an annoying habit of clasping other people by the hand."[28] The *kinaidos*, in short, is considerably more than the juridical subject of deviant sexual acts. To recur to Foucault's terminology, the *kinaidos* represents at the very least a full-blown morphology. As Gleason observes, "Foucault's description of the nineteenth-century homosexual fits the *cinaedus* remarkably well. . . . The *cinaedus* was a 'life-form' all to himself, and his condition was written all over him in signs that could be decoded by those practiced in the art." Gleason hastens to add, however, that "what made [the *cinaedus*] different from normal folk . . . was not simply the fact that his sexual partners included people of the same sex as himself (that, after all, was nothing out of the ordinary), nor was it some kind of psychosexual orientation—a 'sexuality' in the nineteenth-century sense—but rather an inversion or reversal of his gender identity: his abandonment of a 'masculine' role in favor of a 'feminine' one."[29]

Gleason's conclusion has now been massively confirmed by Craig Williams, a specialist in ancient Roman literature, who has undertaken an exhaustive survey of the extant Latin sources. Williams's careful discussion makes it clear that the *cinaedus* does not correspond closely to any type of individual defined by more recent, canonical categories of "sexuality": "When a Roman called a man a *cinaedus*," Williams explains, "he was not ruling out the possibility that the man might play sexual roles other than that of the receptive partner in anal intercourse." Hence,

> the *cinaedus* was not the same thing as a "passive homosexual," since it was neither his expression of sexual desire for other males nor his proclivity for playing the receptive role in anal intercourse that gave him his identity or uniquely defined him as a *cinaedus:* he might engage in sexual practices with women and still be a *cinaedus,* and a man did not automatically become a *cinaedus* simply by being penetrated (victims of rape, for example, would not normally be described as such). A *cinaedus* was, rather, a man who failed to be fully masculine, whose effeminacy showed itself in such symptoms as feminine clothing and mannerisms and a lascivious and oversexed demeanor that was likely to be embodied in a proclivity for playing the receptive role in anal intercourse. *Cinaedi* were, in other words, a prominent subset of the class of effeminate men (*molles*) . . . but hardly identical to that whole class.[30]

Williams goes on to align his own analysis of the *cinaedus* with the tradition of interpretation that extends from Winkler and Gleason to the argument proposed here:

> Likewise I am suggesting that the Roman *cinaedus* was in fact a category of person who was considered "socially deviant," but that his social identity was crucially different from that of the "homosexual," since his desire for persons of his own sex was not a defining or even problematic feature of his makeup as a deviant: his desire to be penetrated was indeed one of his characteristics, but, as we have seen, men called *cinaedi* were also thought capable of being interested in penetrative sexual relations with women.

> Thus the deviance of the *cinaedus* is ultimately a matter of gender identity rather than sexual identity, in the sense that his predilection for playing the receptive role in penetrative acts was not the single defining feature of his identity but rather a sign of a more fundamental transgression of gender categories.[31]

There may well be modern categories of deviance—and there may well be contemporary forms of sexual rebellion, transgression, or affirmation—that correspond in some ways to the ancient figure of the *cinaedus* or *kinaidos*. But such categories would only partly overlap with the category of "the homosexual." And if "homosexuality" today is sometimes understood to *apply* to figures such as the *cinaedus*, that tells us less about the particular characteristics of those figures than it does about the elasticity of the category of homosexuality itself. To capture the defining features of the *kinaidos*, it is necessary to begin, at least, by situating him in his own conceptual and social universe, as I have tried to do here.

One significant difference between the *kinaidos* and "the homosexual" is that the *kinaidos* was defined more in terms of gender than in terms of desire. For whether he was imagined in universalizing or minoritizing terms, the *kinaidos* in any case offended principally against the order of masculinity, not against the order of heterosexuality. As such, the *kinaidos* does not represent a salient example of deviant sexual subjectivity. Although he was distinguished from normal men in part by the pleasure he took in being sexually penetrated, his peculiar taste was not sufficient, in and of itself, to individuate him as a sexual subject. Rather, it was a generic sign of femininity. Even the *kinaidos*'s desire to play a receptive role in sexual intercourse with other men—which was about as close to manifesting a distinctive sexual orientation as the *kinaidos* ever got—represented to the ancients "merely a symptom of the deeper disorder, his gender deviance," as Williams emphasizes, and so it did not imply a different kind of specifically sexual subjectivity.[32] Inasmuch as the ancients did not distinguish systematically between gender and sexuality, the *kinaidos*'s desire to be sexually penetrated could be seen as part and parcel of his singular, transgendered condition: it represented at once a symptom and a consequence of the categorical reversal of his masculine gender identity, and it identified the *kinaidos* as womanly in both his gender identity and his sexual desire. To be "womanly," in such a context, is of course a sexual as well as a gendered trait, and "gender deviance" should not be conceptualized as hermetically sealed off from matters of desire. Nonetheless, the *kinaidos*'s desire did not distinguish him as the bearer of a unique or distinct sexuality as such. Neither did his lust for bodily pleasure, since—far from being considered a deviant desire, as we have seen—such lust was thought common to all men. Nor was there anything peculiar about the *kinaidos*'s sexual object-choice: as Gleason mentions, it was quite possible in the ancient Mediterranean world for a male to desire and to pursue sexual contact with other males without impugning in the slightest his own masculinity or normative identity as a man— just so long as he played an insertive sexual role, observed all the proper phallocentric protocols in his relations with the objects of his desire, and maintained a normatively masculine style of personal deportment. Unlike the modern homosexual, then, the *kinaidos* was not defined principally by his "sexuality." Even without a sexuality of his own, however, the *kinaidos*'s betrayal of his masculine gender identity was so spectacular as to brand him a deviant type of person and to inscribe his deviant identity all over his face and body. To put it very schematically, the *kinaidos* represents an instance of deviant sexual morphology without deviant sexual subjectivity.[33]

: : :

Let's move on, then, from matters of sexual morphology and gender presentation and take up matters of sexual subjectivity itself. My chief exhibit in this latter department will be an ancient erotic fable told by Apuleius in the second century and retold by Giovanni Boccaccio in the fourteenth. The two texts have been the subject of a trenchant comparative study by Jonathan Walters in a 1993 issue of *Gender and History*. I have taken Walters's analysis as the basis of my own, and my interpretation closely follows his, although I have a somewhat different set of questions to put to the two texts.[34]

Here, first of all, in bare outline, is the plot of the erotic fable under scrutiny. A man dining out at the home of a friend finds his dinner interrupted when his host detects an adulterous lover concealed in the house by the host's wife, who had not expected her husband to arrive home for dinner, much less with a guest in tow. His meal abruptly terminated, the disappointed guest returns to his own house for dinner ahead of schedule and tells the story to his righteously indignant wife, only to discover that she herself has hidden in his house a young lover of her own. Instead of threatening to kill the youth, however, the husband fucks him and lets him go. The end. This bare summary does little justice to the artistry and wit with which the two stories are told by their respective authors, but the point I wish to make is a historical one, not a literary one. I trust it will emerge from the following comparison.

Apuleius's tale of the baker's wife in book 9 of *The Golden Ass* begins with a description of her lover. He is a boy (*puer*), Apuleius's narrator tells us, still notable for the shiny smoothness of his beardless cheeks, and still delighting and attracting the sexual attention of wayward husbands (*adulteros*) (9.22). According to the erotic postulates of ancient Mediterranean societies, then, there will be nothing out of the ordinary about a normal man finding him sexually desirable. So the first thing to notice is that Apuleius explains the sexual motivation of the wronged husband by reference to erotic qualities inherent in the sexual object, not by reference to any distinguishing characteristics of the sexual subject—not, in other words, by reference to the husband's own sexual tastes, to his erotic subjectivity. This emphasis on the attractiveness of the boy thereby prepares the way for the ending of the story; it is not necessary for the narrator to invoke any specific sort of erotic inclination, much less a deviant one, on the part of the husband in order to anticipate the denouement of the plot. In fact, as Walters observes, the husband "is not described in any way that marks him out as unusual, let alone reprehensible: he is portrayed as blameless, 'a good man in general and extremely temperate' "; that is in keeping with a story designed, within the larger context of Apuleius's narrative, to illustrate the mischief caused to their husbands by devious, depraved, and adulterous wives.[35] When the baker discovers the boy, he locks up his wife and takes the boy to bed himself, thereby (as Apuleius's narrator puts it) enjoying "the most gratifying revenge for his ruined marriage." At daybreak he summons two of his slaves and has them hold the boy up while he flogs his buttocks with a rod, leaving the boy "with his white buttocks the worse for their treatment" both by night and by day. The baker then kicks his wife out of the house and prepares to divorce her (9.28).

Boccaccio's tale of Pietro di Vinciolo of Perugia, the Tenth Story of the Fifth Day of the *Decameron,* is based directly on Apuleius; its departures from its model are therefore especially telling.[36] Boccaccio's narrator begins further back in time, at the point when Pietro takes a wife "more to beguile others and to abate the general suspect [*la generale oppinion*] in which he was held by all the Perugians, than for any desire [*vaghezza*] of his own" (trans. Payne-Singleton). As Walters remarks, "Boccaccio . . . is at pains to tell us from the beginning that something is wrong with the husband."[37] What Boccaccio marks specifically as deviant about Pietro, or so the foregoing quotation from the *Decameron* implies, is his desire.[38] This turns out to refer to his sexual object-choice and to comprehend, in particular, two different aspects of it: first, the customary objects of his sexual desire are young men, not the usual objects of desire for a man, and, second, Pietro (unlike the baker in Apuleius) has no desire for the usual objects of male desire—namely, women. So he has a non-standard erotic subjectivity, insofar as he both desires the wrong objects and fails to desire the right objects.

Both of these erotic errors are dramatized by the narrative. We are told that his wife's lover is "a youth [*garzone*], who was one of the goodliest and most agreeable of all Perugia," and that when Pietro discovers him he instantly recognizes him as "one whom he had long pursued for his own lewd ends." Understandably, Pietro "no less rejoiced to have found him than his wife was woeful"; when he confronts her with the lad, "she saw that he was all agog with joy because he held so goodly a stripling [*giovinetto*] by the hand." No wonder that, far from punishing his wife, Pietro hastens to strike an obscene bargain with her to share the young man between them. As for Pietro's sexual indifference to women, we are told that his lusty, red-haired, highly sexed young wife, "who would liefer have had two husbands than one," is frustrated by her husband's inattention and realizes that she will exhaust herself arguing with him before she will change his disposition. Indeed, he has "a mind far more disposed otherwhat than to her [*molto più ad altro che a lei l'animo avea disposto*]." At the culmination of the story, Pietro's wife reproaches him for being as desirous of women as "a dog of cudgels [*cosí vago di noi come il can delle mazze*]." [39]

Note that Boccaccio's narrator says nothing to indicate that Pietro is effeminate or in any way deviant in terms of his personal style or sexual morphology. [40] *You wouldn't know he was a paederast or a sodomite by looking at him.* Nothing about his looks or his behavior gives him away— or gives his wife any advance warning about the nature of his sexual peculiarities. As she says, she had supposed he desired what men typically do desire and should desire when she married him; otherwise, she would never have done so. "He knew I was a woman," she exclaims to herself; "why, then, did he take me to wife, if women were not to his mind [*contro all'animo*]?" Nothing in his morphology made her suspect he harbored deviant desires. And why in any case should we presume that the husband would exhibit signs of effeminacy? He no more resembles the ancient figure of the *kinaidos* than does his literary forebear in Apuleius. Far from displaying a supposedly "feminine" inclination to submit himself to other men to be sexually penetrated by them, the husband in Boccaccio plays a sexually insertive role in intercourse with his wife's lover. That, after all, is the point of the story's punchline: "On the following morning the youth was escorted back to the public square not altogether certain which he had the more been that night, wife or husband"—meaning, obviously, *wife to*

Pietro or *husband to Pietro's wife.*[41] What is at issue in Boccaccio's portrait of Pietro di Vinciolo, then, is not gender deviance but sexual deviance.

Finally, in Apuleius's tale the husband's enjoyment of his wife's lover is an incidental component of his revenge and does not express any special or distinctive sexual taste on his part, much less a habitual preference, whereas in Boccaccio's tale the husband is identified as the subject of deviant sexual desires and is only too happy to exploit his wife's infidelity for the purposes of his own pleasure.[42]

A comparison of these two pre-modern texts indicates that it is possible for sexual acts to be represented in such texts as either *more* or *less* related to sexual dispositions, desires, and subjectivities. Whereas Apuleius's text makes no incriminating association between the baker's sexual enjoyment of the adulterous youth and the baker's character, masculinity, or sexual disposition, Boccaccio's text connects the performance of sodomitical acts with a deviant sexual taste and a deviant sexual subjectivity. In order to update Apuleius's plot it seems to have been necessary for Boccaccio to posit a sodomitical disposition or inclination on the husband's part: he seems to have had no other way of motivating the scandalously witty conclusion of the tale as he had inherited it from Apuleius. Pietro's inclination is not the same thing as a sexual orientation, much less a sexual identity or form of life, to be sure. For one thing, his sexual preference seems contained, compartmentalized, and does not appear to connect to any other feature of his character, such as a sensibility, a set of personal mannerisms, a style of gender presentation, or a psychology.[43] Nonetheless, Pietro's sexual taste for young men represents a notable and perhaps even a defining feature of his life as a sexual subject, as well as a distinctive feature of his life as a social and ethical subject. Pietro may not be a deviant life-form, like the ancient Greek or Roman *kinaidos*—a traitor to his gender whose deviance is visibly inscribed in his personal demeanor—but neither is he nothing more than the juridical subject of a sodomitical act. Rather, his sexual preference for youths is a settled feature of his character and a significant fact about his social identity as a moral and sexual agent.[44]

:   :   :

To sum up, I have tried to suggest that the current doctrine that holds that sexual acts were unconnected to sexual identities in European discourses before the nineteenth century is mistaken in at least two different respects. First, sexual acts could be interpreted as representative components of an individual's sexual morphology. Second, sexual acts could be interpreted as representative expressions of an individual's sexual subjectivity. A sexual morphology is not the same thing as a sexual subjectivity: the figure of the *kinaidos,* for example, represents an instance of deviant morphology without subjectivity, whereas Boccaccio's Pietro represents an instance of deviant subjectivity without morphology. Thus, morphology and subjectivity, as I have been using those terms, describe two *different* logics according to which sexual acts can be connected to some more generalized feature of an individual's identity. In particular, I've argued that the ancient figure of the *kinaidos* qualifies as an instance of a sexual life-form or morphology and, therefore, that the property of *kinaidia* (or being a *kinaidos*) is a property of social beings, not merely of sexual acts. Nonetheless, what defines the *kinaidos* is not a unique or peculiar subjectivity but a shameless appetite for pleasure, which is common to all human beings, along with a deviant gender-style, which assimilates him to the cultural definition of woman. By contrast, the sodomitical character of Boccaccio's Pietro di Vinciolo does not express itself through a deviant morphology but through his sexual tastes, preferences, inclinations, or desires—that is, through a deviant subjectivity. Sodomy, in Boccaccio's world, like *kinaidia* in classical antiquity, is a property of social beings, not merely of sexual acts. The relation between the sodomitical act and the subject who performs it is constructed differently in the case of the sodomite from the way that acts and social identities are connected in the case of the *kinaidos.*

Neither the sexual morphology of the *kinaidos* nor the sexual subjectivity of the fourteenth-century Italian sodomite should be understood as a sexual identity, or a sexual orientation in the modern sense—much less as equivalent to the modern formation known as homosexuality. At the very least, popular notions of homosexual identity and homosexual orientation today tend to insist on the *conjunction* of sexual morphology and sexual subjectivity: they presume a convergence in the sexual actor of a deviant personal style with a deviant erotic desire.[45] In addition, what historically distinguishes "homosexuality" as a sexual classification is its unprecedented combination of at least three distinct and previously uncorrelated conceptual entities: (1) a psychiatric notion of a perverted or pathological *orientation,* derived from nineteenth-century medicine, which is an essentially psychological concept that applies to the inner life of the individual and does not necessarily entail same-sex sexual behavior or desire; (2) a psychoanalytic notion of same-sex *sexual object-choice* or desire, derived from Sigmund Freud and his coworkers, which is a category of erotic intentionality and does not necessarily imply a permanent psychosexual orientation, let alone a pathological or deviant one (since, according to Freud, most normal individuals make an unconscious homosexual object-choice at least at some point in their fantasy lives); and (3) a sociological notion of *sexually deviant behavior,* derived from nineteenth- and twentieth-century forensic inquiries into "social problems," which focuses on non-standard sexual practice and does not necessarily refer to erotic psychology or psychosexual orientation (since same-sex sexual behavior is widely distributed in the population, as Kinsey showed, and is not the exclusive property of those with a unique psychology or a homosexual sexual orientation).[46] Despite their several failures to meet the requirements of the modern definition of the homosexual, however, both the *kinaidos* and Boccaccio's Pietro, in their quite different and distinctive ways, challenge the orthodox pseudo-Foucauldian doctrine about the supposedly strict separation between sexual acts and sexual identities in European culture before the nineteenth century.

My argument, then, does not refute Foucault's claim about the different ways male same-sex eroticism was constructed by the discourse of "the ancient civil or canonical codes" and by the discourse of nineteenth-century sexology. Nor does it demolish the absolutely indispensable distinction between sexual acts and sexual identities that historians of homosexuality have extracted from Foucault's text (where the term "identity" nowhere occurs) and that, in any case, antedated it by many years.[47] Least of all does my argument undermine a rigorously historicizing approach to the study of the social and cultural constitution of sexual subjectivity and sexual identity. (Whatever I may be up to in this essay, a posthumous rapprochement with John Boswell is not it.) What my argument does do, I hope, is to encourage us to inquire into the construction of sexual identities before the emergence of sexual orientations and to do this *without* recurring necessarily to modern notions of "sexuality" or sexual orientation. To temper the overly schematic fashion whereby historicist histories of homosexuality have distinguished and sealed off from each other sexual acts and sexual identities is not, I hope, to contribute to an anti-historicist backlash or to imply some permanent, historically invariable relation between particular sexual acts and individual sexual identities. Perhaps we need to supplement our notion of sexual identity with a more refined concept of, say, partial identity, emergent identity, transient identity, semi-identity, incomplete identity, proto-identity, or sub-identity.[48] In any case, my intent is not to reinstall a notion of sexual identity as a historical category so much as to indicate *the multiplicity of possible historical connections between sex and identity,* a multiplicity whose existence has been obscured by the necessary but narrowly focused, totalizing critique of sexual identity as a unitary concept. We need to find ways of asking how different historical cultures fashioned different sorts of links between sexual acts, on the one

hand, and sexual tastes, styles, dispositions, characters, gender presenta-
tions, and forms of subjectivity, on the other.

It is a matter of considerable irony that Foucault's influential distinction between the discursive construction of the sodomite and the discursive
construction of the homosexual, which had originally been intended to
open up a domain of historical inquiry, has now become a major obstacle
blocking further research into the rudiments of sexual identity-formation
in pre-modern and early modem European societies. Foucault himself
would surely have been astonished. Not only was he much too good a
historian ever to have authorized the incautious and implausible claim
that no one had ever had a sexual subjectivity, a sexual morphology, or
a sexual identity of any kind before the nineteenth century (even if he
painstakingly demonstrated that the conditions necessary for having a
sexuality, a psychosexual orientation in the modern sense, did not in fact
obtain until then). His approach to what he called "the history of the
present" was also too searching, too experimental, and too open-ended
to tolerate converting a heuristic analytic distinction into an ill-founded
historical dogma, as his more forgetful epigones have not hesitated to do.

: : :

Of course, the chief thing about Foucault that his self-styled disciples forget is that he did not propound a theory of sexuality. That fact about
Foucault is the more easily forgotten as Foucault has become, especially in
the United States and Britain, the property of academic critical theorists—
the property of those, in other words, whose claim to the professional title
of "theorist" derives from the reflected status, authority, and "theoretical" credentials of the thinkers they study. As one of those thinkers whose
identity as a "theorist" is necessary to ground the secondary and derived
"theoretical" status of others, Foucault is required to have a theory. Theories, after all, are what "theorists" are supposed to have.

Now of course Foucault's *History of Sexuality,* volume 1, is theoretical, in the sense that it undertakes a far-reaching critical intervention in
the realm of theory. It is, more particularly, an effort to dislodge and to
thwart the effects of already-established theories—theories that attempt
to tell us the truth about sexuality, to produce true accounts of its nature,
to specify what sexuality really is, to inquire into sexuality as a positive
thing that has a truth that can be told, and to ground authoritative forms
of expertise in an objective knowledge of sexuality. Foucault's radical theoretical take on sexuality consists in approaching it from the perspective
of the history of discourses, as an element in a larger political-discursive

technology: he treats it accordingly not as a positive thing but as an instru-
mental effect, not as a physical or psychological reality but as a social and
political device; he is not trying to describe what sexuality is but to specify
what it does and how it works in discursive and institutional practice.
That approach to sexuality represents a theoretical intervention insofar
as it engages with already-existing theories of sexuality, but the nature
of the engagement remains purely tactical: it is part of a larger strategic
effort to effect a thoroughgoing evasion of theories of sexuality and to
devise various means of circumventing their claims to specify the truth of
sexuality—not by attempting to refute those claims directly and to install
a new truth in their place but by attempting to expose and to delegitimate
the strategies they employ to construct and to authorize their truth-claims
in the first place. It is this deliberate, ardent, and considered resistance
to "theory" that defines Foucault's own practice of theory, his distinctive
brand of (theoretical) critique.[49]

To undertake such a theoretical critique, to attempt to reorient our
understanding of sexuality by approaching the history of sexuality from
the perspective of the history of discourses, is obviously not to offer a new
theory of sexuality, much less to try to substitute such a theory for those
that already exist. Nor is it an attempt to claim, theoretically, that sexuality *is* discourse or that it is constituted discursively instead of naturally.
It is rather an effort to denaturalize, dematerialize, and derealize sexuality
so as to prevent it from serving as the positive grounding for a theory of
sexuality, to prevent it from answering to "the functional requirements
of a discourse that must produce its truth."[50] It is an attempt to destroy
the circuitry that connects sexuality, truth, and power. And thus it is an
effort to take sexuality away from the experts and make it available to us
as a possible source for a series of scholarly and political counterpractices.
The History of Sexuality, volume 1, in short, does not contain an original
theory of sexuality. If anything, its theoretical originality lies in its refusal
of existing theory and its consistent elaboration of a critical anti-theory.
It offers a model demonstration of how to dismantle theories of sexuality,
how to deprive them of their claims to legitimate authority. *The History
of Sexuality,* volume 1, is a difficult book to read chiefly because we read
it as conveying Foucault's formulation of his theory of sexuality. (There
is no easier way to baffle students than by asking them to explain what
Foucault's own definition of "sexuality" is: it's the worst sort of trick question.) As a theory of sexuality, however, *The History of Sexuality,* volume
1, is unreadable. That may in fact be its greatest virtue.

For our hankering after a correct theory of sexuality seems scarcely
diminished since Foucault's day, least of all among academic practitioners

of so-called queer theory.[51] By juxtaposing to this "theoretical" tendency in queer theory Foucault's own example, by contrasting the queer retheorizing of sexuality with Foucault's strategic undoing of sexual theory, I am not trying to lend aid and comfort to "the enemies of theory" (who would forget not just Foucault but "theory" itself), nor do I mean to contribute to the phobic totalization and homogenization of "theory"—as if there could possibly be any sense in treating theory as a unitary entity that could then be either praised or disparaged. To argue that *The History of Sexuality,* volume 1, contains not a theory but a critical anti-theory is not to argue that the book is "anti" theory, against theory, but rather to indicate that its theoretical enterprise, which is the derealization or desubstantialization of sexuality, militates strenuously against the construction or vindication of any theory of sexuality. Moreover, no inquiry into the deficiencies of contemporary work in lesbian and gay studies or the history of sexuality that pretends to be serious can content itself with mere carping at individual scholarly abuses of "theory" (the notion that scholars nowadays have all been corrupted by "theory" is about as plausible as the notion that lesbian and gay academics have seized control of the universities—and probably derives from the same source); rather, it must take up such institutional questions as how many professors with qualifications in "queer theory" are tenured at major universities and are actually guiding the work of graduate students intending and able to pursue scholarly careers in that field.

Nonetheless, I find the doctrinaire theoretical tendencies in "queer theory" and in academic "critical theory" to be strikingly at odds with the anti-dogmatic, critical, and experimental impulses that originally animated a good deal of the work we now consider part of the canon of "theory." Foucault stands out in this context as one of the few canonical theorists whose theoretical work seems calculated to resist theoretical totalization, premature theoretical closure, and thereby to resist the weirdest and most perverse instance of "the resistance to theory": namely, the sort of resistance to theory that expresses itself *through* the now-standard academic practice of so-called critical theory itself.[52] Foucault's refusal of a theory of sexuality resists the complacencies of the increasingly dogmatic and reactionary resistance to theory that misleadingly and all too often answers to the name of "theory." I believe it is our resistance to Foucault's resistance to this resistance to theory, our insistence on transforming Foucault's critical anti-theory into a theory of sexuality, that has led us to mistake his discursive analysis for a historical assertion—and that has licensed us, on that basis, to remake his strategic distinction between the sodomite and the homosexual into a conceptual distinction between sexual acts and sexual identities, into a bogus theoretical doctrine, and into a patently false set of historical premises. I also believe it is what has led us to convert his strategic appeal to bodies and pleasures as a means of resistance to the apparatus of sexuality into a theoretical specification of the irreducible elements of sexuality. And it is what has made Foucault's intellectual example increasingly and, quite properly, forgettable. If indeed it is as a theorist of sexuality that we remember Foucault, perhaps Baudrillard was right after all: the greatest service we can do to him, and to ourselves, is to forget him as quickly as possible.

Let me give the last word to Foucault, however. In an early essay on Gustave Flaubert, Foucault described an experience of the fantastic that he believed was new in the nineteenth century, "the discovery of a new imaginative space" in the archives of the library.

> This domain of phantasms is no longer the night, the sleep of reason, or the uncertain void that stands before desire, but, on the contrary, wakefulness, untiring attention, zealous erudition, and constant vigilance. Henceforth, the visionary experience arises from the black and white surface of printed signs, from the closed and dusty volume that opens with a flight of forgotten words; fantasies are carefully deployed in the hushed library, with its columns of books, with its titles aligned on shelves to form a tight enclosure, but within confines that also liberate impossible worlds. The imaginary now resides between the book and the lamp. The fantastic is no longer a property of the heart, nor is it found among the incongruities of nature; it evolves from the accuracy of knowledge, and its treasures lie dormant in documents.[53]

The history of sexuality, at its best, should serve as a reminder of the one thing that no one who has been touched by Foucault's writing is likely ever to forget: namely, that the space of imaginative fantasy that the nineteenth century discovered in the library is not yet exhausted and that it may still prove to be productive—both for academic scholarship and for our ongoing processes of personal and cultural self-transformation.

2 The First Homosexuality?

The history and vicissitudes of the term "lesbian," its gradual emergence as the name of a concept or category of erotic experience, dramatize both the challenges and the rewards of work in the history of sexuality. For "lesbian" is at once a very old word and a very new word. It dates back not only to ancient Greece but also to the pre-classical period of Greek civilization. And yet it belongs very much to the modern sciences of sexual orientation, to gay liberation and second-wave feminism, to the jargon of contemporary identity politics.

"Lesbianism" has often appeared to be a kind of afterthought, a supplement to "homosexuality" (which, like all gender-neutral terms, tends to refer more particularly to males than to females). And yet, some recent scholarship has suggested that the category of female same-sex love was constituted earlier than the modern category of homosexuality and may even have been its precursor. The difficulties presented to the historian of sexuality by the multiple temporalities of "lesbianism" are therefore exemplary: they pose basic questions about the ontology of the sexual, about the very nature and mode of being of "sexuality," about the historicity of the modern sexual subject. They also point to a number of methodological problems of considerable and wide-ranging interest: how to distinguish language from experience, categories of thought from forms of subjectivity, continuities from discontinuities in the historiography of sex and gender.[1] In short, any attempt to write the history of lesbianism is bound to raise a series of issues whose complexity and suggestiveness indicate how much we have yet to learn from the nascent project of the history of sexuality, and how broad an intellectual engagement will be necessary in order to learn it.

So just how old is "lesbian"? The word itself is originally the adjectival form of the Greek place-name Lesbos, which refers to a large island in the Aegean Sea six miles off the northwest coast of Asia Minor, probably settled by Aeolian Greeks in the tenth century B.C.[2] That island was the birthplace and home of Sappho, who composed lyric poems in Greek toward the end of the seventh century B.C. and the beginning of the sixth. Many of her poems express love and desire for women and girls. Sappho's work was greatly admired in the male literary culture of classical antiquity, and sufficient numbers of her poems survived by the third century B.C. to fill nine books, although they have come down to us (with one possible exception) only in fragments. Nonetheless, Sappho's poetry and her fame have proved sufficiently powerful to impart to the adjective "lesbian" its now-familiar sexual meaning. "Lesbian" is in that sense by far the most ancient term in our current lexicon of sexuality.

But "lesbian" is also very new. Consider the following scene in *Antic Hay,* a novel by Aldous Huxley published in 1923. Toward the end of the narrative, a young critic, escaping the abuse of one of his friends, whose art exhibition he has snidely reviewed, and avoiding another friend, whose wife he has unknowingly seduced, takes refuge in the home of a society lady, arriving just as she and another guest are embarked on the second course of a long and indolent lunch. The lady greets him rapturously, invites him to join her and her guest at table, and begs him to tell them "all about" his "Lesbian experiences." Which he proceeds to do, launching into an account of his adventures "among the Isles of Greece," as the novelist coyly puts it.[3] The obvious referent of this playful language is heterosexual dalliance. Huxley appears to be invoking the archaic association of the word "Lesbian" with female sexual abandon in order to refer to his character's amorous pursuit of various women. The usage is admittedly precious, by the standards of the day, even arcane. But it is not impossible. Less than eighty years ago, a cultivated social observer could portray a party at which the term "Lesbian" gets thrown about in civilized banter and applied not only to heterosexual love affairs but to the male participant in them without causing the slightest puzzlement or consternation. No such idiom exists today. Sometime between 1923 and the present, then, the word "lesbian" came to mean one thing and one thing only. Despite the antiquity of the term, the mutation of the word "lesbian" into a standard designation for "female homosexual" is a very recent development.

In fact, the transformation of "lesbian" into the proper name of a particular sexual orientation, into a conceptual shorthand for "female homosexual," took a very long time. Neither the island nor the people of Lesbos are associated with "lesbianism" in our sense of the term before the second century A.D. (A possible exception is Anacreon, frag. 358 Page, in the later sixth century B.C., but since scholars dispute both the text itself and its interpretation in terms of this very question—whether or not the mention of Lesbos in this poetic fragment should be understood as a reference to female homosexuality—Anacreon's verses cannot be adduced as evidence either for or against such an association.) In other words, it took nearly a thousand years for a definite link to be made between Lesbos and "lesbianism." The women of Lesbos acquired very early a reputation for sensuality, even licentiousness, but same-sex desire did not initially contribute to it. From at least the fifth century B.C., if not before, the sexual act associated with "lesbianism" in antiquity was fellatio. The Greek verb *lesbiazein,* which is attested for the first time in the classical period, meant "to give head."

The early history of the figure of Sappho herself also defeats modern expectations. It took six centuries for Sappho's same-sex erotic attachments to attract recorded comment. The celebration of the beauty of women by women was at least to some degree conventional in the Greek lyric tradition. In fact, the earliest attestation of female homoerotic desire in a piece of Greek literature occurs in the work of a male author—namely, the late-seventh-century Spartan poet Alcman, who wrote choral odes to be performed (apparently) by a cohort of unmarried girls. In the fragmentary remains of these poems, individual maidens extol the beauty and allure of those whom they especially admire among their leaders and age-mates, and they mention their favorites by name (frags. 1, 3). Far from being a transgression of the laws of desire or of male authority, such same-sex female erotic expressions were scripted for these girls by a male writer. Sappho, too, was greatly esteemed by male readers who, initially at least, do not seem to have regarded her love poetry as irregular or anomalous. At the same time, her expressions of passion for women were not taken to indicate a rejection of men. On the contrary, Sappho was represented in classical Athenian comedies of the fifth and fourth centuries B.C. as the lover of various men, sometimes even as a prostitute. A red-figure Attic hydria, attributed to the Polygnotus Group, from about 440 B.C. portrays Sappho in what may be a female homoerotic setting (Beazley, *Attic Red-*

Figure Vase Painters, 2d ed., 1060, no. 145). But—and this is a fact as curious as it is overlooked—no extant ancient writer of the classical period found the homoeroticism of Sappho's poetry sufficiently remarkable to mention it. So, either Sappho's early readers and auditors saw nothing homoerotic in her poems or they saw nothing remarkable in Sappho's homoeroticism. Neither of those alternatives seems very satisfactory to us, or even very plausible, but this interpretative difficulty ought to force us to consider a new set of questions about what the ancients counted as sex and sexuality, how they understood different erotic practices and identities, and how they distinguished different sexual subjects—questions to which I will return briefly at the conclusion of this essay. In any case, the first writers to touch on the question of Sappho's erotic deviance, so far as we know, were the Roman poets of the late first century B.C. and early first century A.D. (Horace, *Odes* 2.13.24–25; Ovid, *Heroides* 15.15–9, *Tristia* 2.365).[4]

From that period onward, Sappho and Lesbos could be associated at times with certain aspects of female same-sex love and desire, with certain female same-sex sexual practices, and with certain forms of female sex and gender deviance. In addition to being portrayed as an exemplary poetess, a passionate lover of men, and a whore, Sappho could now qualify as a "tribade." This term, an ancient Greek word borrowed by Roman writers and first attested in Latin in the first century A.D. (Phaedrus, 4.15 [16].1, Seneca the Elder, *Controversiae* 1.2.23), was originally understood in antiquity to signify a phallic woman, a hypermasculine or butch woman, and/or a woman who sought sexual pleasure by rubbing her genitals against those of other women. The identification of Sappho as a tribade therefore led to the word "Lesbian" being *applied* to acts or persons we might qualify as "lesbian" today, although neither the referents of that term nor its meaning were identical to those of the modern word "lesbian." Thus, in Lucian's second-century A.D. *Dialogues of the Courtesans,* a character remarks, "They say there are women like that in Lesbos, with faces like men, who are unwilling to let men do it to them, and instead consort with women, as though they themselves were men" (5.2).[5] As Alan Cameron points out, "The Lucian passage proves that the women of Lesbos enjoyed a reputation for same-sex inclination by the Roman period, but *that is not quite the same as using the word Lesbian to mean that.*"[6] In fact, what Lucian refers to would be more accurately described as "tribadism," not "lesbianism," insofar as the speaker fully conflates female same-sex desire with gender deviance or sexual role reversal, and the focus of the passage appears to be women who assume a masculine identity, appearance, and sexual style in their relations with other women, rather than women who desire women, or the women whom they desire.[7] It is not exactly the "homosexuality" of the "women like that in Lesbos" that attracts particular comment, then, but their striking departure from a whole set of social norms governing feminine comportment—norms that conflate gender identity, self-presentation, personal style, erotic inclination, and sexual practice.

By the early tenth century, a Byzantine bishop of Caesarea by the name of Arethas could include the plural noun *Lesbiai* ("Lesbians"), along with "tribades" and other Greek words for female sexual deviants, in a gloss on a text by the second-century Christian writer Clement of Alexandria. But that, once again, is not the same thing as defining *Lesbia* as "lesbian" or "female homosexual," and in any case Arethas himself did not have much understanding of the ancient terminology or its meaning.[8] Similar confusions persisted throughout the medieval period, in which a variety of terms for referring to female-female sex existed, though male sexual practices tended to generate the models for understanding female same-sex relations.

A vocabulary for describing sexual relations between women was gradually consolidated, first in France and then in England, from the sixteenth through the eighteenth centuries. But "lesbian" was not initially the term of choice to designate female same-sex eroticism. "Tribade" and its derivatives came to be the words most commonly used to refer to women who had sex with women, especially in medical or anatomical texts, though also in poetry, moral philosophy, and other learned discourses, from at least 1566 onward.[9] Although early modern authors first employed "tribade" when speaking about those ancient women who had already been labeled tribades in classical texts,[10] the word soon achieved a more contemporary application. But it remained closely tied to specific sexual practices or anatomical features, and it continued to signify a masculine woman, a phallic woman, or a woman who performed genital rubbing with other women. Even when, in the latter part of the sixteenth century, the French libertine writer Pierre de Bourdeille—better known as the Abbé de Brantôme—devoted part of a chapter of the work later called *Les Dames galantes* to a survey of women who had sex with women, and spoke in generic terms of "ces amours femenines [*sic*]," he still organized his discussion not around a category of female homoeroticism per se but around a more particularized topic (namely, did a married woman who made love with another woman thereby commit adultery and cuckold her husband?) and he remained focused on a specific number of traditional commonplaces pertaining to women who sexually desired other women (such as masculine identification, sex-role reversal, hermaphroditism, the use of dildos, and the impossibility of competing with men).[11]

Brantôme also makes substantive use of the adjective "lesbian," speaking startlingly on two occasions of "force telles dames et lesbiennes" and "ces lesbiennes."[12] But the context of his usage ties the word closely to its proper meaning as a place name. In the first passage, the reference to the "many such ladies and lesbians in divers places and regions" follows immediately upon a direct quotation from Lucian about "women like that in Lesbos" and so continues the geographical allusion; in the second passage, Brantôme observes that some of "these lesbians" do not give up sexual relations with men, "even Sappho who was their mistress": here, the speedy mention of Sappho, whose connection to Lesbos and its "lesbian Ladies" Brantôme had duly invoked at the outset of his discussion, serves to reassert the topographical force of the word's meaning. "Lesbian" in this period, then, remained largely a proper name, a place-name, a geographical designation—though, as Brantôme's usage indicates, a name strongly associated with sexual relations between women and often embedded in discourses pertaining to female same-sex erotic practices.[13] For example, a 1646 libertine poem in French by François de Maynard, preoccupied with female finger-fucking, is entitled, in discreet Latin, "Tribades seu Lesbia" ("Tribades, or Lesbia" ["Matters Lesbian"?]). In *The Toast,* a mock epic poem by William King published in 1732, the geographical reference shades into the sexual: "What if *Sappho* was so naught? / I'll deny, that thou art taught / How to pair the Female Doves, / How to practice *Lesbian* Loves." The expanded 1736 edition of the poem refers to "Tribades or Lesbians," thereby demonstrating that " 'Lesbian' could be used both as an adjective and as a noun" in English in the early eighteenth century,[14] though not that it had as yet fully become the name of a sexual rather than a topographical entity. By the end of the eighteenth century in France and England, however, "Sappho," "Sapphic," "Sapphist," "Lesbos," and "Lesbian" had become virtually interchangeable with "tribade" and its derivatives. But even though "Lesbian" could be applied to love between women in the early modern period, it is probably not until the latter part of the nineteenth century that the word acquired an autonomous meaning, becoming almost a technical term, a proper name for a particular kind of erotic practice or sexual orientation. And that meaning did not become dominant or exclusive until the latter part of the twentieth century, as we have seen. Even among lesbians, especially of the less-educated classes, the words "gay" and "queer" continued to be current until the onset of second-wave feminism and the triumph of lesbian-feminism in the late 1960s and early 1970s.

: : :

The historiographic issues raised by the multiple temporalities of "lesbian," as a word, a sexual classification, and a category of erotic experience, emerge with particular clarity from a close reading of Bernadette Brooten's 1996 book, *Love between Women,* a study of female homoeroticism in classical antiquity and the early Christian Church.[15] At certain moments in the book, Brooten emphasizes the gaps that separate ancient sexual discourses from our own. At other moments, she insists on the correspondences between ancient and modern sexual subjects, arguing for the existence in the ancient world of sexual orientations that we would recognize and define as lesbian or homosexual today. The task that Brooten sets herself of surveying all the evidence for how the ancients and early Christians understood erotic relations between women has the effect, perhaps unintended, of dramatizing the historical, theoretical, and interpretative problems that historians of sexuality, and of homosexuality in particular, confront constantly in their daily practice and that endow the history of (homo)sexuality with its considerable theoretical and historiographical interest.

Brooten writes from a lesbian-feminist perspective. Her book is a testimony of the extent to which contemporary political engagements can open up a series of scholarly questions and lead to a new understanding of even very distant historical phenomena. At the same time, the book's focus on what Brooten calls "ancient lesbians" (17) and its invocation of the lesbian category to describe the historical phenomena it studies provides a test of both the benefits and the limits of applying contemporary sexual categories to pre-modern human subjects. It obliges its readers, especially those of us who are classicists, historians of sexuality, queer theorists, or all three at once, to re-examine our ways of understanding the relations of continuity and discontinuity between ancient and modern societies, between pre-modern and modern sexual categories, and between male and female homosexualities. It thereby provokes a reconsideration of the some of the basic conceptual issues surrounding the very definition of the lesbian category as well as the practice of lesbian historiography and the history of (homo)sexuality more generally.

Such a reconsideration is long overdue, but there is nothing astonishing about the fact that we have had to wait so long for an impetus to undertake it. Ancient references to female homosexuality and homoeroticism are not especially numerous, but they are widely scattered. A great many of them occur in the sorts of texts that classicists rarely read, perhaps because they rarely possess the specialized technical competence necessary in order to interpret them. I am referring here to texts that belong to the corpus of obscure, largely neglected, technical, and now-defunct ancient disciplines, such as astrology, magic, dream analysis, physiognomy, and medicine. Many of these texts have not been edited for more than a century, and some have never been translated. The scholarship on them is arcane, of widely varying date and reliability, and, for the most part, not written in English. All of these factors have doubtless contributed to discouraging scholars from attempting to write a history of lesbianism in the ancient world, above and beyond the theoretical, methodological, and historiographic complexities involved in the task of writing the history of an erotic identity at once so old and so new.

It is all the more fortunate that Bernadette Brooten, in the course of a book-length effort to reinterpret the notoriously obscure passage in Paul's *Letter to the Romans* condemning same-sex sexual practices, has gone to the trouble of assembling, for the first time in the history of classical scholarship, nearly all the ancient Greek and Latin sources that bear on the topic of female homosexuality in classical antiquity.[16] Brooten supplements this material with a consideration of ancient Jewish sources and a brief survey of visual representations. She makes all this primary and secondary material available to English-speaking readers and situates it in its original social and discursive context so as to enable them to assess the evidence independently and to draw their own conclusions from it. Her book will be a necessary point of reference for all future investigations of the topic. At the same time, her methods and conclusions are debatable. What makes Brooten's treatment of the ancient material open to criticism is precisely the way she goes about grappling with the conundrum of the oldness or the newness of lesbianism as a sexual category and experience. I would like to see this conundrum resolved by means of a different strategy from the one Brooten employs, but I must acknowledge that any such effort will have to begin by an extended confrontation with Brooten's work. And so that is what I shall undertake in the remainder of this essay. Although I shall have a number of criticisms, often quite sharp, to make of Brooten's readings of the ancient texts, my aim in making them is to further the project of rethinking lesbian history that Brooten's own work has already so powerfully advanced.

: : :

Brooten emphasizes from the outset of her study that the sexual conventions and categories of ancient Greek and Roman civilization were very different from modern ones. She argues, more specifically, that the ancients tended to conceptualize sexual relations in terms of a hierarchy of so-called active and passive sexual roles; by comparison, the sameness or difference of the sexes of the individuals engaged in any particular sexual act was, in and of itself, of minor significance to them. Brooten puts this point as follows in the introduction to her book: "Roman-period writers presented as normative those sexual relations that represent a human social hierarchy. They saw every sexual pairing as including one active and one passive partner, regardless of gender, although culturally they correlated gender with these categories. . . . The most fundamental category for expressing this hierarchy was active/passive—a category even more fundamental than gender for these writers" (2). It was the comparative lack of salience of the relation of gender difference or sameness between the sexual partners that explains in part why the modern meaning of "lesbian" is hard to document in texts from Greek and Roman antiquity. The basic point could be articulated more precisely by saying that the ancients "evaluated sexual acts according to the degree to which such acts either violated or conformed to norms of conduct deemed appropriate to individual sexual actors by reason of their gender, age, and social status" and that those norms presupposed a strict correlation of superordinate and subordinate social status with "active" and "passive" sexual roles. The most salient erotic distinction made by the ancients rested not on a physical typology of anatomical sexes (male vs. female) or even on gender differences (man vs. woman) but on the social articulation of power (superordinate vs. subordinate social identity).[17] The result was a social/conceptual/erotic grid that aligned masculinity, activity, penetration, and dominance along one axis and femininity, passivity, being penetrated, and submission along another. Those two axes corresponded to, but could function independently of, gender differences.

Brooten's analysis of ancient sexual discourses returns to this point a number of times. For example, she observes that for the ancient astrologers "the fundamental division is not between males and females, nor between heterosexual and homosexual, but rather between active and passive" (126–27) and that for Ptolemy in particular "activeness and passiveness are more fundamental than biological maleness and femaleness" (128)—although she quite correctly points out that a passive male is regarded differently from an active female.

At the same time, Brooten tends to treat the ancients' distinctive preoccupation with the relations between sexual role and social status as an idiosyncratic cultural idiom within which the ancients were nonetheless quite able to express their attitudes to "lesbianism" and to "sexuality" more generally, as if these modern categories also prevailed in antiquity and were not made inapplicable by the ancients' habit of classifying erotic actors in terms of sexual role, social status, and gender identity. Again and again Brooten draws on her considerable expertise in decoding the cultural languages of ancient Mediterranean societies in order to translate the perceptions of Greek and Roman writers into the supposedly timeless terms that we currently use today in order to refer to different "kinds" of "sexuality." In effect, then, Brooten treats ancient sexual discourses as though they provide a transparent medium through which the learned interpreter can discern the outlines of the fundamental and universal realities of sexual life. For example, at the beginning of her book, Brooten says that "a strict distinction between active and passive sexual roles . . . shaped the way that people viewed female homoeroticism," as if "female homoeroticism" were a *thing*—a single, stable object, that can be viewed from different perspectives—rather than a social and discursive production in its own right, a culturally constituted category of both erotic arousal and social organization.

Implicit in Brooten's way of thinking and writing is the presumption that we, nowadays, are more or less in possession of the facts of life when it comes to sex. We "know" that there is such a thing as human sexuality; we "know" that sexual orientation is one of the basic categories of human experience. Brooten never explicitly argues that such presumptions are correct or that our current psychological or behavioral models of sexuality are in fact valid. She may actually not believe they are.[18] But her rhetoric has the effect of anchoring modern sexual categories in some transhistorical reality by implying that our understanding of sexuality was shared by the ancients. The opening sentences of her book, for example, insist that "people from various walks of life" in the ancient world "acknowledged that women could have *sexual contact* with women," "knew . . . about *sexual relations* between women," and had "a heightened awareness of *female homoeroticism*" (1; emphasis mine). Later, Brooten speaks of "the awareness of *sexual love* between women on the part of male authors" in antiquity (16; emphasis mine again). These four assertions are all, in their own way, indisputable, thanks in large part to Brooten's own research: numbers of ancient texts cited by Brooten bear out her claim that some women in the ancient Greco-Roman world had erotic and sexual relationships with one another and that numbers of male authors were aware of it. That is a crucially important, and long-overdue, scholarly achievement. Nonetheless, Brooten's fourfold description of what the ancients "knew," although couched in language that strives admirably to be neutral, descriptive, objective, and not culturally loaded, betrays in the unwitting equivalence it constructs between "sexual contact," "sexual relations," "homoeroticism," and "sexual love" the force of the pressure exerted on Brooten's thought by modern sexual concepts.

For "sexual contact" is a behavioral term, which evokes the sexological and sociological language of the Kinsey reports, whereas "sexual relations" is a euphemism for intercourse drawn from the lexicon of the various forensic disciplines, and "homoeroticism" is a coinage of nineteenth-century psychiatry. The amalgamation of behavioral, sexological, sociological, forensic, psychological, psychiatric, and erotic categories into a single unifying idea is a hallmark of the modern concept of sexuality.[19] That all these things are not in fact equivalent is something I learned on the very first day of the very first course in lesbian and gay studies that I ever taught, more than a dozen years ago now. One of the lesbian members of our group declared, in what was obviously intended to be a programmatic rebuke to the implicit assumptions on which the course seemed to be proceeding, "I am not interested in the history of women who *fucked* other women. I'm interested in the history of women who *loved* other women." To which another lesbian in the group mildly rejoined, "Actually, I couldn't care less about the history of women who loved other women, but what I'd really like to find out more about is the history of women who fucked other women." Those differences in stated interest and emphasis effectively point the researcher in two very different directions, toward two very different chronologies, literary traditions, social and political contexts, sets of archival material—in short, toward two very different histories of "lesbianism."[20] Brooten's way of formulating her project neatly elides all such distinctions: by organizing her material, implicitly at least, around the modern concept of homosexuality, she manages to impose a questionable unity and homogeneity on it, to redescribe the ancient phenomena in terms of the modern concept, and to insinuate that sexuality and sexual orientation are more or less objective phenomena, independent of human perception, rooted in some transhistorical reality.

Brooten here more or less explicitly follows in the tracks of the late John Boswell, recapitulating his realist approach to the history of sexuality, his emphasis on seeing through the screen of discourse to the reality of sexual contacts and desire, and his insistence on the objective facts of same-sex sexual attraction.[21] For Brooten, like Boswell, same-sex sexual attraction qualifies as a fact and, thus, lends factuality to homosexuality, which means that no historical falsification occurs when one redescribes the ancient phenomena in terms of the modern concept. The implication appears to be that the modern concept refers to an objective phenomenon that exists apart from us, outside of history and culture—namely, the erotic attraction and conjunction of female bodies. Brooten hastens to concede, like Boswell, that things have changed over time (though only to the extent that "ancient lesbians" did not necessarily think or live like "contemporary lesbians": "For example, I find no evidence of political organizations in antiquity created to promote lesbian rights," she remarks [17]), and she makes it very clear that she sees her task as analyzing "the specific gender constructions and social-sexual arrangements of the Roman and early Byzantine worlds" (18). Nonetheless, without denying that there have been discontinuities in the history of sexuality, she argues that "the historical discontinuities are . . . no greater than with such other terms as 'slavery,' 'marriage,' or 'family,' and yet we have no qualms about applying these terms to historical and cross-cultural phenomena" (18), despite the great variety of institutions to which such terms are applied.

Of course, some of us do have qualms about applying those terms indifferently across historical and cultural boundaries, even if we sometimes fail to be as rigorously historicist in our scholarly practices as we would like or as our historiographical principles might require.²² Here, for example, are some qualms that the historian Henry Abelove once expressed to me and that I invoked many years ago in a book of my own.²³ In response to Boswell's concession that homosexuality was different in the ancient world, but no more different than marriage and family and work, which historians continue to call by those names,²⁴ Abelove had pointed out that just because feudal peasants work with their hands and factory laborers work with their hands, it doesn't follow that feudal peasantry should be described as the form that proletarianism took before the rise of industrial capitalism, because such a description would efface the specificity of proletarianism, its social and definitional dependence on a particular, historical system of economic organization. And yet working with one's hands can certainly be taken to be an objective fact, and as such it would seem to ground the factuality of "proletarianism" in history, just as same-sex sexual attraction or contact can be taken to be an objective fact that would guarantee the transhistorical reality of "homosexuality." And if you really want to describe feudal peasantry as a medieval version of factory labor, well, you can, and the claim will even make a kind of sense: after all, both peasants and factory workers are low on the social and economic ladder; both constitute oppressed and exploited social classes whose labor produces surplus value that enriches the property owners to whom they sell their labor. And both work with their hands. To say that peasants are the proletarians of the feudal system, then, *is not exactly wrong*. It gets at something, something important. But such an approach won't take you very far if what you want to acquire is a historical understanding of the specific, and systematic, economic and social organization of feudalism and capitalism or an understanding of the differences between them. Nor will it yield a concept of "work" that is likely to be of much use as an all-purpose tool for historical analysis.

It is always tempting to highlight correspondences between distant historical periods and more recent ones, to describe the worlds we continually discover in terms of the world we have come to know, and to integrate unfamiliar objects into an existing knowledge of the already familiar. I sympathize with that approach, but I have also learned to be wary of it. On the first day of my first visit to Australia, a country where I was later to live for six years, I kept pointing out to my friend Susan, an American long since transplanted to Australia whom I had come to visit, all the features of the place that I thought I recognized: "Oh, that looks so English," I would say, or "that looks so Californian." To which Susan patiently replied, with a forbearance that I would later come to admire as subsequent visitors to Australia repeatedly tested my own by behaving exactly as I did then, "No, it looks *Australian*." And Susan was right—*not because I was wrong,* not because there were no points of resemblance between Australian architecture or landscape and its English or American analogues, but because, in my haste to bring my initial impressions into focus by assimilating individual elements of the Australian scene to what I already knew, I had overlooked the distinctive cultural system that combined those elements in peculiar ways and that enabled them to cohere according to a unique social and aesthetic logic. While eagerly drinking in all the Australian sights, what I had somehow failed to see was, quite simply, Australia itself. Those historians of sexuality who redescribe in modern conceptual terms the culturally specific phenomena they observe in the distant historical record behave, in effect, like tourists in the archives: they misrecognize the sexual features of the period they study as exotic versions of the already familiar.

: : :

The real threat posed to the history of sexuality by this understandable if overhasty tendency to collapse concrete, local human activities upward into some abstracted, generalized, homogenized, decontextualized, and transhistorical concept—of "work," for example, or "homosexuality"— can be dramatized most vividly by documenting the specific interpretative damage that results from it. For once historians succumb to the lure of the false universals that they themselves have devised or absorbed, the next thing they typically do is take one highly particularized *instance*—of "work" or "homosexuality," such as factory labor or cocksucking—and proceed to despecify it, generalize it, broaden it, and ultimately make it serve as a placeholder for the concept—of "work" or "homosexuality"—as a whole. The social or cultural values that were originally attached to the particular instance are then transposed to the general concept. The dubious outcome that is produced by such a procedure appears plainly enough from the embarrassing record of gaffes committed by otherwise reputable historians of sexual life in classical antiquity who have repeatedly translated what the ancient sources have to say about particular homosexual acts into erroneously totalizing statements of disapproval (or, less often, approval) of "homosexuality" per se.[25] Thus, behind modern scholarly claims about the Romans' supposed condemnation of "homosexuality," as Craig Williams has shown, lies a set of ancient texts that express a much more specific abhorrence of particular practices: for example, receptive anal intercourse on the part of males, or the ostentatious, public, adult male courtship of free, citizen youths.[26] It is interesting, though not altogether surprising, that the same strategy is never used to establish the ancient "disapproval" of "heterosexuality," although since many of the sexual acts that ancient moralists singled out for strong condemnation—from adultery to "luxury," from rape to cunnilingus—involve sexual contact between men and women, it would be no less logical to mine the ancient sources for evidence that ancient Greek and Roman civilization abhorred "heterosexuality." In the case of "heterosexuality," however, scholars seem more reluctant to identify the whole of the sexual phenomenon with highly specific instances of it. No matter how many "heterosexual" practices or desires are frowned on, after all, it remains impossible for modern scholars to imagine that any society could possibly have disapproved of "heterosexuality" itself.

So let's see what would happen if we were to extrapolate "particular, and discursively contingent, instances of disorderly male-female sexuality into the norm or truth of a monolithic system of 'heterosexuality,' "[27] as classical scholars continue to do with instances of same-sex sexual conduct and "homosexuality." A highly instructive exercise of this sort has in fact been undertaken by a scholar of early modern England, working with a documentary record that similarly contains both celebrations and condemnations of specific instances of both same-sex and different-sex erotic desire and confronting a tradition of scholarly commentary that similarly manifests a lopsided tendency to extract totalizing generalities from the available evidence about "homosexuality" but not "heterosexuality." Whence the following attempt to redress the balance:

In early modern England, heterosexuality was considered a shameful and dangerous practice; it was therefore socially and legally proscribed. Laws and local customs punished those people who engaged in premarital sex, had illegitimate children, or committed adultery. Insults like "whore," "cuckold," and "bastard" reveal the opprobrium attached to heterosexual acts. In sonnet sequences and tragedies, heterosexual relations are often represented as anguished, violent, or politically disastrous affairs, structured around male misogyny and possessiveness, female rebelliousness and duplicity, and an overall impasse of communication between the sexes. The prevalence of cuckoldry jokes in comedies suggests that husbands were unable to satisfy or control their sexually promiscuous wives. Indeed, a variety of discourses held that women were problematic sexual partners for men, and that men were compromised, diminished, or endangered by their passion for women. In the aggregate, these sources indicate that heterosexual relations were highly stigmatized, often led to deviant behavior (including "unnatural," nonprocreative, and nonmarital sexual acts, destructive jealousy, and even murder), and hence had to be carefully monitored and circumscribed.[28]

This account is, in its own way, scrupulously accurate and exact. It reproduces, with the very minor shift of register from homosexual to heterosexual, the procedures of much current work on same-sex erotic practices and identities in classical antiquity. As such, it dramatizes vividly the consequences of an approach to the history of sexuality that plays down discontinuities between pre-modern and modern sexual formations and that insists on salvaging from the corrosive effects of historical critique such allegedly transhistorical and transcultural categories of social life as "slavery," "marriage," "the family," "work," "homosexuality," "heterosexuality," and "sexuality."

As this example implies, the theoretical and methodological issues confronting the historian of sexuality cannot be neatly captured by the problematics of reference: they cannot be innocently reformulated in terms of the relation between words and things. It is not simply a matter of determining whether we can apply our word or concept of (homo/hetero)sexuality to the ancients—whether we can discover in the historical record of classical antiquity evidence of behaviors or psychologies that will fit, without too much forcing, the concepts and categories we are accustomed to using nowadays. Nor is it a matter of documenting whether the ancients were able to express within the terms provided by their own conceptual schemes an experience of something approximating to our notions of (homo/hetero)sexuality. As my story about visiting Australia illustrates, and as Henry Abelove's cautionary lesson about the historical category of "working with one's hands" dramatizes, *just because it is possible to construct a non-falsifiable relation of identity or resemblance between two distinct cultural forms does not necessarily mean that it is heuristically or cognitively advantageous to do so.* We should be wary of the seductive objectivism of any method that consists in stripping cultural phenomena of their cultural specificity and then imputing factuality and objectivity to whatever stripped-down transcultural category or concept may result from that strategically despecified redescription. The real question confronting the historian of sexuality is how to recover the terms in which the erotic experiences of individuals belonging to past societies were actually constituted, how to measure and assess the differences between those terms and the ones we currently employ, and how to deal with the conceptual, methodological, political, and emotional consequences of the conclusions we draw from the evidence—the consequences for ourselves, for others, and for the history of sexuality that we hope to create (and, by creating, to be changed by).[29] Ultimately, the hardest issue we face as scholars and activists is how to make a livable world for ourselves out of the tension between identity and identification that structures both our relations with the objects of our historical study and the discursive and institutional practices by which we engage those objects.

That being the case, the last thing I would object to is Brooten's decision to frame her inquiry into the history of sexuality around lesbianism as a concept and a category. In fact, that is precisely what gives her book its compelling interest. Nor is there anything problematic about Brooten's claim to have contributed to lesbian history; indeed, her book is a major event in the growth and consolidation of that burgeoning field. It is surely both inevitable and admirable that an inquiry into the history of the construction of female same-sex love and desire should frame itself in terms of contemporary preoccupations and should address itself to the discursive and political situation from which it emerges. All the recent classical scholarship on the history of male homosexuality (including my own) is entirely framed—some of it quite explicitly, some of it less so—by its engagement with contemporary sexual ideology.

Brooten's work demonstrates the great promise—often denied by traditional classical scholarship and the objectivist hermeneutic theory of which it is both an inheritor and a transmitter—of a situated knowledge, a perspective on the ancient world that emerges from a specific cultural and political location rather than from (supposedly) nowhere at all. At the same time, her work also makes it imperative to draw a distinction that is crucial for the historiography of homosexuality as well as for any historical research that is powered by the force of identification, by the researcher's sense of personal or political engagement with the object of study. And that is the distinction (which, I am well aware, it would be child's play to deconstruct, but perhaps that is not the most interesting thing to do with it) between the present-day concerns which frame all contemporary historical analysis and the historical material framed by them. I believe I can dramatize the usefulness of this distinction by showing that Brooten's work is vulnerable not because it is framed by a modern conception of lesbianism but because that conception tends to break through the frame, to permeate the interior space of the analysis, and to determine the treatment of individual details in it. In order to illustrate this claim, I will need to examine closely a number of Brooten's arguments about individual discourses, authors, and texts.

: : :

I begin with the following example. Brooten contends that "astrologers in the Roman world knew of what we might call *sexual orientation*" (140; emphasis mine). What is the evidence for this already defensively qualified and tentative claim? Well, Ptolemy and Firmicus Maternus, among others, identify certain configurations of stars which cause women who are conceived or born under them to become "tribades" or "viragos," words that generally (although not always) refer to masculine, phallic women who desire and sexually penetrate other women and even boys (e.g., Seneca, *Epistle* 95.21; Martial, 1.90, 7.67, 7.70). Now that fantasized image of gender inversion, that phobic male construction of a hypermasculine woman, does not exactly correspond to any "sexual orientation" I know—nor does it correspond to Brooten's notion of lesbianism, as she makes perfectly clear (7)—but never mind all that for the moment. Brooten concludes that "the stars [according to these ancient astrologers] determined a woman's erotic inclinations for the duration of her life" (140) and, hence, that there was "a category of persons viewed in antiquity as having a long-term or even lifelong homoerotic orientation" (8–9). Of course, the astrologers' sexual system was rather more complicated, as Brooten hastens to point out: "They saw a plethora of orientations" (3), not just two or three. "Ptolemy, for example, distinguished between active and passive orientations, and he also took account of such factors as age, wealth, and whether the person to whom one is attracted is a foreigner" (140; also, 242).

As a persistent if promiscuous expatriate myself, I am hardly in a position to object to the notion of a sexual orientation defined by the love of foreigners. Still, from the perspective of modern sexual categories, such a notion seems bizarre. And the more Brooten explicates it, the more curious Ptolemy's sexual system becomes. Its startling proliferation of "sexual orientations," and its weird focus on tribades to the exclusion of their female or male partners, which Brooten bravely acknowledges (128: "The question of the *tribas*'s partner remains open; Ptolemy devotes no attention to her"), awaken no doubts in Brooten and certainly do not deter her from sticking to her basic conclusion, which is that the ancients—contrary to what Michel Foucault, Arnold Davidson, John J. Winkler, Craig Williams, and I, among many others, have argued—had a concept of sexual orientation and of homosexuality that lesbians and gay men today might recognize as our own.[30]

All this is cause enough for some disquiet on the part of a historian of sexuality. But the problems with Brooten's attempt to translate the ancient astrological categories into modern sexological ones do not end here. For the astral configurations that, according to Firmicus Maternus and others, produced tribades also produced, with only slight astrological variations, female prostitutes—an unexpected contiguity in the ancient sexual spectrum whose logic Brooten spends some time puzzling over (140–41), although the association is a very common one in antiquity. What Brooten does not notice, though, is that, whatever sort of identity is implied by the terms "tribade" and "virago," a *meretrix* or "prostitute" is not the name of a lifelong erotic orientation. Rather, it describes a particular and particularly disgraceful kind of social actor, a deviant from the norms of female social and sexual propriety, a recognizable figure on the fringes of ancient Mediterranean societies. In that sense, *meretrix* may well have designated "a category of persons," as Brooten says. But such a category would not be a category of *erotic subjectivity* of the sort that would *orient* a person's *sexual desires* for the duration of her life, which is what "a lifelong erotic orientation" implies. On the contrary, to invoke the astral signs under which certain women were conceived or born in order to explain why they become prostitutes in later life is to account for the fact that some women turn out to disgrace themselves and their families, not to impute to these women a peculiar sort of sexual interiority, a pathological condition, or distinctive configuration of sexual desire. No doubt, such women, in the eyes of the male astrologers, were bad women and had a whorish disposition. In that sense, they might have been seen as having a sexual identity. But what the term *meretrix* registers is less a subjectivity than a career choice.[31]

The astrologers are accounting for the origin of certain social types. Prostitutes, like tribades, are recognizable and disgraceful exemplars of female sexual impropriety. To trace their origins to the influence of the stars is not to ascribe to such women an innate, fixed, lifelong sexual or erotic orientation—except insofar as social disgrace typically implies some congenital moral depravity. At the very least, it makes no more sense to see in the astrological account of tribades evidence for the ancient notion of a lifelong erotic orientation than it does to see evidence for it in the astrological account of prostitutes, and we would not be likely to infer from reading the astrological texts that the principal meaning of *meretrix* had to do with what Brooten, speaking of the astrological construction of tribades, calls "a woman's erotic inclinations" (140). So in my view the ancient evidence does not support the thesis that Brooten bases on it— namely, that "astrologers in the Roman world knew of what we might call sexual orientation."

My view has lately received some unexpected (and perhaps unintended) support from recent scholarship on prostitution in the Middle Ages, especially the evolving work of Ruth Mazo Karras on medieval *meretrices*. [32] In medieval Europe, according to Karras, to be a prostitute was not merely to engage in an activity but to be a recognizable "type of person." [33] Although Karras goes further, and claims (misleadingly, in my view) that medieval prostitutes were defined by their "sexuality," [34] she does not of course mean that prostitutes were seen as being distinguished from decent women by a deep, inner orientation of their erotic desires. Rather, she argues that a *meretrix* was a woman with a particular sort of sinful, sexually transgressive character and that "prostitute" was therefore an identity category. As Carla Freccero, in the course of a subtle and helpful discussion of Karras's most recent study, points out,

> Karras marshals considerable legal and religious or moral evidence to demonstrate that *meretrices* in the Middle Ages were constituted as an identity by their characterization as "lustful" women, an identitarian category unlike the modern occupational category accorded to the prostitute. "To summarize, medieval people were aware that *meretrices* commonly engaged in sex for money, but this did not identify or define them. Although canonists recognized that *meretrices* operated commercially, they did not consider the acceptance of money to make them *meretrices;* rather, it was the public nature of their sexual activity, the fact that they did not refuse any partner, or the number of partners they had that placed them in that category." Later in her discussion, she notes

that rather than "prostitute," the modern term "whore" might be a more useful translation of *meretrix*, which ostensibly characterizes a certain type of woman rather than a woman who engages in particular activities.[35]

In other words, the label *meretrix* may well have tagged the person to whom that label was attached with something like a social identity, or even a sexual identity, and it certainly branded her as a specific type of person. Karras even goes so far to say—at the risk of engaging in what I would consider tendentious cultural and historical despecification—that a *meretrix* was "permanently marked" by her "essential sinfulness" and in that sense needed to change her "orientation" in order to shed her "identity." Still, even on this account, to be a whore is not to reveal the lifelong configuration of one's erotic desires but to display a sexually depraved character attached to a disreputable social identity. "Whore" is thus a category of persons but not the name of a psychosexual orientation of erotic desire. That medieval understanding of *meretrix* would make the word even more closely comparable to "tribade" or "virago," as I understand the functioning of those terms in the ancient astrological discourses.

The theoretical issues underlying these questions of historical interpretation have been very well articulated by the lesbian literary historian Valerie Traub, in her own review of Brooten. Observing that Brooten conflates "erotic orientation" with "category of person," Traub doubts that the two should be treated as synonymous. Although as an early modernist she is not able to document or confirm her doubts by means of an independent analysis of the ancient sources, she registers what turns out to be a very canny suspicion, to the effect "that the existence of certain nouns that indicate a 'category of persons' does not indicate necessarily 'a belief in long-term or even lifelong homoerotic orientation' " (quoting Brooten, p. 9). Traub goes on to wonder "whether the presence of nouns in the lexicon is adequate to mark such women [*tribades* and *frictrices*] as possessing a stable or self-evident erotic orientation."[36] It is precisely my argument here that the astrologers' usage of both *tribades* and *meretrices* indicates that they conceived the personages designated by those terms as social types but not as the possessors of a lifelong erotic orientation. My argument thus bears out Traub's prescient doubts about the non-coincidence of a category of person (or, as I would prefer, a category of social actor) with a category of erotic orientation. Pre-modern societies may well have had a number of categories of social actor to which sexual characteristics were attached without those categories necessarily approximating to sexual orientations—in the sense of particular configurations of erotic desire—let alone to modern homo- and heterosexual ones. Not every *identity* expresses an *orientation*.

: : :

I turn now to Brooten's account of Aristophanes' famous speech in Plato's *Symposium,* where I find a similarly tendentious (mis)reading of the ancient source. Aristophanes, it will be remembered, defines *erôs* as "the desire and pursuit of the whole" and he offers a myth to support his definition. The human race, according to the myth, was once composed of two-faced, eight-limbed creatures who came in three sexes: male, female, and androgyne. Human beings as we know them were created when Zeus cut our ancestors in two. Each of us is descended from the half of an original whole, and erotic desire is the longing to restore an earlier state of wholeness through union with another individual. Every person we desire is in fact a symbolic substitute for an originary object once loved and subsequently lost in an archaic trauma, and our sexual preferences are determined by the sex of the missing half of our amputated ancestor. Aristophanes mentions a number of contemporary social types whose odd predilections and flagrant behaviors are explained by reference to their genetic origin. Thus, males whose ancestors were double males are eager for adult male lovers when they are boys and become lovers of boys in turn when they become men—and it is they who go into politics: this is the standard Aristophanic joke about the leaders of Athens having all been buggered in their youth. The portion of Plato's text that deals with females whose ancestors were double females is the only Greek text from the classical period that explicitly and unambiguously testifies to the existence of erotic desire among contemporary Greek women (though Plato at least alludes to the possibility again in the *Laws* [636C]); as such, its testimony is unique and precious.[37] But what does Plato's Aristophanes actually say?

According to Brooten, "Aristophanes . . . speaks of *hetairistriai,* women who are attracted to women, as having their origin in primeval beings consisting of two women joined together" (41); when she comes to discuss the use of the same word by the Greek satirist Lucian, some five hundred years later, she writes that "Lucian also presupposes that his readers know the meaning of *hetairistria*. . . . In fact, Lucian's dialogue assumes a familiarity with the phenomenon of sexual love between women" (53). Now since what Lucian's characters relate is the story of the seduction of one Leaena, your average girl, by a wealthy, shaven-headed, hypermasculine woman named Megilla, who claims to be "all man" (as Brooten, 52, notes), what Lucian's readers would seem to be familiar with is nothing so blandly non-specific as "the phenomenon of sexual love between women" but, rather, the stereotype of gender inversion, of sexual role reversal—the phenomenon of "tribadism," that is, not homoeroticism as such—which is the only sort of female same-sex sexual behavior that regularly evokes skeptical or disapproving comment from the ancient pagans. In fact, Arethas, the early tenth-century bishop of Caesarea mentioned earlier, glossed *hetairistria* in this passage of Lucian as "tribade," and in a note on yet another late antique text, the pseudo-Lucianic *Erôtes,* he repeated the conflation of *hetairistria* with "tribade" (although his testimony provides little evidence for the original meanings of these words).[38] In this context, Brooten's assertion that ancient readers were familiar with sexual love between women *in a categorical sense* depends on the exact meaning of *hetairistria* in Plato and Lucian.[39]

Unfortunately for Brooten, no one knows exactly what *hetairistria* means. Its etymology points in two directions, companionship and prostitution—the best we can do to convey a sense of what the word implies is to invoke some rough etymological approximations, such as "companion-izer" (from *hetairos,* "companion") and "courtesanizer" (from *hetaira,* "courtesan")—but its actual meaning is anybody's guess. For the word occurs once and only once in all of extant Greek literature before Lucian, and that one occurrence is in the tantalizing passage from Plato's *Symposium* under discussion. The word evidently refers to *some* social type who represented a case of female same-sex sexual attraction—thus far, Brooten's interpretation of its meaning is indisputable—but the larger context in Aristophanes' speech prohibits any secure inferences as to its precise meaning.

For when Aristophanes mentions the men and women descended from original androgynes, he says that the majority of *moikhoi* and *moikheutriai* come from this race (191D—E). Now, if the meanings of those words had been as utterly lost as the meaning of *hetairistria,* and if we felt justified—as Brooten does—in construing all these words to be categorical designations for forms of erotic attraction defined by sexual object-choice, then we would certainly and confidently take *moikhoi* and *moikheutriai* to signify "male heterosexuals" and "female heterosexuals," or, at least, to borrow Brooten's cautious periphrases, "men who are attracted to women" and "women who are attracted to men." And we would believe that, whatever the words actually meant, our interpretation had to be correct, at least in a general sense. As it happens, however, we do know what those words meant, and it was something altogether different and quite specific. A *moikhos* is a male who has consenting but unauthorized sex with a female under the guardianship of an Athenian citizen ("adulterer" is the standard if misleading translation; "seducer" better captures some of the other dimensions of the word's meaning); a *moikheutria* is the woman he seduces or who seduces him. Both represent instances of "attraction" between women and men, to be sure. But no student of classical Greek would ever think of translating *moikhos* as "heterosexual."

Aristophanes, once again, is making a joke about certain extreme social types who owe their sexual dispositions and their disreputable behavior to the passionate erotic longings they have inherited from their distant ancestors—much as the astrologers traced the origin of certain disreputable types of people to the influence of the stars. Presumably, the reference to *hetairistriai* makes a similar sort of joke, but it is now lost on us. And whatever the point of the joke was, taking *hetairistriai* to mean "women who are attracted to women," or even "lesbians," doesn't produce a terribly witty punchline. The most attractive and ingenious solution to the conundrum has been proposed by T. Corey Brennan, who notes in a review of Brooten's book that, according to the intriguing testimony of the ancient grammarian Moeris (s.v. "hetairistria"), the word "tribade" was avoided in the Attic dialect. The word *hetairistria* was the Attic term, for which the (Koine) Greek language in general employed "tribade."[40] Similarly, as Alan Cameron helpfully points out, in his own critique of Brooten, Timaeus's lexicon to Plato glosses *hetairistriai* as "the so-called tribades."[41] This testimony clearly implies that Attic writers, such as Plato, would have used the term *hetairistria* instead of "tribade." If *hetairistria* was in fact the Attic word used to refer to the same thing that was referred to elsewhere in the Greek world by "tribade," the point of the otherwise baffling joke about *hetairistriai* in the speech of Plato's Aristophanes would be evident: just as the shameless sexual behavior of the rulers of Athens points to their all-male ancestry, and just as seducers and seductresses owe their uncontrollable desires and disgraceful conduct to their genetic make-up, so their descent from a powerful double-female accounts for the nature of those aggressive, commanding women who can make a normal girl forget herself in their arms. Such a hypothesis about the meaning of the word *hetairistria* would also explain why the Atticizing writer Lucian chose it to describe Leaena's hypermasculine lover.

Of course, it's also possible that Moeris's conclusion about the avoidance of "tribade" in Attic merely reflects a conjecture on his part about the meaning of *hetairistria,* based on nothing more than the suggestive textual evidence under discussion here, and it's similarly possible that Lucian didn't understand the point of Aristophanes's joke any better than we do and simply wanted to show off his erudition by putting a five-hundred-year-old word from a classic text into the mouth of contemporary reprobate for humorous effect in a plausible approximation of its original meaning. No doubt it was the very enigmatic and mysterious quality of the term *hetairistria* that grabbed his attention, just as it still grabs ours. Even the Alexandrian lexicographer Hesychius's definition of *dihetairistriai* merely echoes the language of Plato's Aristophanes, plainly revealing that Hesychius, far from possessing independent knowledge of the word's meaning, relied exclusively for his understanding on the Platonic text. Still, even a modest effort to suspend our modern sexual categories when reading the ancient texts opens up their meanings to the possibility of interesting and unforeseen interpretations and makes of the history of sexuality something rather more startling and adventurous than is suggested by the version of *hetairistriai* that emerges from Brooten's reading of Plato. That alone, it seems to me, illustrates the heuristic value of a historicist reading practice.

∴ ∴ ∴

The more conventional advantages of a historicizing approach to the study of the ancient sexual vocabulary, such as scholarly precision and historical accuracy, appear plainly enough in the light of Brooten's tendentious (mis)construal of other ancient terms. For example, she says that "we can define a *kinaidos/cinaedus* as a male who passively receives a male phallus [*sic*] into his body" (24). But in fact we cannot define the term in that way without obliterating the entire basis for the ancient distinction between honorable and dishonorable conduct on the part of a subordinate male partner. Not only is Brooten's definition inaccurate (a victim of male sexual assault would not normally have been described as a *cinaedus*), but it would have been deeply shocking and offensive to the ancients, especially to the classical Greeks (even though they did place great significance on a male's maintenance of his bodily integrity, his physical impenetrability, the question of whether or not he received "a male"—or indeed a female [?]—"phallus into his body").[42] To be sure, it was always at least potentially shaming for a Greek male of any age to be sexually penetrated by anyone. Nonetheless, and perhaps for that very reason, the Greeks made a big deal of distinguishing, in the case of men's male love-objects, between a willing but respectable and virile boy and his debased, sluttish, effeminate opposite.[43]

To characterize a boy who allowed his lover to penetrate him as a *kinaidos* would have indicated that such a boy "submitted" to his lover for the sake of pleasure, that he had pathic desires and enjoyed being fucked— for that is what the insulting word *kinaidos* implied. It was in order to avoid that very implication that the ancients sharply differentiated in the case of males between the mere *fact* of being penetrated and the *desire* to be penetrated. As K. J. Dover and Michel Foucault pointed out long ago, the protocols governing paederasty, especially in classical Athens, were elaborately crafted in such a way as to protect boys from any suggestion that they were motivated in their sexual relations with adult men by sexual desire or sexual pleasure, let alone that they took any pleasure in being sexually penetrated. A boy might well choose to "gratify" (*kharizesthai*), as the Greeks delicately and euphemistically put it, the desire of his older lovers for a variety of motives—ranging from esteem, gratitude, and love (at the respectable end of the scale) to gold digging (at the other end)—so long as he did not act for the sake of sexual pleasure. In this fashion a boy upheld his honor, displayed his sense of decency, demonstrated his masculinity, and helped to preserve his reputation.

A *cinaedus,* by contrast, was a gender-deviant male, an effeminate and lascivious man possessed of a supposedly feminine love of being sexually penetrated or dominated. This was the most disgraceful, the most stigmatized identity a free male could acquire, and it carried with it a number of devastating social disqualifications.[44] As Craig Williams explains, "A *cinaedus* is a man who fails to live up to traditional standards of masculine comportment. . . . Indeed, the word's etymology suggests no direct connection to any sexual practice. Rather, borrowed from Greek *kinaidos* (which may itself have been a borrowing from a language of Asia Minor), it primarily signifies an effeminate dancer who entertained his audiences with a *tympanum* or tambourine in his hand, and adopted a lascivious style, often suggestively wiggling his buttocks in such a way as to suggest anal intercourse." And Williams adds, "The primary meaning of *cinaedus* never died out; the term never became a dead metaphor."[45] Brooten seems to have imported her understanding of the word directly from cultural feminist critiques of "intercourse" that foreground the politics of giving and/or receiving the phallus and that treat homophobia as a by-product of sexism; for once, she seems oblivious to two decades of classical scholarship and social history. Her definition of paederasty as "the male sexual use of children" (56), which conflates it with paedophilia, is equally misleading, tendentious, and inaccurate, and it gratuitously supports the vicious sexual stereotyping of gay male eroticism that has been one of the uglier by-products of historical tensions and misunderstandings between lesbian-feminists and gay men.[46]

Among the contributions that Brooten claims her book makes to the history of sexuality is its establishment of the fact "that nineteenth-century medical writers were not the first to classify homoerotic behavior as dis-

eased" (3). If, on the one hand, Brooten includes within her category of
"homoerotic behavior" *any and all* sexual acts that transpire among two
or more persons of the same sex, as she clearly does, and if she means
that *some* of those acts were classified by the ancients as diseased, then
this contribution is hardly news: it has long been known that at least
some homoerotic behavior—that is, some quite specific same-sex sexual
acts—incurred the disapproval of the ancients and that sometimes the ancients attributed the propensity to commit such stigmatized sexual acts to
a disease-like condition (see, e.g., the much-remarked passage in Aristotle's *Nicomachean Ethics,* 7.5.3–4 [1148b26–35]).[47] Indeed, a number of
Brooten's claims to originality are inflated.[48] If, on the other hand, Brooten
means that ancient medical writers occasionally classified as diseased *all
homoerotic behavior as such,* as she also does, her claim is highly misleading. Here, once again, we see how interpretative problems are produced
by the historian's practice of taking quite specific same-sex sexual acts or
relations and generalizing them in such a way that they come to stand in
for the totalizing, undifferentiated category of "homoerotic behavior" as
a whole. Let us have a closer look at the hermeneutic procedure by which
Brooten arrives at this questionable result.

First of all, Brooten tends to neglect the historical specificities that distinguish ancient medical discourses and the attitudes to sexual behavior
manifested in them. For example, a study of the applications of the word
"disease" (Latin *morbus*) by Roman writers reveals that it did not imply
the same kind of disqualification that a modern diagnosis of pathology
does. Instead, it could be used to refer generally to the character traits responsible for an individual's immoral or disreputable habits—to depravity, in other words, not necessarily to a morbid or unhealthy condition.
As Craig Williams shows, "A predilection for various kinds of excessive
or disgraceful behavior was capable of being called a disease" by the Romans and therefore "*cinaedi* were not said to be *morbosi* in the way that
twentieth-century homosexuals have been pitied or scorned as 'sick.' "[49]
Medicalizing language, in other words, does not operate in the two cultures in the same way, nor does it mean quite the same thing. The point is
an important one: the ancient usage is disapproving, but it is not wholly
pathologizing; indeed, it could hardly be, in the absence of modern technical understandings of the "normal" and the "pathological."

Next, in her analysis of one particularly revealing medical text—a
chapter of an obscure treatise *On Chronic Diseases* by Caelius Aurelianus,
a fifth-century A.D. translator of the Greek physician Soranus—Brooten
quite explicitly refuses to distinguish between the author's disapproval of

certain stigmatized homoerotic behaviors and all "homoerotic behavior" as such: she insists on treating his comments on some homoerotic behavior as if they referred to all homoerotic behavior. She begins by claiming categorically that "same-sex desire and behavior did fall within the realm of medical theory" in antiquity (144), and she criticizes me in particular for maintaining in *One Hundred Years of Homosexuality* that Caelius Aurelianus is "unconcerned about same-sex love per se" (162).[50] Yet she admits that Caelius is interested "only in sexually passive men (and not in the active male partners in anal intercourse)" and that he presumes "penetrating males to be healthy" (148). In short, Caelius implies that "while adult men's desire for boys may be seen as healthy, boys' passive sexual behavior is not" (162). But if that is indeed the position that Caelius takes, if he does in fact apply different standards of judgment to different same-sex sexual acts, considering some of them to be healthy and others not, what else does that indicate, if not precisely that, in the case of males at least, Caelius is "unconcerned about same-sex love per se"?

Brooten goes on to say that Caelius "explicitly defines the passivity of boys as diseased" (162). But of course it is not the fact of a boy's sexual penetration by a man that Caelius regards as a symptom of a mental or moral disease but rather a boy's desire (*passio*) to be penetrated (*On Chronic Diseases* 4.9.137), a desire that is by no means characteristic of all boys who are sexually penetrated by men. Moreover, it is only the boy's temporary lack of sufficient virility to play an "active" sexual role that, when viewed by Caelius according to the standards of adult manhood, is problematic, because this transient lack of virility, entirely normal and natural in a boy, will, if not remedied by the onset of maturity, become incapacitating in an adult male and will afflict him with *mollitia,* the unnatural, inverted condition of "softness" or effeminacy. Brooten's conclusion— that "according to the system of *On Chronic Diseases,* there exists no same-sex encounter in which both partners are disease-free" (162)—is not only wrong in the case of men and boys (since both "active" men and boys who don't desire to be penetrated are in fact disease-free, according to Caelius) but is beside the point.[51] After all, the ancients did not consider both partners in a sexual encounter to share or participate in the same "sexuality"; rather, they regarded sex as an intrinsically non-relational act, a miniature drama of polarization in which the participants expressed and acted out the relevant hierarchical distinctions between them in social status and sexual role.[52]

When it comes to Caelius's treatment of tribades, moreover, Brooten notes, as I do, that Caelius "emphasizes their bisexuality over their same-sex preference" (151n), and she agrees with me that "the text is concerned with reversing proper sex roles or with alternating between behaviors and characteristics proper to women and to men respectively" (161–62). She objects to my reading of the text on the grounds that Caelius sees no way "for women to have sexual contact with other women other than to take on male sex roles or to alternate between characteristics and practices proper to women and those proper to men," which means that, on Brooten's reading, Caelius ends up condemning *all* forms of homoeroticism *in the case of women*, if not in the case of men. A lesbian-oriented interpretation of Caelius, then—one that treats his account of female same-sex relations as central, primary, and defining, instead of treating it as a mere afterthought, a supplement to his account of men and boys—has the potential to disclose dimensions of his text that a gay male reading may overlook, according to Brooten (that is a point with which I would, in principle at least, register strong agreement). But, in the present instance, even this modified objection to my reading of Caelius—namely, that Caelius does indeed pathologize all same-sex love in the case of women (insofar as women, unlike men, cannot both play their socially assigned roles and engage in same-sex sexual acts, and insofar as women "cannot both respect phallocentric protocols and obtain sexual pleasure from contact with other females" [161])—fails on obvious grounds. In fact, it is neatly disposed of by Brooten herself. For Brooten also emphasizes that "the women whom the *tribades* pursue are of no interest to the text"; in other words, the female partners of tribades are not regarded as diseased (151). So, despite what Brooten claims, women *can* have sexual contact with other women while respecting all the phallocentric protocols: all they have to do is to get themselves seduced by a tribade.[53]

The woman whom a tribade seduces will obtain sexual pleasure from contact with another woman while conforming to her proper (passive, receptive, feminine) role in the phallocentric system. Indeed, the pagan sources Brooten examines do not contain a single instance in which a conventionally feminine female partner of a tribade is unambiguously and categorically treated as deviant or diseased.[54] That does not mean that women who had non-tribadic sex with each other were necessarily beyond reproach. The Hellenistic poet Asclepiades, in his seventh epigram, which Brooten discusses briefly (42), voices disapproval of two women who prefer women to men. A sixteenth-century Cretan humanist scholar by the name of Marcus Musurus, in a gloss on this poem, called the two women "tribades," which would certainly help to explain the poet's hostility to them and bring it into line with the dominant patterns of ancient sexual discourse.[55] But this remark isn't of much use in establishing what Asclepiades intended nearly two thousand years earlier. Brooten appears to take this comment to imply that the two women were having a sexual relationship *with each other,* which may well be what the humanist thought, but nothing in the poem or in the accusation that they were both tribades implies this: they might both have been imagined as separately pursuing other women, which seems indeed to be the likely reading of the epigram. If the two women in Asclepiades' poem are imagined as having a sexual relationship with each other, and are also imagined not to be tribades themselves, then this text would indeed constitute a counterexample to the usual discursive pattern: an instance of pagan sources morally problematizing non-tribadic participants in female same-sex eroticism. Such a reading, however, seems far-fetched. In any case, whether Asclepiades' poem is an exception to the general pattern or not, the basic point remains: to be fucked by a tribade was not necessarily to assume a deviant identity.

In short, Brooten seems to have forgotten all about the femme.[56] Like Amy Richlin, who makes similar errors in her reading of ancient texts and who seems to believe that, in the case of men, there is something *more homosexual* about getting fucked by one than fucking one,[57] Brooten seems to believe that there is something *more lesbian* about being butch than being femme.[58]

So what about that femme? Brooten herself appears to be of several minds about how the female partners of tribades were viewed. Caelius himself says nothing about them. Certainly, being seduced by a tribade does not necessarily make you a tribade yourself. Some texts do refer to the partner of a tribade as a tribade, but they are highly exceptional (cf. 6–7, 18, 128).[59] Brooten argues, rather theoretically, that "women who derive sexual pleasure from contact with women . . . have to be medically problematic" (161). Here Brooten quite uncharacteristically steps into the realm of pure speculation, into a hypothetical world quite beyond the limits of the evidence. Why do the female partners of tribades *have to be* medically problematic? So that sexual asymmetries can be banished from the ancient record and the undifferentiated category of "female homoeroticism" can be upheld as an ancient concept? *Even at the cost of pathologizing some "ancient lesbians"?* Brooten asserts that there is "no positive evidence that passive sexual behavior by adult women in relations with other adult women was societally acceptable" (161n), but she presents no positive evidence from pre- or non-Christian sources to show that it was considered sexually abnormal in and of itself. Lucian's portrayal of Leaena as an ordinary girl testifies eloquently to the contrary, but Brooten does not seem to notice. In sum, Brooten's argument that Roman-period medical writers considered women who responded to the erotic advances

of a tribade to be "medically problematic" is based on nothing but the silence of our sources, on the absence of statements explicitly endorsing the
behavior of such women. But such endorsements are hardly to be expected
from ancient Greek and Roman writers.

Brooten's recurrent imprecision in interpreting the ancient texts is regrettable especially because it could so easily have been avoided without
affecting her basic claims about the existence and knowledge of love between women in classical antiquity: earlier research had already indicated
the traps into which unwary modern students of ancient sexual discourses
were likely to fall. Although these mistakes mar Brooten's interpretation
of the ancient texts, they do not invalidate her general descriptive survey of
the pagan Greek and Latin sources (Brooten's interpretations are in general
much more sound and reliable than Boswell's, for example). Nonetheless,
since Brooten bases large-scale conclusions about the history of sexuality
on matters of semantics, claiming about "tribade," "virago," *hetairistria,*
and other such words that "all of these nouns demonstrate that people in
the ancient Mediterranean had the concept of an erotic orientation with
respect to women" (5), her tendency to reformulate the meanings of the
ancient terms to conform with modern sexual concepts has the effect of
begging the very questions she sets out to answer, and it thereby under-
mines the larger project of her book.[60]

: : :

The consistent anachronisms in Brooten's approach to the ancient evidence
are all the more bizarre because almost all the evidence with which she
has to deal reflects, as she points out (16), not the experiences of ancient
women but the fantasies, jokes, abuse, or moral judgments of hostile male
authors. "This study contributes to the history of male ideas about lesbians
far more than to women's history," she writes; "the sources bear witness to
male constructions of female homoeroticism, rather than to lesbians' perceptions of themselves" (25). We might have expected Brooten to bring
out the ideological and cultural specificity of these male constructions,
their oddity and remoteness from commonly accepted modern notions. We
might have expected her to foreground the opacity of the ancient sexual
discourses and, instead of trying to see through them to the "real women"
who are so bizarrely represented in them and whose own experiences of
same-sex desire and same-sex eroticism have left only exiguous traces in
the surviving record of classical antiquity, to make those discourses reflect
on the men who produced and maintained them. Brooten, however, would
rather highlight the continuity of male incomprehension, prejudice, and

hostility to lesbians than historicize its discursive and institutional manifestations.

In adopting this approach, Brooten makes one extremely important point about the history of homosexuality with which I vigorously agree (in fact, it may have come to her, indirectly, from me). She suggests that there may be fewer turning points in the history of lesbianism than in the history of male homosexuality (21–25). This has got to be right. As Gayle Rubin brilliantly argued more than twenty-five years ago, the subordination of women to men in society—in all its "endless variety and monotonous similarity, cross-culturally and throughout history"—and the asymmetrical sex/gender systems that it produces entail radically different social experiences of sex for women and for men.[61] The massive, universal or near-universal fact of male dominance, the corresponding kinship structures, the sexual division of labor, and the traffic in marriageable women that results from it mean, in particular, that women must submit to a system of compulsory heterosociality, in which they are not permitted to have a social existence apart from men, whereas men are permitted various forms of homosociality so long as they have occasional sex with women. The dominating feature of women's sexual lives is not so much heterosexual desire as the inescapability of sexual relations with men, the inability to deny men sexual access to themselves, whereas the dominating feature of men's sexual lives is merely the requirement to desire women some of the time, which leaves a good deal of men's erotic life available for various other sorts of social and sexual uses.[62]

The effects of this asymmetrical system are various and complex: sexual relations among women represent a perennial threat to male dominance, especially whenever such relations become exclusive and thereby take women out of circulation among men, but they also represent a perennial option for women, so long as women otherwise submit to the requirements of the kinship system, do not attempt to deny men access to themselves, and do not resist male control. As Valerie Traub says (she is speaking specifically about early modern England, but her words may have a more general application), "Only when women's erotic relations with one another threaten to become exclusive and thus endanger the fulfillment of their marital and reproductive duties, or when they symbolically usurp male sexual prerogatives, are cultural injunctions levied against them."[63] Sexual relations among men remain open to many more specific sorts of social elaboration and construction.

The conclusion we should derive from this model is not that the social construction of sexuality applies only to men and not to women. On the contrary, one of the great virtues of Rubin's model is that it accounts for the near-universal fact of male dominance in constructionist terms—that is, without essentializing it, naturalizing it, or treating it as necessary, uniform, or inevitable. That is why Rubin's approach is superior to Catharine MacKinnon's, which also tries to account for structural, transhistorical continuities in the oppression of women, but which—despite MacKinnon's intentions—lends itself more readily to an essentializing interpretation: it is highly indicative, therefore, that Brooten invokes MacKinnon's model, instead of Rubin's, to highlight "the long-term structures of male dominance and female subordination" (23–24).[64]

Nonetheless, a social-constructionist approach to sexuality that is derived from the study of men will not succeed in bringing into precise focus the history and diversity of sexual relations among women.[65] To see the historical dimensions of the social construction of same-sex relations among women, we need a new optic that will reveal specific historical variations in a phenomenon that necessarily exists in a constant and inescapable relation to the institutionalized structures of male dominance. Perhaps we even need to rethink our notions of chronology and entertain the possibility that those very notions have been gendered: it may be that the history of lesbianism exists in a different relation to time—a different relation to linear, developmental temporality—from the history of male homosexuality.[66] In any case, it is this constant and inescapable coexistence with a social structure that varies relatively little, both historically and culturally, which endows female same-sex eroticism with a greater degree of continuity, of thematic consistency, over time and space, making each historical instance both different and the same, both old and new. Histories of lesbianism need to reckon with this quite specific dimension of lesbian existence, which has potentially far-reaching implications for how we understand the different temporalities of female and male homosexuality.

It is also the threat that love between women can pose to monopolies of male authority that lends plausibility to the hypothesis that a notion of female-female eroticism may have been consolidated relatively early in Europe, even before similar notions emerged that could apply to all forms of male homoeroticism. Perhaps lesbianism was the first homoeroticism to be conceptualized categorically as such. Perhaps, in that sense, lesbianism should be seen, historically, as the first homosexuality. That is a hypothesis that will require considerably more knowledge than we presently possess in order to confirm or disprove. In the meantime, lesbian history certainly deserves to be studied in all its specificity, by means of an independent set of conceptual and historiographic tools, according to a different periodization, and even perhaps according to a different model of temporality. Whatever else the current and ongoing explorations of lesbian history have to offer us, one of their most startling benefits will be a much-enhanced understanding of the different historicities of female and male homosexuality.[67]

3

Historicizing the Subject of Desire

First: the good news. On January 19, 1990—in one of the
darkest hours of those sex-hating, Helms-ridden times—
the U.S. Postal Service officially issued a homosexual love
stamp. It is a curious production. The stamp displays in
its uppermost register the heading "love" in large, widely
spaced black lettering. Underneath that rubric is a symmetrical design featuring two identical lovebirds, or doves,
outlined in profile, facing each other, and blocked out in
solid blue; centered between and below them is a solid
red valentine-shaped heart, and beneath it is a symmet-
rically arranged vine tendril in solid green. The inspiration
for this design—to judge from U.S. Postal Service Poster
669 (fig. 1), which advertises the stamp and which exhorts
us, moreover, to "Add a little Love to [our] collection"—
apparently derives from traditional European-American
quilting patterns. I say that the stamp promotes "homosexual" love, because in conformity, no doubt, with age-old
quilting conventions the two birds are not depicted in an
anatomically explicit manner, and so it is not easy to determine whether they represent specifically a lesbian or a gay
male couple: their blue coloring, along with my own partisan sentiments, incline me to favor the gay male possibility,
but the customary assignment of quilting work to collec-
tives of women, the traditional association of lovebirds with
women's domestic world, the poster's acknowledgment of

FIGURE 1

one Dora B. Hamlin as the source of the quilt against which the stamp is photographed and its crediting of one Renee Comet as the photographer—all of those considerations combine to argue, perhaps, for the lesbian inter-pretation. Whether the birds are gay or lesbian, however, they are clearly identical to each other in every respect, and they are in love: the heading "love," the red, valentine-shaped heart, and (most important of all) the requirements of the symmetrical design, taken in conjunction, leave no room for escape from that queer conclusion.

Now: the bad news. My conclusion, inescapable though it may be, is one that almost nobody else seems to have drawn, so far as I am aware—neither the Postal Service, the public at large, nor lesbians and gay men in particular.[1] As if by magic, each person who views the stamp—no mat-ter what her or his social location—instantly and unreflectively reconfig-ures the image, constructing the pair of lovebirds not only as male and female but as a heterosexual and, presumably, monogamous couple (the stamp is not easily taken to represent a one-night stand). The viewer may also perform a number of other, subsidiary operations on this visual text, such as installing the "male" bird on the right-hand side of the field and even magnifying "his" size in relation to that of "his" mate, so as to motivate as well as to justify a heterosexist reading. But nothing in the text itself—nothing, at least, that I have been able to detect—provides the slightest impetus for such collective hallucinations. Rather, the apparently universal and unconquerable urge to read off gendered, heterosexualized meanings from the innocent surface of this unoffending text springs— as the text's source in the figural repertory of European-American folk art implies—from the traditional codes or conventions for representing "love" in European-American culture. Those codes, which also govern the culture's visual rhetoric, restrict the use of erotic symbols, such as the valentine-shaped heart, to heterosexual contexts and employ exemplary animals, such as lovebirds, to typify and thereby to naturalize contemporary human social and sexual arrangements, such as monogamous, heterosexual marriage. Common to all those rhetorical practices is a representational strategy whose effect is to (re)produce "love" as an exclusively heterosexual institution and to convert, under the sign of "love," all pairs of identically figured bodies into heterosexual couples (compare the image on the cover of the *New Yorker*'s 1991 Valentine's Day issue, reproduced here as fig. 2). It takes nothing less than a combination of masculine names, explicitly gay identities, and matching fezzes to withstand the weight of heterosexual presumption, if one is to judge by the example of Matt Groening's Akbar and Jeff (see the cover of the 1991 Valentine's Day issue of *The Advocate*, reproduced here as fig. 3, with accompanying story)—though inasmuch as "Life in Hell," the cartoon in which they appear, is routinely syndicated in college newspapers without stirring the slightest breath of scandal, perhaps even that odd couple's resistance to heterosexual presumption is less successful than one might have supposed.[2]

The point of this perverse little exercise has been to recall the currently trendy (if still undervalued) precept that the body is not only a thing but a sign: it functions as a site for the inscription of gendered and sexual meanings, among a great many other meanings. Instead of treating the body as the "really real," after the fashion of various scientific positivists, or as that which lies outside of language, or meaning, or subjectivity, or discourse, or representation, or power, after the sentimental fashion of various post-structuralists, it might be more profitable to regard the body, after the constructionist fashion of Donna Haraway, as "a

Feb. 18, 1991 THE NEW YORKER Price $1.75

FIGURE 2

'material-semiotic actor' " in "the apparatus of bodily production." [3] Haraway's project is to denaturalize the body and to deconstruct the bourgeois concept of "self," which has so closely attached to it, through a radical critique of scientific and, specifically, immunological discourse. My own considerably more modest project in this essay is to denaturalize the sexual body by historicizing it, by illuminating its multiple determinations in historical culture, and thereby to contest the body's use as a site for the production of heterosexual meanings and for their transformation into timeless and universal realities. To that end, I propose to take advantage of the happy accident of my training in classical scholarship—for it turns out that classical scholarship, if properly deployed, can in fact provide abundant ammunition against the powerful cultural magic that continually (re)produces the sexual body as a heterosexual body, and against the homophobic logic that ineluctably constructs "love" in exclusively heterosexual terms.

FIGURE 3

: : :

How does one write a history of the body? At one point in his career, Michel Foucault seemed about to offer us an exemplary answer to that question. In the first volume of his unfinished *History of Sexuality*, Foucault promised that his own study would not be "a 'history of mentalities' that would take account of bodies only through the manner in which they have been perceived and given meaning and value; but a 'history of bodies' and [of] the manner in which what is most material and most vital in them has been invested" by knowledge and power.[4] In the second volume, published eight years later, Foucault enlarged his project and spoke of his work as a "genealogy" of desire—and a genealogy of man as a desiring subject.[5] Despite Foucault's initial insistence on writing the history of sexuality as a history of bodies, and his later redescription of that project as a history of erotic subjectivity, the history of sexuality he founded is often understood as a history neither of bodies nor of subjects but as a history of categories or representations, a history of the different ways that different historical cultures have put "sexuality" (understood as some natural and timeless fact of life) into "discourse" (understood as language, or articulate speech). In a word, Foucault is thought to have demonstrated that "sexuality" is, within the horizons of any particular historical culture, a "discourse."

I confess that I have never understood how anyone could seriously believe that sexuality is a discourse or how anyone could attribute such a notion to Foucault. To be sure, Foucault's inaugural lecture at the Collège de France, "The Order of Discourse," is accessible in English only in a catastrophic translation by Rupert Swyer, which makes almost no sense on its own terms and can only have exercised a disastrous influence on English-language standards of acceptable theory-speak.[6] But a more decisive factor is doubtless our penchant for assimilating unfamiliar conceptual innovations to earlier, deeply entrenched habits of thought. If there is a tide in the affairs of men, as Shakespeare's Brutus says, there is something like an undertow or a backwash in the fortunes of critical terms and concepts. New critical vocabularies are helplessly overwhelmed and reabsorbed— or "recuperated," as we used to say, before that term lost its conceptual specificity—by older and more familiar ones, while prior epistemologies and methodologies continually resurface within the intellectual framework of even the most radical innovations.

Those of us who typically depend for our understanding of contemporary critical concepts on what Northrop Frye once called "the psychology of rumor"[7] may often find ourselves tempted to believe that we can infer the meaning of a new term from its recognizable lexical associations, from its ostensible semantic adjacency to other words with which we are already conversant. That tendency produces a kind of terminological drift whereby the vocabulary coined to articulate conceptual advances is gradually resignified until it ultimately comes to designate the very concepts it was invented to displace. The most spectacular recent casualty of such a process is of course Deconstruction, which in its current usage has come to mean very nearly the same thing as the New Criticism: common academic parlance has detached the verb "to deconstruct" from its original meaning and invested it instead with a series of progressively—or, perhaps it would be more accurate to say, regressively—normalizing significations, starting with "demystify," ranging through "dismantle," "criticize," and "analyze," and devolving finally into "unpack," "explicate," or even simply "explain." Likewise, "intertextuality" has become little more than a pretentious equivalent to "literary allusion" or "source criticism," as Julia Kristeva complained already two decades ago.[8]

Foucault, of course, did not claim that sexuality was a discourse. He argued for treating it as a novel social apparatus composed of a vast and seemingly heterogeneous mass of discourses, social practices, disciplinary mechanisms, institutional structures, and political agencies, all of which arose, out of different circumstances and different contexts, in Europe during the modern period. These heterogeneous discourses, practices, mechanisms, structures, and agencies came to form a vast and complex network, the formation of which corresponded to a dominant strategic function (which Foucault called "bio-power," the administration of life). It is this dominant strategic function, uniting and connecting these otherwise disparate elements, that provides Foucault with his basis for claiming that the whole network constitutes a single *dispositif,* a single "device" or "apparatus."[9] Nonetheless, Foucault's notion has been widely understood in such a way as to salvage the non-technical, pre-theoretical meanings of both "sexuality" and "discourse," thereby preserving and even reanimating those meanings within an ostensibly Foucauldian framework of analysis.

Thus, many historians, as well as many scholars working in the interdisciplinary field of lesbian and gay studies, have tended to assume that the principal achievement of Foucault's *History of Sexuality* was to have provided a precise and detailed account of how various societies *represent* sexuality *in* their discourses, as if sexuality were some ubiquitous natural reality outside of, or even prior to, discourse and as if discourse itself were some wholly transparent cognitive or linguistic medium, rather than a highly specialized, evolved, and evolving technology for producing truths. That tendency to treat Foucault's startling determination to write the history of sexuality "from the viewpoint of a history of discourses"[10] as if such a project amounted to nothing more than a banal preoccupation with the *representation* of sexuality *in* discourse has had the effect of authorizing the (re)production, under the apparent aegis of Foucauldian historicism, of an entire series of ancient positivistic distinctions between material things and mental representations, objects and words, bodies and minds, nature and culture—precisely those metaphysical dichotomies that Foucault's radical holism had in fact enabled him, and might have enabled other historians of sexuality, to evade. A second effect of attributing to Foucault such pre-Foucauldian conceptions of both sexuality and discourse has been to allow his would-be followers to resume their old habit of situating historical ruptures merely within sexual categories rather than within sexual subjects themselves and thus to license them to continue speaking and thinking of pre-modern sexual formations as "sexualities"— as quaint historical variants, that is, of a timeless and universal entity.

And yet Foucault himself famously contended that what we call sexuality nowadays is in fact a distinctively modern, bourgeois production, that it is not some biological or physiological reality but an unprecedented, historically specific device (*dispositif*) for the organization of subjectivities, social relations, and knowledges—"a great surface network," as he puts it, "in which the stimulation of bodies, the intensification of pleasures, the incitement to discourse, the formation of special knowledges, the strengthening of controls and resistances, are linked to one another, in accordance with a few major strategies of knowledge and power." [11]

Foucault's attempt to refute what he calls "the repressive hypothesis" is continuous with that claim. The targets of his anti-Lacanian critique are not limited to the conventional image of the Victorian era as a period in which the discourses of sex were oppressively silenced instead of explosively produced or to the conceptualization of power as a force of negation and prohibition instead of as a force of production and possibility. What Foucault also aimed to contest by means of his attack on "the repressive hypothesis" was the common representation of sexuality as an eternal, universal presence in history, a cultural invariant, the flamboyant historical variations of which supposedly reflected only the differential impact on sexuality of the various mechanisms employed in different societies to repress it; such a representation of sexuality, as Foucault remarks in *The Use of Pleasure,* has the unfortunate effect of situating desire outside the field of human history altogether. [12] By contrast, Foucault refused to consider sexuality or desire exterior to historical configurations of power, knowledge, and subjectivity.

The history of sexuality, as Foucault conceived it, then, is not a history of the representations, categories, cultural articulations, or collective and individual expressions of some determinate entity called sexuality but an inquiry into the historical emergence of sexuality itself, an attempt to explain how it happened that in the eighteenth and nineteenth centuries sexuality gradually came into existence as a conjunction of strategies for ordering social relations, authorizing specialized knowledges, licensing expert interventions, intensifying bodily sensations, normalizing erotic behaviors, multiplying sexual perversions, policing personal expressions, crystallizing political resistances, motivating introspective utterances, and constructing human subjectivities. Sexuality, in the last analysis, is thus an apparatus for constituting human subjects. It is Foucault's concern with the constitution of the subject rather than with the production of sexual categories or classifications, his resolve to use the history of sexuality as a means of inquiry into the modalities of human subjectivation—as an exercise in *historicizing the subject of desire*—that imparts to his project as a whole its distinctive shape and its fundamentally radical design.[13] Such a conception still represents almost as decisive a rupture with customary modern ways of thinking about sexuality as it did when Foucault first formulated it nearly three decades ago.

To be sure, Foucault himself was not always so unambiguous about these matters as one might have liked. In the earlier and more accessible portions of the first volume of his *History of Sexuality,* he speaks freely of "the *mise en discours* of sex," of "regulating sex through useful and public discourses," and more generally of "discourse on" or "about sex"— thereby giving his incautious reader the possible impression that sex somehow pre-exists the discourses of sexuality.[14] Later in the same volume, however, he goes out of his way to argue that "sex" itself, far from being a pre-discursive fact—the raw material of sexuality, as it were—is a product of sexuality, an element internal to its discursive operation: "We must not situate sex on the side of reality, and sexuality on that of confused ideas and illusions; sexuality is a very real historical configuration"; indeed, "the apparatus of sexuality, with its different strategies, was what put in place" the very notion of sex.[15]

: : :

In order to demonstrate that the history of sexuality, at its most adventurous, can be a history of erotic subjectivity, not simply of sexual classifications, categories, or representations, and in order to anchor a history of the body in the history of erotic subjectivity, I propose to look at some literary texts from the ancient world whose potential contribution to the history of sexuality has yet to be fully realized. My chief exhibit will be a late antique Greek text, entitled the *Erôtes* (the "Loves," the "Forms of Desire," or, as A. M. Harmon somewhat quaintly renders it, the "Affairs of the Heart"), which has been preserved in medieval manuscripts among the writings of Lucian. Stylistic considerations, however, apparently prohibit ascribing the work to the authorship of that well-known Greek satirist; the text's most recent editor and translator, M. D. Macleod, attributes it to a late antique imitator of Lucian and assigns it to the early fourth century A.D., although his dating of the text has been disputed.[16] Detached at one stroke by this scholarly sleight of hand from any specific geographical, political, or cultural context, and long relegated to the academic oblivion of Latin dissertations, to the embarrassed silences of classical philologists, or to the recreational reading of bored graduate students in classics (which is how I first encountered it), this anonymous little work deserves nonetheless to acquire a prominent place in our emerging histories of sexuality, and in

1984 it in fact provided Foucault with the vehicle for a characteristically subtle and brilliant analysis in a late chapter of *Le souci de soi*.[17] Foucault's chief purpose was to contextualize the *Erôtes,* along with the opinions expressed in it, in the philosophical currents of late antiquity—the only possible historical and cultural context for it that can now be recovered. I have a different, and admittedly cruder, purpose in view, as will appear presently.

The *Erôtes* is a notably sophisticated and elegant specimen of late antique luxury literature. Taking the form of a philosophical dialogue, but designed to mock the moral pretensions and austere postures of traditional philosophers (especially the supposedly high-minded, Platonizing advocates of boy-love[18] who by late antiquity had become stock figures of fun in the erotic literature of Greece),[19] the work features a debate between two men, Charicles and Callicratidas, over the relative merits of women and boys as vehicles of male sexual pleasure. As such, it belongs to a widely distributed genre of erotic writing, which is represented in the surviving literature of the ancient world by Plutarch's *Eroticus* and by an extended passage in *Leucippe and Cleitophon,* a late Greek romance, or novel, by Achilles Tatius.[20] Similar debates can be found in medieval European and Arabic literatures, in late imperial Chinese literature, and in the literature of "the floating world," the luxury literature of town life in seventeenth-century Japan.[21]

In the ancient Greek context, however, the existence of such a genre raises a number of provocative issues. For one thing, most Greeks seem routinely to have assumed that most adult Greek men—whatever their particular tastes—were at least capable of being sexually aroused both by beautiful women and by beautiful boys; as I have noted elsewhere, "it would be a monumental task indeed to enumerate all the ancient documents in which the alternative 'boy or woman' occurs with perfect nonchalance in an erotic context, as if the two were functionally interchangeable."[22] In fact, an instance of precisely such a nonchalant approach to matters of sexual object-choice can be found in the opening chapter of the *Erôtes,* in which one adult male speaker urges the other not to omit "mention of any of your passions, whether male or even female" (1).[23] One question it may be interesting to put to the pseudo-Lucianic text, then, is this: how do exclusive sexual preferences on the part of men get conceptualized and represented in a culture that neither expects nor enforces exclusive sexual object-choice in the case of men? A second question springs immediately from the first. Since the dialogue in the *Erôtes* is about as close as an antique Greek text ever gets to producing a discussion about the relative values of homosexuality and heterosexuality, how should a modern interpretation deal with the issues of identity and difference that it raises? It is fairly evident (as I hope to show) that the dialogue in question cannot be understood straightforwardly or unproblematically as a debate over the relative merits of "homosexual and heterosexual love."[24] At the same time, it is clearly difficult for those of us who are (or who at least function as if we were) the inheritors of the Kinsey scale to conceive of exclusive preference for male or female sexual contacts except in terms of sexual orientation.[25] Is it possible for us to think exclusive sexual object-choice outside the terms of "sexuality"? Are their other ways of conceptualizing sexual preference? And how can a reading of the *Erôtes* today manage to preserve a sense of the cultural specificity of the sexual system reflected in it, and prevent that system from being overwhelmed and colonized by modern notions of sexuality, without at the same time reducing the *Erôtes* to a mere antiquarian curiosity and preventing it from functioning positively in the context of contemporary anti-homophobic politics?

A third question presents itself more particularly to the historian of sexuality. How can a historically precise reading of a pre-modern text help us to arrive at a more systematic conceptual distinction between an individual's established sexual object-choice, or even a conscious erotic preference for a sexual object of one sex rather than another, and homosexuality and heterosexuality, conceived as categories of psychosexual orientation? Can we use the text of the *Erôtes* to document historical instances or representations of sexual object-choices, and conscious erotic preferences, that nonetheless do not satisfy modern criteria for sexual orientation or "sexuality"? If so, we would be able to document a historical transformation not only in the classifications or categories of "sexuality," but in the very mode of being of sexuality, and in the historical forms of erotic subjectivity themselves.

It is with these questions in mind that I turn to a reading of the pseudo-Lucianic text. My reading, light-hearted as it is, will be an "engaged" one, and as such, it will have a very limited scope. I am not going to attempt to provide a balanced description of the *Erôtes* as a whole or to convey much in the way of aesthetic appreciation of the work's admittedly numerous formal and stylistic accomplishments. Nor is it my intention—and, I trust, my reading will not produce this effect—to champion the ancients at the expense of the moderns or to promote a rhetoric of erotic self-fashioning over a rhetoric of sexuality; after all, it is not possible to reinstitute the ancient Greek sociosexual system, nor, if it were, would I wish to live under it—for reasons that will emerge shortly. Finally, I am not about to undertake a critique (which it would be easy enough to do) of male sexual privilege as it permeates the world of the text or to analyze the operations of gendered, social power as it expresses itself in the adult male objectification of both women and boys. What I want to do, instead, is to bring out the cultural specificity of ancient sexual experiences and to throw into relief the ideological contingency of what we lightly call "our own" sexual practices and institutions.[26] The point is not to devise a popularity contest between the ancients and the moderns but to contrast them in order to distinguish more systematically the peculiar features of their respective sexual regimes. Furthermore, I want to bring the *Erôtes* into the arena of late twentieth-century ideological struggles over sexual definition and to dramatize the multiple temporalities that the historian of sexuality inhabits. By attempting to make this text contemporary, I wish to place its testimony at the service of various current radical critiques of sexual identity.[27] At the same time, by exploiting the text's cultural distance from the world that I move in, I wish to problematize some twentieth-century assumptions about sexual preference, erotic identity, and the linkages between them. In short, by confronting the modern Western bourgeois distinction between hetero- and homosexuality with the Greek distinction between boys and women as objects of male sexual pleasure, and thereby calling attention both to thematic continuities and to discursive ruptures in the history of sexuality, I aim to demonstrate the play of identity and difference in queer historiography. The ultimate effect of this stereoscopic—or dialectical—procedure, I hope, will be to defamiliarize current sexual behaviors and attitudes and to destabilize the binary opposition between heterosexuality and homosexuality that so decisively structures contemporary discourses of homophobia. I will leave more weighty theoretical reflections to the conclusion.

: : :

The dialogue between Charicles and Callicratidas in the pseudo-Lucianic *Erôtes* sounds a number of themes that will be immediately familiar to modern readers from contemporary debates over the morality, or immorality, of homosexuality. Charicles argues, for example, that men should favor sex with women over sex with boys because it conduces to reproduction, renews life, and preserves the human race from annihilation (19). Callicratidas replies that the very instrumentality of cross-sex sexual intercourse for species reproduction is a mark of its unworthiness: "Anything cultivated for aesthetic reasons in the midst of abundance," he maintains, "is accompanied with greater honor than things which require for their existence immediate need, and beauty is in every way superior to necessity" (33). Connected to the argument about reproduction is another familiar one about the supposed naturalness of sex between men and women and the supposed unnaturalness of sex between men and boys, an argument borrowed in this case directly from Plato's *Laws* (835D—842A, esp. 836C, 839A).[28] Calling "luxury" (*tryphê*) what Callicratidas had called "beauty," Charicles associates boy-love with eunuchs, with the surgical construction of gender, and he goes on to appeal, in the Platonic manner, to animal behavior for a standard of alleged naturalness in matters of sex (20–22).[29] Callicratidas, however, is unmoved by the analogy from animals; he claims that male animals eschew sex with one another and copulate with females precisely *because* they are mindless;[30] otherwise, he remarks, "they would not be satisfied with solitary lives in the wilderness, nor would they feed on one another, but just like us they would have built themselves temples and . . . would live as fellow citizens governed by common laws" (36). And to Charicles' assertion that anatomy is destiny, that sex between men and boys is necessarily one-sided in its distribution of sexual pleasure whereas sex between men and women is mutually enjoyable (27), Callicratidas retorts that true reciprocity consists in the shared erotic life of an ongoing, long lasting relationship (48), not in who does what to whom. Some of those answers to moral objections against gay sex may still prove to be, within certain limited contexts, rhetorically useful today.

But despite the various points of correspondence between the pseudo-Lucianic debate and modern polemics, or between ancient misogyny and its twentieth-century gay male equivalent, a number of factors militate against interpreting the argument between Charicles and Callicratidas unproblematically as a dispute over the relative merits of heterosexuality and homosexuality. Chief among these factors is the dialogue's focus on paederasty to the virtual exclusion of any mention of either female or adult male homosexuality. The text contains only one mention of female homosexuality, wholly negative in intent (if subversively potent in effect), and even that does not refer to lesbianism in the modern sense of the word but rather to what the writer calls "tribadism"—that is, to the sexual penetration of women by other women.[31] "If males find intercourse with males acceptable," exclaims Charicles (the partisan of women), playing what he clearly considers to be his trump card in the argument, "henceforth let women too love one another. . . . Let them strap to themselves cunningly contrived instruments of wantonness, those mysterious monstrosities devoid of seed, and let woman lie with woman as does a man. Let wanton tribadism—that word seldom heard, which I feel ashamed even to utter—freely parade itself, and let our women's chambers . . . defile themselves with sexually indeterminate amours" (28). Needless to say, Callicratidas (the partisan of boys) does not rise to his opponent's challenge and endorse such forward-looking proposals.

Within the realm of male eroticism, correspondingly, the *Erôtes* makes absolutely no allowance for the possibility of sexual relations among adult men—for the possibility, that is, of "homosexual" rather than merely paederastic love. Both Charicles and Callicratidas seem to agree that adult males hold not the slightest sexual appeal to other men; the terms in which they express that shared assumption are revealing, I believe, of the distance that separates the aesthetic and sexual conventions of ancient Mediterranean paederasty from the canons of modern American middle-class gay male taste. "If a man makes attempts on a boy of twenty," Charicles (the partisan of women) remarks, "he seems to me to be pursuing an equivocal love.[32] For then the [boy's] limbs, being large and manly, are hard; the chins that once were soft are rough and covered with bristles, and the well-developed thighs are as it were sullied with hairs. And as for the parts less visible than these, I leave knowledge of them to you who have tried them" (26).[33] Each detail in this description of overripe boyhood is intended to evoke revulsion and disgust; it is telling that Charicles' opponent, Callicratidas, has nothing to say by way of refutation of it. No muscle boys or leather daddies welcome here.

I should pause at this point and describe more fully the two rivals in the debate. Callicratidas, the partisan of boys, is an Athenian. He is a man of mature age, well established in life; his sexual taste bespeaks a stable and settled disposition, not a transition from one identity to another or a mere "phase" in his psychosexual development. His sexual "acts" express a well-established erotic "identity." Far from being socially marginalized by his openly acknowledged erotic preference, however, Callicratidas is a leading figure in Athenian public life. Far from being effeminized by his sexual predilection for boys, as the modern "inversion model" of homosexual desire would have it (whereby a man exclusively attracted to males has "a woman's soul in a man's body" or represents a "sexual intermediate" or member of a "third sex"), Callicratidas's inclination renders him hypervirile: he excels, we are told, at those activities traditionally marked in Greek culture as exclusively and characteristically masculine—namely, political life, public oratory, gymnastics (9, 29), and philosophy—and he takes as his role models the heroes and philosophers of old (46–49).[34] Callicratidas's sexual desire for boys, then, makes him more of a man; it does not weaken or subvert his male gender identity but rather consolidates it.[35]

By contrast, Charicles, the partisan of women, is young and handsome; he hails from Corinth, a city as traditionally renowned for its courtesans as Athens is renowned for political rhetoric and philosophy. Although Charicles asserts that nature, in implanting in men and women a desire for one another, sought to polarize the sexes and to distinguish masculine from feminine styles, making males masculine and women feminine (19, 28), his own comportment belies that claim. Just as Callicratidas's habit of consorting with boys represents either a symptom or a cause of his hyper-masculinity, so Charicles' erotic preference for women seems to have had the corresponding effect of effeminizing him: when the reader first encounters him, for example, Charicles is described as exhibiting "a skillful use of cosmetics, so as to be attractive to women" (9). Indeed, Greek women, if one is to credit the desires imputed to them by male authors, seem to have liked men who looked young.[36] (No one in this world, apparently, would appear to find adult men sexually appealing—which, to my mind, furnishes a very good reason for not trying to revive ancient Greece.) Now cosmetic adornment is itself an indicatively feminine practice (38–41), and so Charicles would seem to have been infected by femininity from his long habit of associating with women.[37] His passionate encomium of women, moreover—his defense of their claims to be loved by men and his praise of their sexual attractiveness—signals to the jaundiced eye of Callicratidas that Charicles has simply enslaved himself to the cause of women and is entirely at their beck and call: if he were a real man, the implication seems to be, he would not allow himself to be so dominated by women as to be obliged to defend their interests in public. According to the terms of Greek misogynistic discourse, there would appear to be no distinction between being the champion of women and being their slave (30). Compared to Callicratidas, then, it is Charicles who is a traitor to his gender, having been led to betray his masculine identity by the very vehemence of his sexual preference for women: he has become woman-identified. In short, the sharply polarizing tendencies of Greek sexual discourse would seem to require that excessive liking for women on the part of a man be interpreted as a sign of deviant, specifically effeminate identity. Such an outlook is plainly at odds with modern constructions of hetero- and homosexuality (which of course is not to say that it is unheard of today).[38]

: : :

As the preceding account implies, neither Callicratidas nor Charicles is entirely conventional, by Greek standards, in the matter of his sexual tastes. Rather, each man is something of an extremist (5), a zealot whose fanatical attachment to his own erotic object-choice—and whose correspondingly violent revulsion against the sexual objects favored by his opponent—mark him out as peculiar and manifest themselves in his entire style of

life. Moreover, each man's sexual inclination, if not exactly "written im-
modestly on his face and body" (as Foucault says of the nineteenth-century
homosexual),[39] is at least visibly inscribed in his domestic arrangements.
Callicratidas, the narrator points out, "was well provided with handsome
slave-boys and all of his servants were pretty well beardless. They remained
with him till the down first appeared on their faces, but, once any growth
cast a shadow on their cheeks, they would be sent away to be stewards
and overseers of his properties at Athens." Charicles, by contrast, "had in
attendance a large band of dancing girls and singing girls and all his house
was as full of women as if it were the Thesmophoria [a women's religious
festival], with not the slightest trace of male presence except that here and
there could be seen an infant boy or a superannuated old cook whose age
could give even the jealous no cause for suspicion" (10). Callicratidas and
Charicles do not represent, then, spokesmen for abnormal and normal
sexualities, respectively: rather, they are both a bit queer.

Nonetheless, each man demonstrates a certain connoisseurship in
speaking about the good and bad features of the sexual objects favored by
his rival, a knowingness that bespeaks a broader range of erotic sympa-
thies or a wider sexual experience than one might initially have imputed to
such self-styled sexual purists. I have already cited one instance: Charicles'
vivid and sensuously precise evocation of the physical attributes of a boy
past his prime. Charicles' taste in boys, his ability to judge when a boy
is no longer desirable, his standards for discriminating smoothness and
hairiness in youthful cheeks and thighs are confirmed in their inerrancy
by the institutional arrangements of Callicratidas's household, which (as
the passage just quoted makes clear) has well-established procedures for
"graduating" overage, hirsute lads. Charicles evidently understands what
Callicratidas likes and dislikes in a boy. Conversely, Callicratidas betrays
an intimate knowledge of women. His violent denunciation of women's
cosmetic practices (38–41) implies so extensive an acquaintance with them
that one might imagine him to be a professional beautician—were it not
that his accusations belong to the arsenal of traditional Greek misogyny.[40]
Still, the intensely visceral terms in which he avows his disgust (he claims
that "every man [who gets out of a woman's bed] is in immediate need of a
bath" [42]) seem intended to indicate at least passing personal familiarity.
And his acceptance, however reluctant, of the necessity of having sexual
relations with women in order to beget offspring (38) demonstrates that
he does not regard himself as incapable of consummating a sexual union
with a woman, should the situation call for it.

On rare occasions, in fact, both Charicles and Callicratidas are able
to agree about the attractiveness of a sexual object. Their desires coin-

cide, interestingly enough, in the case of the famous statue of Aphrodite at Cnidus, by the sculptor Praxiteles. Callicratidas, of course, is initially reluctant to view this world-renowned masterpiece, because it has the form of a female figure (11), but even he is struck dumb by the sight of it, while Charicles raves over it and even kisses the statue (13). When the two men inspect the rear of the figure, however, it is Callicratidas's turn to rave, while Charicles stands transfixed with tears pouring from his eyes (14). "Heracles!" Callicratidas exclaims,

> what a well-proportioned back! What generous flanks she has! How satisfying an armful to embrace! How delicately moulded the flesh on the buttocks, neither too thin and close to the bone, nor yet revealing too great an expanse of fat! And as for those precious parts sealed in on either side by the hips, how inexpressibly sweetly they smile![41] How perfect the proportions of the thighs and the shins as they stretch down in a straight line to the feet! So that's what Ganymede looks like as he pours out the nectar in heaven for Zeus and makes it taste sweeter. For I'd never have taken the cup from Hebe if she served me.
>
> (14)

Charicles is hardly in a state to disagree. Such passages leave one with the impression that what endears boys to Callicratidas and women to Charicles is not a preferred sex or gender but merely certain favorite parts of the human anatomy.

That impression is strengthened when the two men go on to discover that a discoloration of the marble they have noted on the back of the statue was caused by a young man who fell in love with it and who, having arranged to be locked up alone with the statue at night, had sex with it by stealth (15–16).[42] Charicles concludes that the feminine evokes love even when carved in stone. Callicratidas, however, observes that although the amorous youth had the opportunity to glut his entire passion for the goddess during an uninterrupted night of love, he chose to make love to her "as if to a boy" (*paidikôs*)—that is, from the rear—in order not to be confronted by the female part of her (17). (Face-to-face intercourse would have been pretty hard to bring off, in any case, even if the lover had desired it, since Praxiteles' statue—in addition to being made of marble—was far from anatomically correct. Callicratidas's rejoinder, then, provides one more indication of the playful, highly sophistical tenor of the whole debate.) These passages confirm that the quarrel between Charicles and Callicratidas comes down not to a difference in sexual object-choice, to

differing sexual preferences or orientations, but rather to a differential liking for particular human body parts, independent of the sex of the person
who possesses them.

The specific arguments that the two men use in order to establish the
putative superiority of their preferred sexual object display, accordingly,
what modern middle-class readers will be apt to find not only unpersuasive
but positively bizarre styles of reasoning. That is because most bourgeois
Westerners nowadays tend to think of sexual object-choice as an expression of individual "sexuality," a fixed sexual disposition or orientation,
over which no one has much (if any) control and for which reasons cannot
be given: any reasons one might give for one's sexual object-choice seem to
be mere afterthoughts, adventitious rationalizations, late cognitive arrivals
on the scene of sexual speciation; reasons follow the fact of one's sexual
being and do not determine or constitute it. Thus, sexual preference is not
something that one can be argued logically out of or into—least of all by
considerations of utility or convenience. And yet, those are precisely the
sorts of considerations that Charicles invokes in order to demonstrate that
women are superior vehicles of male sexual pleasure. For example, women
have more sexual orifices than do boys, Charicles observes; hence, it is
possible for men to make use of women "even more like boys than boys"
(*paidikôteron*—i.e., by two methods of penetration instead of merely one),
thereby availing themselves of "twin paths to sexual pleasure," whereas
"a male has no way of bestowing the pleasure a woman gives" (27).[43]
And here is yet another consideration of a practical nature: women, unlike
boys, can be enjoyed for a protracted period of time. "From maidenhood
to middle age, before the time when the last wrinkles of old age spread
over her face, a woman is a pleasant armful for a man to embrace," Charicles points out (25), adding—a bit wishfully, perhaps—that a woman's
body (unlike a boy's) remains attractively hairless as she grows older (26).
Callicratidas does not dispute those assertions, but counters instead with
a lengthy polemic about the superiority of art to nature (33–36: I quoted
an excerpt from it at the outset of my discussion).[44]

What all this evidence indicates, finally—and here is the pay-off for the
historian—is that the anonymous author of the pseudo-Lucianic *Erôtes*
approaches the question of male sexual object-choice not as a matter of
sexual orientation but rather as a matter of taste: the sort of thing that, as
everyone knows, there's no disputing, and that everyone just loves to dispute. (As W. H. Auden wrote in 1936, "Who can ever praise enough The
world of his belief?")[45] The quarrel between Charicles and Callicratidas
over the relative merits of women and boys as vehicles of male sexual pleasure is not an argument about the relative merits of heterosexuality and

homosexuality in the modern sense but a disagreement over the respective advantages and disadvantages of different "avenues of sexual pleasure" (cf. 27) and different stylistics of personal life. The alternatives presented by the two disputants delineate sexual options apparently available, in principle at least, to any free adult Greek male, such that anyone—no matter how set in his ways—might plausibly be thought at least capable of entertaining those options, if not necessarily eager to explore them.

Here, then, are nine considerations we can derive from the pseudo-Lucianic text that combine to make it look very queer indeed, especially if we view it as a debate about the relative merits of homosexuality and heterosexuality: (1) the text's emphasis on paederasty to the exclusion of homosexuality (whose existence, apparently, is not even recognized); (2) the masculinization of the paederast and the effeminization of the lover of women; (3) the paederast's lack of social marginalization; (4) the shared queerness of both interlocutors; (5) the ability of each interlocutor to put himself in the erotic subject position of the other; (6) their common know-ingness about both women and boys; (7) the paederast's capacity to eroti-cize elements of the human anatomy independently of the sex of the person whose anatomy is being eroticized; (8) the lover of women's utilitarian appeal to quantitative factors as a basis for calculating relative sexual value; and, finally, (9) both men's treatment of sexual object-choice as a matter of taste. The conjunction of all nine of those considerations (which, taken individually, might be paralleled in modern bourgeois experience) suggests that what one is dealing with in the *Erôtes* is something quite different from a system of "sexuality," in the modern sense of that modern word. And so our reading of the text ought to caution us against identifying stable sexual object-choice or conscious erotic preference with contemporary notions of sexuality or sexual orientation.

: : :

In order to make sense of the quarrel between Charicles and Callicrati-das in modern terms, it may be helpful to think of it somewhat along the lines of a passionate debate over dietary object-choice between a commit-ted vegetarian and an unreconstructed omnivore—or, to employ a more ludicrous (and therefore a more exact) analogy, between someone who eats nothing but vegetables and someone who eats nothing but meat. It is a quarrel that springs not from fundamental differences in kind among human beings but from the dissimilar values, ideals, and preferred styles of life that otherwise similar human beings happen (for whatever reason) to have espoused.[46] It is therefore a dispute about the very sorts of things that people tend to argue about most heatedly—namely, their basic commitments. No matter how basic such commitments may be, however, they are susceptible of being criticized or debated precisely because they derive from what people believe and value, not from what or who they are. The probability of one disputant actually convincing the other to alter his basic commitments, and to alter the behavior that follows from them, is admittedly slim, but by citing various reasons or adducing various considerations each disputant can nurture the (no doubt foredoomed) hope that his interlocutor may come one day to look at things from his own perspective. Without the conviction that the available options admit of right choices and wrong choices, that those choices are open to everyone to make, and that one's own choice is indeed the correct one, one has little motive to get worked up over the issue—and uncommitted onlookers have little cause to find the dispute amusing or entertaining. Such is not the case with sexuality nowadays. That is why modern debates over the respective merits of various sexual orientations, even when they take place (if they ever do) without an explicit or implicit element of anti-gay violence, tend to have an entirely different character from the sexual debates staged by ancient Greek writers: modern arguments are more like arguments about whether it is better to be a peasant or a king—matters possible to dispute in principle but impossible to do anything about in actual practice. The practical outcome of such arguments, in other words, is always foreclosed from the start, which makes them, at best, "forlorn / Yet pleasing," as Shelley puts it, "such as once, so poets tell, / The devils held within the dales of Hell, / Concerning God, freewill and destiny."[47]

What exactly is at stake in the quarrel between Charicles and Callicratidas may be easier to grasp if the *Erôtes* is situated in its wider generic context and compared to another text from an analogous cultural tradition, namely, *The Great Mirror of Male Love* by the seventeenth-century Japanese writer Ihara Saikaku. Published in Osaka and Kyoto on New Year's Day, 1687, *The Great Mirror* contains forty tales of exemplary love between men and boys. Its opening chapter justifies the choice of subject by means of twenty-three comparisons of women to boys, each of them designed to champion the latter at the expense of the former and to establish the relative advantages of boys as vehicles of male pleasure. What sets off these alternatives from the arguments of Callicratidas is that they are couched entirely in negative terms. That is, instead of purporting to demonstrate straightforwardly that the love of boys is superior to the love of women, Saikaku's comparisons show that when affairs go badly, boy-love is on the whole less vexatious. Here is how Saikaku's argument begins:

Which is to be preferred: A girl of eleven or twelve scrutinizing herself in a mirror, or a boy of the same age cleaning his teeth?

Lying rejected next to a courtesan, or conversing intimately with a kabuki boy who is suffering from hemorrhoids?

Caring for a wife with tuberculosis, or keeping a youth who constantly demands spending money?

Having lightning strike the room where you are enjoying a boy actor you bought, or being handed a razor by a courtesan you hardly know who asks you to die with her?

The choice is evidently not a difficult one: "In each case above," Saikaku concludes with a partisanship so extreme as to be ludicrous and therefore self-canceling, "even if the woman were a beauty of gentle disposition and the youth a repulsive pug-nosed fellow, it is a sacrilege to speak of female love in the same breath with boy love. . . . The only sensible choice is to dispense with women and turn instead to men."[48]

What the pseudo-Lucianic *Erôtes* shares with *The Great Mirror of Male Love,* besides its evident misogyny, is its combination of literary gamesmanship and sexual connoisseurship: it playfully explores various possibilities of sexual pleasure, presenting the (implied male) reader with specific sets of alternative options for achieving erotic enjoyment and personal satisfaction. Perhaps the final surprise that the *Erôtes* has to offer the modern historian of sexuality is its dramatization of the absurdity of the very notion of exclusive sexual object-choice, whether homo- or hetero-. It is not that Greek males exhibited on the whole a different "sexuality" from modern American men of the professional classes, if one may judge solely on the basis of this one text (which, of course, it would be extremely hazardous to do in the absence of corroborating documentation).[49] Rather, the Greeks exhibited no "sexuality" at all, in the modern sense. Not only are the very notions of "sexuality" and "sexual orientation" entirely foreign to the world of this text: to the extent that the text can even accommodate such notions—to the extent that it can represent human types who roughly approximate modern hetero- and homosexual males— it treats them as outlandish and bizarre. Merely to have a fixed sexual object-choice of any kind is to be some sort of freak, apparently—a figure of fun whose foredoomed efforts at rationalizing his exclusive preference provide amusement and relaxation for one's fellow man (5, 29, 53).[50]

Despite all the sound and fury of their polemics, then, Charicles and Callicratidas actually agree about the fundamentals. They certainly resemble each other more than either resembles a modern homosexual or heterosexual male (who, correspondingly, resembles his modern counterpart

more than he resembles either Charicles or Callicratidas). Like the putative differences of gender that supposedly distinguish the two lovebirds
represented on the United States "LOVE" stamp, the putative differences
of sexual orientation that seem to distinguish Charicles and Callicratidas
are largely an optical (that is, a semiotic) illusion—an effect of cultural perspective: the two disputants, like the two lovebirds, are mirror-opposites,
which is to say that their basic outlook on the relation between sexual
preference and erotic identity is pretty much the same. Charicles and Callicratidas are doubtless a very odd couple, but in their own way they are
made for each other.[51]

: : :

If my interpretation of the pseudo-Lucianic *Erôtes* proves to be persuasive, I shall have managed to provide at least some support for Michel
Foucault's proposition that sexuality is not lodged in our bodies, in our
hormones, or in our genitals but resides in our discursive and institutional
practices as well as in the experiences that they construct. Bodies do not
come with ready-made sexualities. Bodies are not even attracted to other
bodies.[52] It is human subjects, rather, who are attracted to various objects,
including bodies, and the features of bodies that render them desirable to
human subjects are contingent on the cultural codes, the social conventions, and the political institutions that structure and inform human subjectivity itself, thereby shaping our individual erotic ideals and defining for
us the scope of what we find attractive. Modern cultural modes of inter-
pellating European and American bourgeois subjects typically occlude that
process of sexual subjectivation, prompting us to misrecognize it as a bio-
physical process—and thus to interpret the "sexuality effects" produced
in our bodies as the collective sign of an intrinsically and irreducibly bodily event. As D. A. Miller has reminded us, "All the deployments of the
'bio-power' that characterizes our modernity depend on the supposition
that the most effective take on the subject is rooted in its body, insinu-
ated within this body's 'naturally given' imperatives. *Metaphorizing the
body begins and ends with literalizing the meanings the body is thus made
to bear.*"[53]

But just because that deployment of bio-power which we call sexuality
makes use of our bodies as sites for the production of sexuality effects—
in the form of literalized bodily meanings—we need not therefore assume
that sexuality itself is a literal, or natural, reality. Rather, sexuality is a
mode of human subjectivation that operates in part by figuring the body
as the literal and by pressing the body's supposed literality into the service

of a metaphorical project. As such, sexuality represents a seizure of the body by a historically unique apparatus for producing historically specific forms of subjectivity. What I have tried to do through my reading of the pseudo-Lucianic *Erôtes* is to confront the ancient discourses of erotic self-fashioning with the modern discourses of sexuality in order to dramatize the differences between them and to make visible the historical dimensions of that supposedly ahistorical and universal entity called "the body"—to historicize that discursive space in which modern bio-power constructs "the body" as the "natural" ground of the desiring subject. One aim, and (I hope) one effect, of my interpretative strategy will be to contribute, insofar as scholarship can, to the task of reconstituting the body as a potential site of cultural activism and political resistance. If the sexual body is indeed historical—if there is, in short, no orgasm without ideology— perhaps ongoing inquiry into the politics of pleasure will serve to deepen the pleasures, as well as to widen the possibilities, of politics.

4

How to Do the History of Male Homosexuality

The history of sexuality is now such a respectable academic discipline, or at least such an established one, that its practitioners no longer feel much pressure to defend the enterprise—to rescue it from suspicions of being a palpable absurdity. Once upon a time, the very phrase "the history of sexuality" sounded like a contradiction in terms: how, after all, could *sexuality* have a *history?* Nowadays, by contrast, we are so accustomed to the notion that sexuality does indeed have a history that we do not often ask ourselves what *kind* of history sexuality has. If such questions do come up, they get dealt with perfunctorily, in the course of the methodological throat clearing that historians ritually perform in the opening paragraphs of scholarly articles. Recently, this exercise has tended to include a more or less obligatory reference to the trouble once caused to historians, long long ago in a country far far away, by theorists who had argued that sexuality was socially constructed—an intriguing idea in its time and place, or so we are reassuringly told, but one that was taken to outlandish extremes and that no one much credits any longer.[1] With the disruptive potential of these metahistorical questions safely relegated to the past, the historian of sexuality can get down, or get back, to the business at hand.

But this new consensus, and the sense of theoretical closure that accompanies it, is premature. I believe that it is more useful than ever to ask how sexuality can have a history. The point of such a question, to be sure, is no longer to register the questioner's skepticism and incredulity (as if to say, "How on earth could such a thing be possible?") but to inquire more closely into the modalities of histori-cal being that sexuality possesses: to ask how exactly—in what terms, by virtue of what temporality, in which of its dimensions or aspects—does sexuality have a history?

That question, of course, has already been answered in a number of ways, each of them manifesting a different strategy for articulating the relation between continuity and discontinuity, identity and difference, in the history of sexuality. The constructionist-essentialist debate of the late 1980s should be seen as a particularly vigorous effort to force a solution to this question, but even after constructionists claimed to have won it, and essentialists claimed to have exposed the bad scholarship produced by it, and everybody else claimed to be sick and tired of it, the basic question about the historicity of sexuality has remained. In fact, current work in the history of sexuality still appears to be poised in its emphasis between the two poles of identity and difference, which in my view represent merely reformulated versions of the old essentialist and constructionist positions. Nonetheless, it may be prudent to recast the question in less polemical or old-fashioned terms by acknowledging that any adequate attempt to describe the historicity of sexuality will have to fix on some strategy for ac-commodating the aspects of sexual life that seem to persist through time as well as the dramatic differences between historically documented forms of sexual experience. Current analytic models that attempt to do this by map-ping shifts in the categories or classifications of an otherwise unchanging "sexuality," or by insisting on a historical distinction between pre-modern sexual acts and modern sexual identities, simply cannot capture the com-plexity of the issues at stake in the new histories of sexual subjectivity that are available to us.[2]

The tensions between interpretative emphases on continuity and dis-continuity, identity and difference, appear with almost painful intensity in the historiography of homosexuality. They reflect not only the high political stakes in any contemporary project that involves producing rep-resentations of homosexuality but also the irreducible definitional uncer-tainty about what homosexuality itself really is.[3] Perhaps the clearest and most explicit articulation of the consequences of this uncertainty for his-torians is found in the introduction to *Hidden from History*, the path-breaking anthology of lesbian and gay history published in 1989: "Same-sex genital sexuality, love and friendship, gender non-conformity, and a certain aesthetic or political perspective are all considered to have some (often ambiguous and always contested) relationship to that complex of attributes we today designate as homosexuality. . . . Much historical research has been an effort to locate the antecedents of those characteristics a given historian believes are constitutive of contemporary gay identity, be they sodomitical acts, cross dressing, or intimate friendships."[4] If contemporary gay or lesbian identity seems to hover in suspense between these different and discontinuous discourses of sodomy, gender inversion, and same-sex love, the same can be said even more emphatically about homosexual identity as we attempt to trace it back in time. The essence of the constructionist approach to the history of homosexuality, after all, was to argue that homosexuality is a modern construction, not because no same-sex sexual acts or erotic labels existed before 1869, when the term "homosexuality" first appeared in print, but because no single category of discourse or experience existed in the pre-modern and non-Western worlds that comprehended exactly the same range of same-sex sexual behaviors, desires, psychologies, and socialities, as well as the various forms of gender deviance, that now fall within the capacious definitional boundaries of homosexuality. Some earlier identity categories attached to same-sex sexual practices occupied some of the discursive territory now claimed by homosexuality; others cut across the frontier between homosexuality and heterosexuality. A number of these identity categories persisted in various forms for thousands of years before the modern term or concept of homosexuality was invented. It is quite possible that the current definitional uncertainty about what homosexuality is, or the uncertainty about what features are constitutive of lesbian or gay male identity, is the result of this long historical process of accumulation, accretion, and overlay. The history of discourses pertaining to forms of male intimacy may be especially revealing, because such discourses have been extensively and complexly elaborated over time, and they condense a number of the crosscutting systems of thought at whose intersection we now find ourselves.

: : :

In what follows I offer what I believe is a new strategy for approaching the history of sexuality in general and the history of male homosexuality in particular. My strategy is designed to rehabilitate a modified constructionist approach to the history of sexuality by readily acknowledging the existence of transhistorical continuities, reintegrating them into the frame of the analysis, and reinterpreting their significance within a genealogical understanding of the emergence of (homo)sexuality itself. A constructionist history of (homo)sexuality, in my view, can easily accommodate such continuities and need not be afraid of or embarrassed by them.

I begin where all histories of homosexuality must begin (like it or not), namely, with the modern notion of homosexuality, which, explicitly or implicitly, defines the horizons of our immediate conceptual universe and inevitably shapes our inquiries into same-sex sexual desire and behavior in the past. If we cannot simply escape from the conceptual tyranny of homosexuality by some feat of scholarly rigor (as I once thought we could)—by an insistent methodological suspension of modern categories, by an austerely historicist determination to identify and bracket our own ideological presuppositions so as to describe earlier phenomena in all their irreducible cultural specificity and time-bound purity—we can at least insist on taking our categories so seriously as to magnify their inner contradictions to the point where those contradictions turn out to be analytically informative. And if we really try hard to make our modern definitions of homosexuality apply to the past, we will place so much heuristic pressure on them that they will dissolve to reveal the shape of other, earlier categories, discourses, logics, coherences.

To follow the disintegration of our own concepts as we trace them backward in time can be the start of an inquiry into the alterity of the past. A genealogical analysis of homosexuality begins with our contemporary notion of homosexuality, incoherent though it may be, not only because such a notion inevitably frames all inquiry into same-sex sexual expression in the past but also because its very incoherence registers the genetic traces of its own historical evolution. In fact, it is this incoherence at the core of the modern notion of homosexuality that furnishes the most eloquent indication of the historical accumulation of discontinuous notions that shelter within its specious unity. The genealogist attempts to disaggregate those notions by tracing their separate histories as well as the process of their interrelations, their crossings, and, eventually, their unstable convergence in the present day.

Of course, to speak of "convergence" in this context is merely to describe how the modern concept of homosexuality functions; it is not to subscribe to a belief in that functioning. It is therefore not to reduce the heterogeneities of queer existence in the present or the past to an "overarching principle that speaks for an already given whole" but, rather, to demonstrate how the modern notion of homosexuality has come to perform the role of such a principle.[5] I wish to avoid the implication that by analyzing the triumphalism of a modern discursive category I am in any way participating in that triumphalism. On the contrary, I wish to bring out the particularity of "homosexuality" as a singular, distinctive formation that pretends to represent all same-sex sexual expression, a partial perspective that claims to encompass the whole. My response is to deidealize homosexuality, so as to return it to its cultural specificity and contingency.

To that end, I shall try to describe, very tentatively, very speculatively, some important pre-homosexual discourses, practices, categories, patterns, or models (I am really not sure what to call them) and to sketch their similarities with and differences from what goes by the name of homosexuality nowadays. I do so by way of gesturing toward a larger genealogical project that others, I hope, will correct and complete. The project I envision needs to be systematic in distinguishing those earlier, pre-homosexual traditions of homosexual discourse both from one another and from the modern discourses of homosexuality, while also noting overlaps or commonalities among them. It needs to describe these different categories in all their positivity and build as much specificity as possible into each of them, while also accounting for their interrelations. And it needs to identify ruptures within each of these discursive traditions—breaks, transformations, reconfigurations—so as to take account of heterogeneities contained within the long histories of their respective evolutions. Such a project, if successful, would be able to capture the play of identities and differences *within* the synchronic multiplicity of different but simultaneous traditions of discourse that have existed through the ages as well as the play of identities and differences *across* the various diachronic transitions within each of them over the course of time, while foregrounding the significant break effected during the past three or four centuries by the emergence of the discourses of (homo)sexuality itself.

The project I have imagined and described is not an entirely original invention of my own. Previous historians and sociologists have identified four principal models according to which same-sex sexual behaviors are culturally constructed around the world (age-differentiated, role-specific, gender-crossing, and homosexual), and these four models reveal some obvious correspondences with the categories employed in the genealogy of male homosexuality I am about to outline.[6] My own approach is distinguished, I believe, by being explicitly genealogical rather than sociological or behavioral (or even, in a strict sense, historical) and by making visible a series of discursive figures immanent in the social and cultural traditions of Europe in particular. (I focus here on the history of European discourses, because I am attempting to construct the genealogy of a European notion—that is, homosexuality—but I include non-European material in my survey whenever it seems pertinent.) My most immediate precursors, it turns out, are the editors of *Hidden from History* quoted above: the three models of homosexuality that they enumerate—"same-sex genital sexual-

ity" (or "sodomitical acts"), "love and friendship" (or "intimate friendships"), and "gender non-conformity" (or "cross-dressing")—closely anticipate the divisions I will be proposing here.

I will argue, in any case, that there is no such thing as a history of male
homosexuality. At least, there is no such thing as a singular or unitary history of male homosexuality. Instead, there are histories to be written of at
least four different but simultaneous categories or traditions of discourse
pertaining to aspects of what we now define as homosexuality. Each of
these traditions has its own consistency, autonomy, density, particularity,
and continuity over time, though each also undergoes various breaks or
ruptures. Each has subsisted more or less independently of the others, although they have routinely interacted with one another, and they have
helped to constitute one another through their various exclusions. Their
separate histories, as well as the history of their interrelations, have been
obscured *but not superseded* by the recent emergence of the discourses of
(homo)sexuality. In fact, what "homosexuality" signifies today is an effect
of this cumulative process of historical overlay and accretion. One result
of that historical process is what Eve Kosofsky Sedgwick memorably calls
"the unrationalized coexistence of different models" of sex and gender in
the present day.[7] I believe I am now in a position to offer, as a hypothesis, a
historical explanation for the phenomenon that Sedgwick has so brilliantly
described.

I suggest that if our "understanding of homosexual definition . . . is
organized around a radical and irreducible incoherence," owing to "the
unrationalized coexistence of different models" of sex and gender, as Sedgwick says, it is because we have retained at least four pre-homosexual
models of male sexual and gender deviance, all of which derive from an
age-old system that privileges gender over sexuality, alongside of (and despite their flagrant conflict with) a newer homosexual model derived from
a more recent, comparatively anomalous system that privileges sexuality
over gender.[8] If that explanation is correct, then a genealogy of contemporary homosexual discourse—which is to say, a historical critique of the
category of homosexuality, such as I propose to undertake here—can significantly support and expand Sedgwick's influential discursive critique of
the category of homosexuality in *Epistemology of the Closet* and provide
it with an overdue and much-needed historical grounding.[9]

The four pre-homosexual categories of male sex and gender deviance
that I have identified so far can be described, very provisionally, as categories of (1) effeminacy, (2) paederasty or "active" sodomy, (3) friendship
or male love, and (4) passivity or inversion. A fifth category, the category of
homosexuality, is—despite occasional pre-figurations in earlier discourses

(which it would be valuable to trace, though I cannot do so here)—a recent addition. Each of these five categories requires a separate analysis. I will concentrate on the history of discourses, because what I am attempting to map out is a genealogy of the modern discourses of homosexuality, but, as will become evident, I do not mean to exclude the history of practices, whose relation to the history of discourses remains to be fully considered. In any case, my principal aim is to produce a model, to articulate a patterning of discourse, not to write a social history or a descriptive survey of sexual practices. And even so I will make no attempt here to recover the variety of discursive silences, the subjugated knowledges, the non-represented voices that must figure significantly, or at least be taken into account, in any substantive history of male homosexuality. The preliminary genealogy offered here will inevitably overrepresent dominant or elite discourses, though it is not entirely limited to them, and as such it will be admittedly partial and incomplete. A fully realized genealogical inquiry would need to overcome, to the greatest possible degree, such limitations.

Let me emphasize at the outset that the names I have chosen for the first four of these categories are heuristic, tentative, and ad hoc. My designations are not proper historical descriptors—how could they be, since the first four categories cut across historical periods, geographies, and cultures? Nor will my definitions of the first four categories explicate the historical meanings of the names I have called them. For example, "sodomy," "that utterly confused category," [10] was applied historically to masturbation, oral sex, anal sex, and same-sex sexual relations, among other things, but my second category refers to something much more specific—not because I am unaware of the plurality of historical meanings of "sodomy" but because I use the term "active sodomy" specifically in a transhistorical fashion to denominate a certain model or structure of male homosexual relations for which there is no single proper name. That is unfortunate, but for the moment I see no alternative. With that as a final warning, let me now begin.

: : :

Effeminacy has often functioned as a marker of so-called sexual inversion in men, of transgenderism or sexual role reversal, and thus (according to one very specific and historically contingent cultural logic) of homosexual desire. Nonetheless, it is useful to distinguish effeminacy from male passivity, inversion, and homosexuality. In particular, effeminacy should be clearly distinguished from homosexual object-choice or same-sex sexual preference in men—and not just for the well-rehearsed reasons that it is possible for men to be effeminate without being homosexual and to be homosexual without being effeminate. Rather, effeminacy deserves to be treated independently because it was for a long time defined as a symptom of an excess of what we would now call heterosexual as well as homosexual desire. It is therefore a category unto itself.

Effeminacy did not always imply homosexuality. In various European cultural traditions men could be designated as "soft" or "unmasculine" (*malthakos* in Greek, *mollis* in Latin and its Romance derivatives) either because they were inverts or pathics—because they were *womanly,* or transgendered, and liked being fucked by other men—or because, on the contrary, they were *womanizers,* because they deviated from masculine gender norms insofar as they preferred the soft option of love to the hard option of war. In the culture of the military elites of Europe, at least from the ancient world through the Renaissance, normative masculinity often entailed austerity, resistance to appetite, and mastery of the impulse to pleasure. (The once fashionable American ideal of the Big Man on Campus, the football jock who gets to indulge limitlessly his love of hot showers, cold beer, fast cars, and faster women, would appear in this context not as an emblem of masculinity but of its degraded opposite, as a monster of effeminacy.) A man displayed his true mettle in war, or so it was thought, and more generally in struggles with other men for honor—in politics, business, and other competitive enterprises. Those men who refused to rise to the challenge, who abandoned the competitive society of men for the amorous society of women, who pursued a life of pleasure, who made love instead of war—they incarnated the classical stereotype of effeminacy. This stereotype seems to live on in the American South, where "a redneck queer" is defined as "a boy from Alabama who laks girls better'n football."[11] It is also alive and well in Anglo-Celtic Australia, where a real bloke supposedly avoids the company of women and prefers to spend all his time with his mates: that's how you can be sure that he's straight.

This stereotype, which admittedly sorts out rather oddly with recent notions of hetero- and homosexuality, goes far back in time. For the ancient Greeks and Romans, a man who indulged his taste for sexual pleasure with women did not necessarily enhance his virility but often undermined it. To please women, such a man was likely to make an effort to appear smooth instead of rough, graceful instead of powerful, and might even compound that effeminate style by using makeup and perfumes, elaborate grooming, and prominent jewelry. In the late antique dialogue ascribed to Lucian discussed in the previous chapter, which features a debate between two men as to whether women or boys are better vehicles of male erotic pleasure, it is the advocate of boys who is portrayed as hypervirile, whereas the defender of women, a good-looking young man, is described as exhibiting "a skillful use of cosmetics, so as to be attractive to women."[12] Similarly, the stereotype of an adulterer in the ancient Greek literary tradition can be judged from the following description, in a romance by the Greek prose writer Chariton, of a man who flagrantly exhibits all the canonical identifying markers of adultery: "His hair was gleaming and heavily scented; his eyes were made up; he had a soft cloak and fine shoes; heavy rings gleamed on his fingers."[13] Effeminacy has traditionally functioned as sign of heterosexual excess in men.

It was men, evidently, who liked men to be rough and tough. They may have liked their women and boys to be soft and smooth, but they did not respect these qualities in a mature man. Women, by contrast, seem to have found the soft style of masculinity more appealing. This has created a certain tension between gender norms and erotic pleasure in traditional male cultures. The paradigmatic instance, which illustrates the traditional clash between hard and soft styles of masculinity, can be found in the figure of Hercules. Hercules is a hero who oscillates between extremes of hypermasculinity and effeminacy: he is preternaturally strong, yet he finds himself enslaved by a woman (Queen Omphale); he surpasses all men at feats of strength, yet he is driven mad by love, either for a woman (Iole) or for a boy (Hylas).[14] Hercules sets the stage for such modern figures as Shakespeare's Mark Antony, who claims Hercules as his literal ancestor in *Antony and Cleopatra* and who incurs similar charges of effeminacy when he takes time out from ruling the Roman Empire to live a life of passion and indulgence with Cleopatra. The roles of ruler and lover are made to contrast from the very opening of the play, when Antony is described as "the triple pillar of the world transform'd / Into a strumpet's fool" (1.1.12–13).

Antony is not unique in Shakespeare. Othello also voices anxieties about the incapacitating effects of conjugal love on a military leader. But this tension is best represented for our purposes by Shakespeare's Romeo, who may nowadays figure as an icon of male heterosexuality but who once saw his own romantic ardor in a less normative light. Berating himself for a lack of martial strength, reluctant as he is to fight Juliet's cousin Tybalt, and invoking the traditional opposition between the cold, wet melancholia of love and the hot, dry nature of masculine virtue, Romeo exclaims:

> O sweet Juliet,
> Thy beauty hath made me effeminate,
> And in my temper softened valour's steel![15]
>
> (3.1.113–15)

The survival and interplay of these different notions of effeminacy may help explain the persistent sexual ambiguity that attaches, even today, to predominantly male institutions, such as fraternities, the armed forces, the church, the corporate boardroom, or Congress: Is the sort of manhood fostered and expressed there to be considered the truest and most essential form of masculinity, virility in its highest and purest form, or an exceptional and bizarre perversion of it?

: : :

In short, effeminacy needs to be distinguished from homosexuality. This brings me to the second pre-homosexual category I want to describe: paederasty or "active" sodomy. These terms, as I will use them, refer to the male sexual penetration of a subordinate male—subordinate in terms of age, social class, gender style, and/or sexual role.[16] Such a notion of subordination reflects the widespread social symbolization of phallic penetration as an exercise of hierarchical power. Accordingly, the discourses of paederasty or active sodomy are shaped by a crucial distinction between the male desire *to penetrate* and the male desire *to be penetrated* and, thus, between paederasty or "active" sodomy, on one side of the hierarchical equation, and male passivity or inversion, on the other. (My differentiation between the second and the fourth of the five categories conforms to that distinction.)

The nineteenth-century sexologists, who inherited that traditional opposition and then systematically elaborated it into the distinction between paederasty ("Greek love") and passivity ("contrary sexual feeling" or "inversion of the sexual instinct"), based their division on a psychiatric distinction between "perversity" and "perversion," according to which an inverted, transgendered, or passive sexual orientation always indicated "perversion" in a man, whereas the sexual penetration of a subordinate male might qualify merely as "perversity." These Victorian medical writers, who were still largely untouched by the distinction between homo- and heterosexuality (which had yet to assert its ascendancy over earlier modes of sexual classification), were at pains to determine whether deviant sexual acts proceeded from an individual's morally depraved character (i.e., perversity)—whether, that is, they were merely the result of vice, which might be restrained by laws and punished as a crime—or whether they originated in a pathological condition (i.e., perversion), a mental disease, a perverted "sexuality," which could only be medically treated.

The distinction is expounded by Krafft-Ebing as follows: "*Perversion* of the sexual instinct . . . is not to be confounded with *perversity* in the sexual act; since the latter may be induced by conditions other than psychopathological. The concrete perverse act, monstrous as it may be, is clinically not decisive. In order to differentiate between disease (perversion) and vice (perversity), one must investigate the whole personality of the individual and the original motive leading to the perverse act. Therein will be found the key to the diagnosis."[17] The male sexual penetration of a subordinate male certainly represented a perverse act, but it might not in every case signify a perversion of the sexual instinct, a mental illness affecting "the whole personality": it might indicate a morally vicious character rather than a pathological condition.

Implicit in this doctrine, and highly significant for the purposes of my analysis, is the premise that there was not necessarily anything sexually or psychologically abnormal in itself about the male sexual penetration of a subordinate male. If the man who played an "active" sexual role in sexual intercourse with other males was conventionally masculine in both his appearance and his manner of feeling and acting, if he did not seek to be penetrated by other men, and/or if he also had sexual relations with women, he might not be sick but immoral, not perverted but merely perverse. His penetration of a subordinate male, reprehensible and abominable though it might be, could be reckoned a manifestation of his excessive but otherwise normal male sexual appetite. Like the somewhat earlier, aristocratic figure of the libertine or rake or roué, such a man perversely refused to limit his sexual options to pleasures supposedly prescribed by nature and instead sought out more unusual, unlawful, sophisticated, or elaborate sexual experiences to gratify his jaded sexual tastes.[18] In the case of such men, paederasty or sodomy was a sign of an immoral character but not of a personality disorder, "moral insanity," or psychological abnormality.[19]

The sexologists' distinctions between the perverse and the perverted, between the immoral and the pathological, between the merely vicious and the diseased, may strike us as quaintly Victorian, but prominent psychologists, sociologists, and jurists today continue to draw similar distinctions between "pseudo-homosexuality" and "homosexuality," or between "situational," "opportunistic" homosexuality and what they call, for lack of a better term, "real" homosexuality.[20] The acts of homosexual penetration performed on men in prison by men who lead heterosexual lives out of prison, for example, are often regarded not as symptoms of a particular psychosexual orientation, as expressions of erotic desire, or even as "homosexuality," but as mere behavioral adaptations by men to a society without women. Such behavior, it is often believed nowadays, simply vouches for the male capacity to enjoy various forms of perverse gratification[21] and, further, to eroticize hierarchy—to be sexually aroused by the opportunity to play a dominant role in structured relations of unequal power. But the underlying notion is that a conventionally masculine man who sexually penetrates a subordinate partner of either sex is acting out a conventional male role. That notion has a long history.

In fact, the distinction between a quasi-normal, non-homosexual homosexuality and an absolutely deviant sexual inversion—the distinction that was systematically elaborated in nineteenth-century psychiatry and that lives on today—did not originate in the Victorian period. It reflects an age-old practice of classifying sexual relations in terms of penetration versus being penetrated, superordinate versus subordinate status, masculinity versus femininity, and activity versus passivity—in terms of *hierarchy* and *gender,* that is, rather than in terms of *sex* and *sexuality.* Possible evidence for an age-structured, role-specific, hierarchical pattern of sexual relations among males can be found in the Mediterranean basin as early as the Bronze Age civilizations of Minoan Crete in the late second millennium B.C. and as late as the Renaissance cities of Italy in the fourteenth and fifteenth centuries A.D.[22] The best known and most thoroughly documented historical instances of this pattern are probably ancient Greek and Roman paederasty and early modern European sodomy, but the pattern itself seems to have pre-existed them, and it also has outlived them.[23]

The evidence from judicial records in fifteenth-century Florence is sufficiently detailed to afford us a glimpse of the extent and distribution of sodomitical activity in one (admittedly notorious) pre-modern European community. Between 1432 and 1502 as many as seventeen thousand individuals in Florence, most of them males, were formally incriminated at least once for sodomy, out of a total population of forty thousand men, women, and children: two out of every three men who reached the age of forty in this period were formally incriminated for sodomy. Among those who were indicted, approximately 90 percent of the "passive" partners (including, according to Florentine notions, the insertive partners in oral copulation as well as the receptive partners in anal intercourse) were eighteen years old or younger, and 93 percent of the "active" partners were nineteen or older—the vast majority of them under the ages of thirty to thirty-five, the time of life at which men customarily married.[24]

This is sex as hierarchy, not mutuality, sex as something done to someone by someone else, not a common search for shared pleasure or a purely personal, private experience in which larger social identities based on age or social status are submerged or lost. Here sex implies difference, not identity, and it turns on a systematic division of labor. It is the younger partner who is considered sexually attractive, while it is the older one who experiences erotic desire for the younger. Although love, emotional intimacy, and tenderness are not necessarily absent from the relationship, the distribution of erotic passion and sexual pleasure is assumed to be more or less lopsided, with the older, "active" partner being the *subject* of desire and the recipient of the greater share of pleasure from a younger partner who figures as a sexual *object,* feels no comparable desire, and derives no comparable pleasure from the contact (unless he is an invert or pathic and therefore belongs to my fourth category). The junior partner's reward must therefore be measured out in currencies other than pleasure, such as praise, assistance, gifts, or money. As an erotic experience, an experience of passion or desire, paederasty or sodomy refers to the "active" partner only.[25]

This traditional, hierarchical model of male sexual relations represents sexual preference without sexual orientation (in the case of the "active" partner, who is still the point of reference here). Numbers of texts going back to classical antiquity testify to a conscious erotic preference on the part of "men," even to the point of exclusivity, for sexual intercourse with members of one sex rather than the other; indeed, a venerable subgenre of erotic literature consists of formal debates between two "men" about whether women or boys are superior vehicles of male sexual gratification.[26] (By "men" I refer to adult, socially empowered males, as opposed to subordinate men or "boys.") Such playful debates are widely distributed in the luxury literatures of traditional male societies: examples can be found in Greek prose works from late antiquity, in medieval European and Arabic poetry and prose, in late imperial Chinese writings, and in seventeenth-century Japanese literature.[27]

But the explicit and conscious erotic preferences voiced in such contexts should not be equated with declarations of sexual orientation, for at least three reasons. First, they are presented as the outcome of conscious choice, a choice that expresses the male subject's values and preferred way of life, rather than as symptoms of an involuntary psychosexual condition. The men who voice such preferences often see themselves as at least nominally capable of responding to the erotic appeal of both good-looking women and good-looking boys. This is sexual object-choice as an expression of ethics or aesthetics, as an exercise in erotic connoisseurship, not as a reflex of sexuality. It is more like vegetarianism than homosexuality. Second, same-sex sexual object-choice in and of itself does not necessarily function in this context as a marker of difference. It does not individuate men from one another in terms of their "sexuality." Finally, same-sex sexual object-choice in this case does not mark itself visibly on a man's physical appearance or inscribe itself in his personal mannerisms or deportment. Nor does it impugn his masculinity.[28]

Nonetheless, paederasty or sodomy did provide an opportunity and a context for men to express and discuss their sexual tastes, to explore their erotic subjectivities, and to compare their sexual preferences. It is in the context of erotic reflection by socially empowered, superordinate, conventionally masculine males that men have been able to articulate conscious erotic preferences, sometimes to the point of exclusivity, for sexual relations with boys or women, as well as for sexual relations with certain kinds of boys or women. The highly elaborate, ritualistic, conspicuously public practice of courtship and lovemaking provided socially empowered males with a traditional, socially sanctioned discursive space for articulating such preferences and for presenting themselves as conscious subjects of desire.

This point is an important one for historians, and it has long been obscured. John Boswell, who influentially defined as "gay sexuality" all same-sex "eroticism associated with a conscious preference," thought that if he could find in pre-modern Europe evidence of conscious erotic preferences by some males for others, he would have documented the existence of "gay sexuality" in that period as well.[29] Of course, evidence of conscious erotic preferences does exist in abundance throughout the surviving documentary record, but it tends to be found in the context of discourses linked to the senior partners in hierarchical relations of paederasty or sodomy. It therefore points not to the existence of "gay sexuality" per se but to one particular discourse and set of practices constituting one aspect of what counts as gay sexuality nowadays, an aspect of gay sexuality that no gay man would identify with the totality of gay sexuality. Declarations of conscious erotic preferences are rarely, if ever, to be found in the contexts of the three other traditional discourses of male same-sex eroticism and gender deviance discussed here. And so conscious same-sex erotic preference ought not be equated with the whole of gay sexuality or male homosexuality. It represents merely one historical tradition among several.[30]

: : :

Far removed from the hierarchical world of the sexual penetration of subordinate males by superordinate males is the world of male friendship and love, which can claim an equally ancient discursive tradition. To be sure, hierarchy is not always absent from social relations between male friends: from the heroic comradeships of Gilgamesh and Enkidu in the Babylonian *Epic of Gilgamesh,* David and Jonathan in the biblical Books of Samuel, and Achilles and Patroclus in the *Iliad,* to the public displays of royal affection by England's James I and his male courtiers, to the latest American biracial cop thriller, male friendships often reveal striking patterns of asymmetry.[31] Precisely to the extent, however, that such friendships *are* structured by social divisions or by inequalities of power, to the extent that they approximate patron-client relationships in which the two "friends" are assigned radically different duties, postures, and roles, to just that extent are such friendships opened up to the possibility of being interpreted, then as now, in paederastic or sodomitical terms.[32] Within the horizons of the male world, as we have seen, hierarchy itself is *hot:* it is indissociably bound up with at least the potential for erotic signification. Hence, disparities of power between male intimates take on an immediate and inescapable aura of eroticism. Conversely, what often looks to us nowadays like eroticism may have served in the past to constitute, to dramatize, and to identify as "friendships" routine relationships of dependence between unequals.[33]

No wonder, then, that three and four centuries after the composition of the *Iliad,* some Greeks of the classical period interpreted Achilles and Patroclus as a paederastic couple (although they could not always agree on who was the man and who was the boy), while more recently scholars have disputed whether James I was homosexual or whether David and Jonathan were lovers. Such disputes, which often have a long history, tend to conflate notions of friendship first with notions of erotic hierarchy, paederasty, or sodomy, and then with notions of homosexuality. It may be useful therefore to distinguish friendship both from erotic hierarchy and from homoerotic desire.

It should be noted that in addition to the tradition of the heroic warrior with his subordinate male pal or sidekick (who inevitably dies), in addition to the patron-client model of male friendship, which may well have been the dominant model of friendship in the early modern period, there is another tradition that emphasizes equality, mutuality, and reciprocity in love between men.[34] Such an egalitarian relation can obtain only between two men who occupy the same social rank, usually an elite one, and who can claim the same status in terms of age, masculinity, and social empowerment. In the eighth and ninth books of his *Nicomachean Ethics,* Aristotle championed precisely such a reciprocal model of friendship between male equals, and he wrote, most influentially, that the best sort of friend is "another self," an *allos autos* or alter ego (9.4 [1166a31]). The sentiment is echoed repeatedly down through the centuries: a true friend is part of oneself, indistinguishable from oneself. True friends have a single mind, a single heart in two bodies. As Montaigne writes in his essay *On Friendship,* "Our souls mingle and blend with each other so completely that they efface the seam that joined them, and cannot find it again."[35]

The friendship of virtuous men is characterized by a disinterested love that leads to a merging of individual identities and hence to an unwillingness to live without the other, a readiness to die with or for the other. We find the theme of the inseparability of male friends in both life and death repeated time and again from representations of Achilles and Patroclus, Orestes and Pylades, Theseus and Pirithous in the ancient world to *Lethal Weapon*'s Mel Gibson and Danny Glover in the modern world.

The language used to convey such passionate male unions often appears to modern sensibilities suspiciously overheated, if not downright erotic. Thus Montaigne can write:

> If you press me to tell why I loved him, I feel that this cannot be expressed, except by answering: Because it was he, because it was I . . . it is I know not what . . . which, having seized my whole will, led it to plunge and lose itself in his; which, having seized his whole will, led it to plunge and lose itself in mine, with equal hunger, equal rivalry. [Note that Montaigne's insistence on perfect equality in friendship is emphasized even at the syntactical level of his prose, by the parallelism and mutual correspondence of the clauses that refer to the reciprocal devotion of the two friends.] I say lose, in truth, for neither of us reserved anything for himself, nor was anything either his or mine. . . . Our souls pulled together in such unison, they regarded each other with such ardent affection, and with a like affection revealed themselves to each other to the very depths of our hearts, that not only did I know his soul as well as mine, but I should certainly have trusted myself to him more readily than to myself.[36]

Similarly, in a 1677 drama on a Roman theme by Dryden, *All for Love*, Antony can say about his noble friend Dolabella:

> I was his soul, he lived not but in me.
> We were so closed within each other's breasts,
> The rivets were not found that joined us first.

[Compare Montaigne's "Our souls mingle and blend with each other so completely that they efface the seam that joined them, and cannot find it again."]

> That does not reach us yet: we were so mixed
> As meeting streams, both to ourselves were lost;

> We were one mass; we could not give or take
> But from the same, for he was I, I he.[37]
>
> (3.90–96)

It is difficult for us moderns—with our heavily psychologistic model of the human personality, our notion of unconscious drives, our tendency to associate desire with sexuality, and our heightened sensitivity to anything that might seem to contravene the strict protocols of heterosexual masculinity—it is difficult for us to avoid reading into such passionate expressions of male love a suggestion of "homoeroticism" at the very least, if not of "latent homosexuality," those being the formulations that often act as a cover for our own perplexity about how to interpret same-sex emotions that do not quite square with canonical conceptions of sexual subjectivity. But quite apart from the difficulty of entering into the emotional lives of pre-modern subjects, we need to reckon with the discursive contexts in which such passionate declarations were produced.

The thematic insistence in the two texts quoted above on mutuality and the merging of individual identities, although it may invoke in the minds of modern readers the formulas of heterosexual romantic love (e.g., Cathy's "I am Heathcliff"), in fact situates avowals of reciprocal love between male friends in an honorable, even glamorous tradition of heroic comradeship: precisely by carefully removing any hint of subordination on the part of one friend to the other and, thus, any suggestion of hierarchy, the emphasis on the fusion of two souls into one actually distances such a love from erotic passion. Montaigne even expresses despair about the impossibility of combining the two kinds of emotion within the confines of a single relationship.[38] He certainly never betrays the slightest doubt, in writing about his love for Etienne de La Boétie, that the sentiments he expresses are entirely normative, even admirable and boastworthy (although of course unique in their specifics). Far from offering us clues to his psychopathology, inadvertently revealing to us traces of his suppressed or unconscious desires, or expressing his erotic peculiarities (something he freely does elsewhere in his *Essays*), Montaigne deliberately immunizes his account of that friendship from disreputable interpretation by elaborately presenting his love as egalitarian, non-hierarchical, and reciprocal. For by such means he detaches it from the erotic realms of difference and hierarchy, setting it explicitly *against* the sexual love of men and women as well as the male sexual enjoyment of boys.

That doesn't mean that male lovers couldn't appeal to the friendship tradition as a cover for, or as a means of ennobling, erotic passion: "Why shouldst thou kneel?" Edward II asks Gaveston in Marlowe's recreation of the story; "knowest thou not who I am? / Thy friend, thy self, another Gaveston!" (1.1.141–42). (Dryden's Antony might be invoking this very precedent.) But it does indicate that sexual love, at least as it is viewed within the cultural horizons of the male world, is all about penetration and therefore all about position, superiority and inferiority, rank and status, gender and difference. Friendship (of the non-patronage sort), by contrast, is all about sameness: sameness of rank and status, sameness of sentiment, sameness of identity. It is this very emphasis on identity, similarity, and mutuality that distances the friendship tradition, in its original social and discursive context, from the world of sexual love. Sexual love, in the light of the male friendship tradition, actually sounds like a contradiction in terms: sexual penetration is not the sort of thing you would do to someone you really love.

So if the tradition of male friendship maintains a certain distance from the world of sexual difference and sexual relations, why include an account of that tradition here, in a genealogy of male homosexuality? Because the friendship tradition provided socially empowered men with an established discursive venue in which to express, without social reproach, sentiments of passionate and mutual love for one another. And such passionate, mutual love between persons of the same sex is an important component of what we now call homosexuality. So if we are to devise a complete and satisfactory genealogy of male homosexuality, we will have to find room in it for a history of male love.

: : :

Both paederasty/sodomy and friendship/love are consonant with masculine gender norms, with conventional masculinity as it has been defined in a number of European cultures. If anything, paederasty and friendship are both traditionally *masculinizing,* insofar as they express the male subject's virility and imply a thoroughgoing rejection of everything that is feminine. Both can therefore be seen as consolidating male gender identity (although not, of course, in every instance). As such, they belong to a different conceptual, moral, and social universe from what the Greeks called *kinaidia,* the Romans *mollitia,* and the nineteenth-century sexologists "contrary sexual feeling" or "sexual inversion." All these terms refer to the male "inversion" or reversal of masculine gender identity, a wholesale surrender of masculinity in favor of femininity, a transgendered condition expressed in everything from personal comportment and style to physical appearance, manner of feeling, sexual attraction to "normal" men, and preference for a receptive or "passive" role in sexual intercourse with such men.

The mere fact of being sexually penetrated by a man is much less significant for the sexual classification of passives or inverts than the question of the penetrated male's pleasure. In the pre-modern European systems of paederasty and sodomy, boys may be sexually penetrated, but they do not supposedly derive much pleasure from the act: they are the more or less willing objects of adult male desire, but they are not conventionally assigned a share of desire equal to that of their senior male partners, nor are they expected to enjoy being penetrated by them. Although they are "passive" in terms of their behavior, then, they are not passive in their overall erotic temperament or attitude: they are not aroused by the prospect or the act of submission. They have to be motivated to submit to their male lovers by a variety of largely non-sexual inducements, such as gifts or threats. So their "passivity" does not extend to their desire, which remains unengaged and can therefore claim to be uncontaminated by any impulse to subordination, any hint of "femininity." In that respect, they uphold and embody, even while playing a "passive" sexual role, traditional standards of virility.

Kinaidoi (*cinaedi* in Latin) and inverts, by contrast, actively desire to submit their bodies "passively" to sexual penetration by men, and in that sense they are seen as having a woman's desire, subjectivity, and gender identity. The category of male passive or invert applies specifically to subordinate males whose willingness to submit themselves to sexual penetration by men proceeds not from some non-sexual motive (including love for their partner) but from their own erotic desires and/or from their assumption of a feminine gender identity.

Although the pleasure he takes in being sexually penetrated may be the most flagrant, the most extreme expression of the overall gender reversal that characterizes the male invert, inversion is not necessarily, or even principally, defined by the enjoyment of particular sexual acts. Nor does it have to do strictly with homosexual desire, because inverts may have insertive phallic sex with women without ceasing to be considered inverts. Rather, inversion has to do with deviant gender identity, sensibility, and personal style, one aspect of which is the "womanly" liking for a "passive" role in sexual intercourse with other men. Therefore notions of inversion do not tend to make a strict separation between specifically sexual manifestations of inversion and other, equally telling deviations from the norms of masculinity, such as the adoption of feminine dress. The emphasis falls on a violation of the protocols of manhood, a characterological failure of grand proportions that cannot be redeemed (as sodomy can) by the enjoyment of sexual relations with women. Inversion is not about sexuality but about gender, to the extent that it makes sense to separate the two.[39]

What, then, is the difference between effeminates and passives? What distinguishes those men (belonging to my first category) who affect a "soft" style of masculinity and prefer making love to making war from those men (belonging to this fourth category) who have effeminate mannerisms and wish to submit their bodies, in "womanly" fashion, to the phallic pleasures of other men? The distinction is a subtle one, and it is easily blurred. After all, some stigma of gender deviance, of effeminacy, attaches to both types of men. And polarized definitions of the masculine and the feminine, along with the hyperbolic nature of sexual stereotyping, enable the slightest suggestion of gender deviance to be quickly inflated and transformed into an accusation of complete and total gender treason. From *liking* women to wanting to be *like* women is, according to the phobic logic of this masculinist ideology, only a small step—which is why both effeminates and passives (or "pathics") can be characterized as soft or unmasculine. The common application of the vocabulary of gender deviance to both effeminates and passives complicates for the modern interpreter the problem of distinguishing them.

One way to describe the difference between effeminates and passives is to contrast a universalizing notion of gender deviance with a minoritizing one. "Softness" either may represent the specter of potential gender failure that haunts all normative masculinity, an ever-present threat to the masculinity of every man, or it may represent the disfiguring peculiarity of a small class of deviant individuals.[40] Effeminates belong to the former category—they are men who succumb to a tendency that all normal men have and that all normal men have to guard against or suppress in themselves—whereas passives are men who are so unequal to the struggle that they can be seen to suffer from a specific constitutional defect, namely, a lack of the masculine capacity to withstand the appeal of pleasure (especially pleasure deemed exceptionally disgraceful or degrading) as well as a tendency to adopt a specifically feminine attitude of surrender in relations with other men. Passives therefore belong to a minoritizing category of male gender deviance.

It is these latter features that define the invert, even more than his desire or his sexual object-choice, because neither his desire nor his sexual object-choice is unique to him. The desire for a male partner, for example, is something the invert has in common both with the paederast and with the heroic male friend, figures vastly removed from him in social and moral status. Similarly, the desire to be penetrated by other men is something the invert has in common with the male homosexual, although many gay men who like to be penetrated do not necessarily qualify as inverts, either in their own eyes or in those of others. Inversion also differs from paederasty and friendship in that the love of boys and the love of friends are not necessarily discreditable sentiments, and they may well be confessed or even championed by the subjects themselves. Inversion, by contrast, is a shameful condition, never proclaimed about oneself (until relatively recently, that is, when a certain camp effrontery has become possible for some men), and almost always ascribed to some other person by an accuser whose intent is to demean and to vilify.

Moreover, traditional representations of "active" paederasts or sodomites do not necessarily portray them as visibly different in their appearance from normal men. You can't always tell a paederast or a sodomite by looking at him. An invert, by contrast, usually stands out, because his reversal of his gender identity affects his personal demeanor and shapes his attitude, gestures, and manner of conducting himself. Unlike the active penetration of boys, which might differentiate the lover of boys from the lover of women in terms of erotic preference but may not mark him as a visibly different sort of person, passivity or inversion stamps itself all over a man's social presentation and identifies him as a spectacularly deviant social type. It is in the context of inversion that we most often find produced and elaborated representations of a peculiar character type or stereotype, a phobic caricature embodying the supposedly visible and flagrant features of male sexual and gender deviance. Although this type is attached to homosexual sex, it is not attached to homosexual sex absolutely, for it is connected much less regularly, if at all, with paederasty or "active" sodomy; rather, it seems to be associated with passive or receptive homosexual sex, seen as merely one aspect of a more generalized gender reversal, an underlying betrayal of masculinity.[41] There is a remarkably consistent emphasis throughout the history of European sexual representation on the deviant morphology of the invert, his visibly different mode of appearance and dress, his feminine style of self-presentation. Inversion manifests itself outwardly.

It doesn't take one to know one. Everybody seems to know what an invert looks like and how he behaves, even if no normal man could possibly impersonate one. As a character in an ancient Greek comedy says, "*I have absolutely no idea how to use a twittering voice or walk about in an effeminate style, with my head tilted sidewise like all those pathics that I see here in the city smeared with depilatories.*"[42] Similarly, the Roman orator Quintilian speaks of "the plucked body, the broken walk, the female attire" as "signs of one who is *mollis* [soft] and not a real man."[43] Ancient physiognomists, experts in the learned technique of deciphering a person's character from his or her appearance, provide a more detailed description of the type: "You may recognize him by his provocatively melting glance and by the rapid movement of his intensely staring eyes. His brow is furrowed while his eyebrows and cheeks are in constant motion. His head is tilted to the side, his loins do not hold still, and his slack limbs never stay in one position. He minces along with little jumping steps; his knees knock together. He carries his hands with palms turned upward. He has a shifting gaze, and his voice is thin, weepy, shrill, and drawling."[44] All attempts at concealment are useless: "For it is by the twitching of their lips and the rotation of their eyes, by the haphazard and inconsistent shifting of their feet, by the movement of their hips and the fickle motion of their hands, and by the tremor of their voice as it begins with difficulty to speak, that effeminates are most easily revealed."[45]

But the ability to unmask an invert is hardly limited to specialist gender detectives. The Roman leader Scipio Aemilianus, consul in 147 B.C. and censor in 142, had no difficulty branding an opponent with all the telltale signs: "For the kind of man who adorns himself daily in front of a mirror, wearing perfume; whose eyebrows are shaved off; who walks around with plucked beard and thighs; who when he was a young man reclined at banquets next to his lover, wearing a long-sleeved tunic; who is as fond of men as he is of wine: can anyone doubt that he has done what *cinaedi* are in the habit of doing?"[46] The unmentionable deed of the *cinaedi*, of course, is passive bodily penetration.

The particular markers of inversion are culture-bound and therefore susceptible to change over time. In fact, it is in the context of inversion that we need to be particularly alert to breaks in historical continuity, to ruptures in the long traditions of representing and conceptualizing male passivity and gender deviance. Unfortunately, an analysis of discontinuities within these traditions falls outside the scope of the very rough and approximate genealogical outline offered here. Some differences will be evident from the citations that follow. What is striking, however, is the consistent *legibility* of inversion, which remains one of its perennial features. The medieval and early modern "catamite" (a word sometimes presumed, on the basis of dubious etymological reasoning, to signify the passive partner of a sodomite) is another highly "overt" type, and he clearly belongs in something like the same sort of category as the ancient Mediterranean *cinaedus* already described.

Here, for example, is a retrospective account of the goings-on at the court of the English king William Rufus, at the turn of the twelfth century, by a monastic chronicler named Orderic Vitalis: "At that time effeminates set the fashion in many parts of the world: foul catamites,

doomed to eternal fire, unrestrainedly pursued their revels and shame-
lessly gave themselves up to the filth of sodomy. They rejected the traditions of honest men, ridiculed the counsel of priests, and persisted in
their barbarous way of life and style of dress. They parted their hair
from the crown of the head to the forehead, grew long and luxurious
locks like women, and loved to deck themselves in long, over-tight shirts
and tunics."[47] Note that nothing in this passage establishes that the "effeminates" excoriated in it are being condemned specifically for sexual
passivity (although the use of the word "catamite" clearly points in that
direction). It would be easy enough for an incautious (or essentialist) historian to construe Orderic's reference to "the filth of sodomy" as implying the opposite—namely, that the "effeminates" are also being accused
of playing an "active" role in homosexual intercourse. But I think it is
possible to determine more precisely what Orderic is talking about. It
is because there is admittedly no way to settle the question on the basis
of a literary analysis alone that the approach I am advocating here can
aid decisively in the accurate decipherment of historical texts. Although
there is probably no way to settle the matter definitively, it should be
possible to resolve some ambiguities and narrow the interpretative options. In Orderic's case, the text's insistence on the visible deviance of
the catamites, its ascription to them of an effeminate morphology, situates it in a discursive tradition considerably more specific than that of
merely "gay male representation." Instead, Orderic's account would seem
to belong to a particular European tradition of discourse, a particular
discursive mode of representing male inverts or passives, which emphasizes their extravagantly feminine appearance. The more we know about
the discursive rules and regularities that control the production of statements about historical sexual actors, the easier it may be to figure out
what is going on in a particular passage even in the absence of explicit
linguistic indicators. In this way, attentiveness to the discursive context of
Orderic's text makes it possible, I believe, to extract from his ambiguous
and indeterminate language a better idea of the transgression for which
the "effeminates" are being condemned than we could ever do on the basis
of his words alone.

From Orderic we leap across another gap in time to the Renaissance
court of the French king Henri III, where in July 1576 one observer, com-
menting indignantly on the "effeminate, lewd make-up and adornments"
of the king's *mignons*—minions, or darlings (a synonym for "catamite")—
remarked that "these fine *mignons* wear their hair long, curled and re-
curled by means of artifice, with little velvet bonnets on top of it, like
the whores of the brothels."[48] Here is another example of male gender

deviance that discloses itself visibly even to the eyes of more properly masculine men—and carries with it an unmistakable sexual implication.

A century and a half later Londoners painted a vivid portrait of the
"mollies," the effeminate men who gathered privately in certain taverns
called "molly houses." Samuel Stevens, a religious crusader for the refor-
mation of morals, furnished a description in November 1725: "I found
between 40 and 50 men making love to one another, as they called it.
Sometimes they would sit in one another's laps, kissing in a lewd manner
and using their hands indecently. Then they would get up, dance and make
curtsies, and mimic the voices of women. . . . Then they would hug, and
play, and toy, and go out by couples into another room on the same floor to
be married, as they called it." Another firsthand account of a molly house
includes a description of a costume ball held there: "The men [were] calling one another 'my dear' and hugging, kissing, and tickling each other
as if they were a mixture of wanton males and females, and assuming
effeminate voices and airs. . . . Some were completely rigged in gowns,
petticoats, headcloths, fine laced shoes, furbelowed scarves, and masks;
some had riding hoods; some were dressed like milkmaids, others like
shepherdesses with green hats, waistcoats, and petticoats; and others had
their faces patched and painted and wore very extensive hoop petticoats,
which had been very lately introduced."[49] A literary echo of this stereotype can be found in the figure of Captain Whiffle, in Tobias Smollett's
novel *Roderick Random* (1748). But it is a character in John Cleland's
Memoirs of a Woman of Pleasure (also 1748) who makes the traditional
insistence on the visibility of the male invert in terms that look forward
to the pathologizing discourses of the modern era. There is, she says, "a
plague-spot visibly imprinted on all that are tainted" with this passion.[50]

For it was precisely this visibly disfigured victim of erotic malignancy
who provided neurologists and psychiatrists in the latter part of the nineteenth century with the clinical basis for the first systematic scientific conceptualization and definition of pathological (or perverted) sexual orientation. In August 1869, the same year that witnessed the first printed
appearance of the word "homosexuality," Karl Friedrich Otto Westphal,
a German expert on "the diseases of the nerves" or "nervous system,"
published an article on "contrary sexual feeling" or "sensibility" [*conträre
Sexualempfindung*], which he presented as a symptom of a neuropathic or
psychopathic condition.[51] Specialists continued to argue over the proper
scientific designation for this condition, and already by 1878 an Italian
specialist by the name of Arrigo Tamassia could speak of "inversion of the
sexual instinct," a designation that ultimately proved more popular than
Westphal's formula.[52] But we should not be deceived by all this fervor of

terminological innovation. Despite the newfangled names, the condition that the doctors were busy constructing as a perverted orientation shared a great many features with the deviant character that had been ascribed from time immemorial to the stigmatized figure of the *kinaidos* or *cinaedus,* the *mollis,* the "catamite," "pathic," "minion," or "molly."[53] It was this ancient figure, this venerable category of "folk" belief that was reconstructed by means of the sophisticated conceptual apparatus of modern sexology into a new scientific classification of sexual and gender deviance, a psychosexual orientation.

But sexual inversion, if it was indeed an orientation, still did not equate to homosexuality. "Contrary sexual feeling," for example, was intended to signify a sexual feeling contrary to the sex of the person who experienced it—that is, a feeling of belonging to a different sex from one's own, as well as a feeling of erotic attraction at odds with the sex to which one belonged (because its object was a member of the same sex as oneself and because it expressed a masculine or feminine attitude proper to members of a sex different from one's own). Westphal, like many of his contemporaries, did not distinguish systematically between sexual deviance and gender deviance. Attraction to members of one's own sex indicated an identification with the opposite sex, and an identification with the opposite sex sometimes expressed itself as a feeling of sexual attraction to members of one's own sex. In this Westphal was reproducing the assumptions of his own culture, but he had also been influenced by the arguments of Karl Heinrich Ulrichs, the first political activist for the emancipation of sexual minorities, whom he cites in his article, and who in a series of writings composed from about 1862 on described his own condition as that of an *anima muliebris virili corpore inclusa,* a "woman's soul confined by a male body."[54]

Similarly, the concept of sexual inversion treated same-sex sexual desire and object-choice as merely one of a number of pathological symptoms exhibited by those who reversed, or "inverted," the sex roles generally thought appropriate to their own sex. Such symptoms, indicating masculine identification in women and feminine identification in men, comprised many different elements of personal style, ranging from the ideologically loaded (women who took an interest in politics and campaigned for the right to vote) to the trivial and bizarre (men who liked cats), but the thread that linked them was sex-role reversal or gender deviance.[55] Sexual preference for a member of one's own sex was not clearly distinguished from other sorts of non-conformity to one's gender identity, as defined by prevailing cultural norms of manliness and womanliness. One implication of this model, which differentiates it strikingly from notions of homosexuality, is that the conventionally masculine and feminine same-sex partners of inverts are not necessarily abnormal or problematic or deviant themselves: the straight-identified male hustler, or the femme who allows herself to be pleasured by a butch, is merely acting out a proper sexual scenario with an improper partner and may well be sexually normal in his or her own right (as Krafft-Ebing himself had emphasized in the passage previously quoted), however criminal their actual conduct may be.[56]

If paederasty or sodomy was traditionally understood as a sexual preference without a sexual orientation, inversion by contrast was defined as a psychological orientation without a sexuality. In a footnote at the end of his article Westphal emphasized "the fact that 'contrary sexual feeling' *does not always coincidentally concern the sexual drive as such* but simply the feeling of being alienated, with one's entire inner being, from one's own sex—a less developed stage, as it were, of the pathological phenomenon."[57] For Westphal and his colleagues, "contrary sexual feeling" or sexual inversion was an essentially psychological condition of gender dysphoria that affected the inner life of the individual, an *orientation* not necessarily expressed in the performance or enjoyment of particular (homo)sexual acts. In fact, Westphal's star example of contrary sexual feeling in a male was an individual who strictly avoided—or at least claimed to avoid—all sexual contact with members of his own sex, who expressed a distinct sexual desire for women, and who was diagnosed as suffering from contrary sexual feeling on the basis of his gender style alone, not on the basis of homosexual desire.[58]

This personage turned out to be one "Aug. Ha.," who had been arrested at a train station in Berlin in the winter of 1868, at the age of twenty-seven, while wearing women's clothes. He had worked as a servant for several households, often wearing female attire and even owning fake breasts at some point; he had also stolen women's clothing and toiletries from his employers and had been imprisoned for using false identities. Medical records had noted the "almost effeminate conduct of the patient, who speaks with a lisping voice in an effeminate tone." Westphal met him and examined him personally. He described Ha. as "powerfully built" and "well fed," tall, clean-shaven, with well-developed muscles and body fat, regular features, and thick, long, blond, slightly curly hair—though Westphal thought it might be possible to discern "something feminine" in the patient's facial characteristics. Anatomically, Aug. Ha. was hardly exotic. Physical examination revealed "no particular deformity" in the ears (although the earlobes bore traces of piercing), and abundant body hair, with pubic hair reaching up to the navel. The scrotum and skin of the penis were strongly pigmented and wrinkled; the testicles were "only of moderate size"; the anus showed "nothing special."

More to the point, Ha. maintained that he "never let himself be used by men and never busied himself with them in a sexual way, even though many offers in this direction reached him." He had simply had a strong "inclination" or a "drive" (his own words [*Neigung, Trieb*]) to dress up as a woman since he was eight years old and had often been punished by his mother for getting into her clothes. He had always had good relations with women and in his youth he had gone out dancing with them while wearing women's clothes himself. He had an "inclination [again, his own word, *Neigung*] to cultivate sexual relations with women, though rarely, for fear of becoming repulsive." He continued to occupy himself with needlework, embroidering cloths and manufacturing small women's hats, while under observation in the hospital. Westphal applied for and succeeded in obtaining his release, but, when his true identity became known, Ha. was rearrested and rearraigned in the light of his earlier thefts, and at the time of writing was serving a two-year sentence for recidivism in the Brandenburg prison.[59]

Sexual inversion, then, does not represent the same notion as homosexuality because same-sex sexual object-choice, or homosexual desire, is not essential to it. One can be inverted without being homosexual, and one can have homosexual sex, if one is a paederast or sodomite, without qualifying as sexually inverted: according to nineteenth-century psychiatric criteria, one would be merely perverse, not perverted. Hence, as Kinsey (who was versed in these concepts) insisted, "Inversion and homosexuality are two distinct and not always correlated types of behavior."[60] Instead, the notions of contrary sexual feeling and sexual inversion seem to glance back at the long tradition of stigmatized male passivity, effeminacy, and gender deviance, which focuses less on homosexual sex or homosexual desire per se than on an accompanying lack of normative masculinity in one or both of the partners.[61]

: : :

Now, at last, we come to homosexuality, a category whose peculiar and distinctive features and ramifications will, I hope, stand out more clearly in contrast to the four discursive traditions already discussed. The word "homosexuality" appeared in print for the first time in German in 1869, in two anonymous pamphlets published in Leipzig by an Austrian translator of Hungarian literature who took the name of Karl Maria Kertbeny. Although Kertbeny claimed publicly to be "sexually normal" himself, his term "homosexuality" can be considered an originally pro-gay coinage, insofar as Kertbeny used it in the course of an unsuccessful political campaign to prevent homosexual sex from being criminalized by the newly formed Federation of North German States.

Unlike "contrary sexual feeling," "sexual inversion," and "Uranian love," "homosexuality" was not coined to interpret the phenomenon it described or to attach a particular psychological or medical theory to it, and Kertbeny himself was vehemently opposed to third-sex or inversion models of homosexual desire. "Homosexuality" simply referred to a sexual drive directed toward persons of the same sex as the sex of the person who was driven by it. Indeed, it was the term's very minimalism, when viewed from a theoretical perspective, that made it so easily adaptable by later writers and theorists with a variety of ideological purposes. As a result, the term now condenses a number of different notions about same-sex sexual attraction as well as a number of different conceptual models of what homosexuality is.

Specifically, "homosexuality" absorbs and combines at least three distinct and previously uncorrelated concepts: (1) a psychiatric notion of perverted or pathological *orientation,* derived from Westphal and his nineteenth-century colleagues, which is an essentially psychological concept that applies to the inner life of the individual and does not necessarily presume same-sex sexual behavior; (2) a psychoanalytic notion of same-sex *sexual object-choice* or desire, derived from Freud and his coworkers, which is a category of erotic intentionality and does not necessarily imply a permanent sexual orientation, let alone a deviant or pathological one (since, according to Freud, most normal individuals make an unconscious homosexual object-choice at some point in their fantasy lives); and (3) a sociological notion of *sexually deviant behavior,* derived from nineteenth- and twentieth-century forensic inquiries into "social problems," which focuses on non-standard sexual practice and does not necessarily refer to erotic psychology or sexual orientation (since same-sex sexual behavior, as Kinsey showed, is not the exclusive property of those with a homosexual sexual orientation, nor is it necessarily pathological, since it is widely represented in the population). So neither a notion of orientation, nor a notion of object-choice, nor a notion of behavior alone is sufficient to generate the modern definition of "homosexuality"; rather, the notion seems to depend on the unstable conjunction of all three. "Homosexuality" is at once a psychological condition, an erotic desire, and a sexual practice (and those are three quite different things).

Furthermore, the very notion of homosexuality implies that same-sex sexual feeling and expression, in all their many forms, constitute a single thing, called "homosexuality," which can be thought of as a single integrated phenomenon, distinct and separate from "heterosexuality." "Homosexuality" refers to *all* same-sex sexual desire and behavior, whether hierarchical or mutual, gender-polarized or ungendered, latent or actual, mental or physical. And, perhaps most important of all, it makes *homosexual object-choice itself* function as a marker of sexual and social difference.

The originality of "homosexuality" as a category and a concept appears more vividly in this light. Earlier discourses, whether of sodomy or inversion, referred to only *one* of the sexual partners: the "active" partner in the case of sodomy, the effeminate male or masculine female in the case of inversion. The other partner, the one who was not motivated by sexual desire or who was not gender-deviant, did not qualify for inclusion in the category. "Homosexuality," by contrast, applies to *both* partners, whether active or passive, whether gendered normatively or deviantly. The hallmark of "homosexuality," in fact, is the refusal to distinguish between same-sex sexual partners or to rank them by treating one of them as more (or less) homosexual than the other.

Kinsey can be taken as representative of this modern outlook. Dismissing as "propaganda" the tendency of some men to define their own sexual identity according to a role-specific, pre-homosexual model—to consider themselves straight because they only had fellatio performed on them by other men and never performed it themselves—Kinsey wrote that all "physical contacts with other males" that result in orgasm are "by any strict definition . . . homosexual."[62] According to Kinsey, in other words, it doesn't matter who sucks whom. Same-sex sexual contact is all that is required.

In this way homosexuality, both as a concept and as a social practice, significantly rearranges and reinterprets earlier patterns of erotic organization, and as such it has an additional number of important practical consequences. First, under the aegis of homosexuality, the significance of gender and of gender roles for categorizing sexual acts and sexual actors fades.[63] So one effect of the concept of homosexuality is to detach sexual object-choice from any necessary connection with gender identity, making it possible to ascribe homosexuality to women and to men whose gender styles and outward appearance or manner are perfectly normative.

To be sure, this conceptual transformation has not been either total or absolute. Many people nowadays, both gay and non-gay, continue to draw a direct connection between gender deviance and homosexuality. Despite the dominance of the categories of homosexuality and heterosexuality, active women and passive men, as well as effeminate men and masculine women, are still considered somehow *more homosexual* than other, less flamboyantly deviant, persons who make homosexual object-choices. Here we can discern the force with which earlier, pre-homosexual sexual categories continue to exert their authority within the newer conceptual universe of homo- and heterosexuality.

A second effect of the hegemony of the recent homo-/heterosexual model has been to downplay the taxonomic significance of sexual roles. Even the most asymmetrical behaviors can get trumped for the purposes of sexual classification by the sameness or difference of the sexes of the persons involved. Witness the anxiety expressed in the following anonymous letter to the sex advice columnist of an alternative newspaper:

> I'm a 200 percent straight guy, married with children. About six months ago, I went to a masseur who finished things with a terrific blow job. If you wonder why I didn't stop him, the truth is, I couldn't, because he was massaging my asshole with his thumb while blowing me. It was so good that I've been going back to this guy just about every week, not for the massage but for the blow job. Now I'm starting to worry that this might label me as gay. I have no interest in blowing this guy, but I wonder if the guy who gets the blow job is as guilty as the one who does it.[64]

The letter writer's worry is a direct effect of the emergent discourses of sexuality and of the recent changes in sexual classification that they have introduced. No such anxieties assail those as yet untouched by the discourses of sexuality.[65]

The homo/heterosexual model has other consequences as well. Homosexuality translates same-sex sexual relations into the register of sameness and mutuality. Homosexual relations no longer necessarily imply an asymmetry of social identities or sexual positions, nor are they inevitably articulated in terms of hierarchies of power, age, gender, or sexual role—which, again, is not to claim that such hierarchies do not continue to function meaningfully in lesbian or gay male societies and sexualities or that they do not structure the relations of many different sorts of lesbian and gay male couples: in some quarters it still matters a lot who sucks—or fucks—whom.[66] Nonetheless, homosexual relations are not *necessarily* lopsided in their distribution of erotic pleasure or desire. Rather, like that of heterosexual romantic love, the notion of homosexuality implies that it is possible for sexual partners to bond with one another not on the basis of their difference but on the basis of their sameness, their identity of desire and orientation and "sexuality." Homosexual relations cease to be compulsorily structured by a polarization of identities and roles (active/passive, insertive/receptive, masculine/feminine, or man/boy). Exclusive, lifelong, companionate, romantic, and mutual homosexual love becomes possible for both partners. Homosexual relations are not organized merely according to the requirements or prescriptions of large-scale social institutions, such as kinship systems, age classes, or initiation rituals; rather, they function as principles of social organization in their own right and give rise to freestanding social institutions.[67]

Homosexuality is now set over against heterosexuality. Homosexual object-choice, in and of itself, is seen as marking a difference from heterosexual object-choice. Homo- and heterosexuality have become more or less mutually exclusive forms of human subjectivity, different kinds of human sexuality, and any feeling or expression of heterosexual desire is thought to rule out any feeling or expression of homosexual desire on the part of the same individual, with the exception of "bisexuals" (who are therefore thought of as belonging to an entirely separate "sexuality"). For sexual object-choice attaches to a notion of sexual orientation, such that sexual behavior is seen to express an underlying and permanent psychosexual feature of the human subject. Hence people are routinely assigned to one or another sexual species on the basis of their sexual object-choice and orientation.

In short, homosexuality is more than same-sex sexual object-choice, more even than conscious erotic same-sex preference. Homosexuality is the specification of same-sex sexual object-choice in and of itself as an overriding principle of sexual and social difference. Homosexuality is part of a new system of sexuality, which functions as a means of personal individuation: it assigns to each individual a sexual orientation and a sexual identity. As such, homosexuality introduces a novel element into social organization, into the social articulation of human difference, into the social production of desire, and ultimately into the social construction of the self.

: : :

It may be easier to grasp some of the overlapping and distinguishing features of our five discursive traditions in the history of (homo)sexual classification by consulting table 1. As this schematic comparison indicates, each of the five traditions is irreducible to the others. I am not interested in defending the rightness or wrongness of the individual answers I have given to my own set of questions (I acknowledge that my answers are debatable); rather, I wish to show by the way my affirmatives and negatives are scattered across the chart that the patterns I have sketched do not reduce to a single coherent scheme.

One way to make sense of this table is to note the radical difference between the initial category ("homosexuality") and the four others. All of the

TABLE 1. THE FIVE CATEGORIES

	homosexuality	effeminacy	sodomy	friendship	inversion
Is it an orientation	Yes	No	Not really	No	Yes (?)
Does it involve gender-deviance?	Maybe	Yes	No (?)	No	Yes
Does it involve same-sex genital contact	Mostly	Not necessarily	Mostly	No (?)	Sometimes
Is it a sexual preference?	Yes	No	Sometimes	No	Not really
Does it represent a character type?	Maybe	Yes	No (?)	No	Yes
Does it involve homoerotic desire?	Yes	Sometimes	Yes, at least for one partner	Maybe	Not necessarily
Does it classify women and men together?	Yes	No	No	No (?)	Yes
Is it constant across sex or gender transition?	Maybe	No	No	No	No

final four traditional, post-classical, or long-standing categories ("effem-inacy," "paederasty/sodomy," "friendship/love," "passivity/inversion") depend crucially on notions of gender. This is obvious in the case of effem-inacy and passivity/inversion, but it is also true of paederasty/sodomy and friendship/love, since they are defined by the male subject's embodiment and performance of traditionally masculine and masculinizing norms, just as effeminacy and passivity/inversion are defined by the male subject's vi-olation of them. In these traditional systems of sex and gender, the notion of "sexuality" is dispensable because the regulation of conduct and social status is accomplished by the gender system alone.

Of course, social status and class also contribute to the production of the final four categories. For example, effeminacy applies especially to those men who are high enough in rank and status to be susceptible of suffering a loss or reduction in rank by comporting themselves at variance with the behavior expected of the elite. Friendship/love demands an equality of rank between the partners, whereas paederasty/sodomy depends on a socially significant difference between the partners in age, status, and sexual role. Passivity/inversion defines itself in relation to the gender hierarchy. With the arrival of homosexuality, the systems of difference that were internal to the structure of the earlier four categories find themselves externalized and reconstituted at the border between homosexuality and heterosexuality, categories that now represent in and of themselves new strategies of social differentiation and regulation and new ways of regulating and enforcing gender norms. The homo/hetero categories function not to maintain an already existing hierarchy of gender and status but to manage, by differentiating and disciplining them, unranked masses of notionally identical "individuals." One name for that technique of governing individuals en masse by comparing and differentiating them is normalization.[68]

: : :

There is an irony in sex. I refer to a different irony from the familiar ones produced by all the tragicomic disproportions between love and its objects, between feeling and expression, between desire and demand. The irony I have in mind is etymological. For the word "sex" itself may derive from the Latin *secare*, "to cut or divide": it originally signified the sharpness and cleanness of the division between the natural categories of male and female. And yet "sex" has had the fine edge of its meaning so blunted by historical shifts and rearrangements in the concepts and forms of sexual life that it now represents what is most resistant to clear classification, discrimination, and division.

More particularly, the emergence of homosexuality as a category has not only made it difficult for us to grasp earlier kinds or classifications of sex and gender in all their positivity and specificity. It has also complicated for us the task of understanding the significance of various present-day asymmetries *within* homosexual relations, patterns of preference or practice that deviate from the ideal standards of reciprocity, equality, and gender identity imposed by the crypto-normative force of the homosexual category itself. How do we now understand the role that perceived differences in age, gender style, sexual role, body type, social class, ethnicity, race, religion, and/or nationality play in structuring, however partially, the relations of some lesbian and gay male couples? Such differences between the partners often turn out to be richly meaningful, both to the partners themselves and to those who come into contact with them, but it's no longer clear exactly how those differences function to construct actual forms of lesbian and gay life or what their structural significance is in fashioning contemporary lesbian or gay male sexualities.

In the "History" chapter of his book on Oscar Wilde, arguably the most brilliant and original exploration of how to do the history of male homosexuality, Neil Bartlett ponders the relation between past and present formations of homosexual existence in these very terms, and I can think of no better way to conclude than by quoting him.

> *"What kind of man was he?"*
>
> That is, what kind of men were we?
>
> . . . Watching that man in the high-heeled shoes, the black dress falling off one shoulder (it is late in the evening), I remember that he and his sisters have been making their own way as ladies of the night [in London] since 1870, when Fanny and Stella were doing the Strand.[69] His frock is handed down, second-hand, part of a story, part of a tradition. And that man buying his younger boyfriend (slightly embarrassed, but happily drunk) another drink—I remember the bizarre twisting of mythologies that Wilde used to justify his adoration of young men, the mixing of a pastiche of Classical paederasty with a missionary zeal for "the criminal classes," the sense that they, not the boys he left sleeping in [his home in] Chelsea, were his true sons—should I forget all that, should I be embarrassed myself? Should I look the other way? Should I dismiss all that simply because now, as then, one man is paying for another? Isn't there an attempt to create a new kind of relationship, an affair of the heart somehow appropriate to the meeting of two very different men? That's our real history, the one we're still writing.[70]

Appendix: Questions of Evidence

It is a pleasure to have the opportunity to comment on three papers that represent something of the state of the art of current research into male same-sex eroticism in the ancient Mediterranean world.[1] The three papers range over a period of some fifteen hundred years, and they span the disciplines of archaeology, iconography, philology, and the history of religion—not to mention classical scholarship, cultural studies, and the history of sexuality more generally. Together they demonstrate the great gains in knowledge, sophistication, and confidence that have been made in the study of male same-sex eroticism in ancient Mediterranean societies since Kenneth Dover and others renewed scholarly investigation of that topic twenty years ago. I shall have little to say by way of criticism of the three papers, partly because each of them is so solid and authoritative, and partly because each of the speakers knows so much more than I do about the particular field in which he works: Bronze Age art and archaeology in the case of Professor Koehl, Greek vase-painting in the case of Professor DeVries, and Roman sexual discourse in the case of Professor Williams. Still, I have some general observations to make, as well as a few doubts and questions to raise about what each speaker has said.

Each of the three scholars has quite properly focused his remarks on the evidence for male sexual expression in a specific society, a single culture narrowly circumscribed by language, time, and place. Each of the ancient cultures discussed not only differs from the others in all of those departments but is also separated from them linguistically, temporally, and spatially by considerable removes. Nonetheless—and this seems to me to be the great interest of the three papers taken as a group—there remain striking correspondences among these otherwise quite distinct ancient cultures in their structuring of male same-sex sexual behavior. The evidence presented for sexual relations among males in these three cultures reveals a common pattern, one long familiar from the classical period of Athenian civilization in the fifth and fourth centuries B.C. but often assumed to be peculiar to it. Now instead we seem to have at least some evidence, the most startling (because the least expected) provided by Koehl, for a certain consistency or regularity in the social patterning of male same-sex eroticism in the ancient Mediterranean world from the Bronze Age to the end of the Roman Empire in the West—a period of roughly two thousand years. That is an extraordinary and astonishing conclusion for scholarship to have reached. It is real news.

To be very schematic about it, each of the three of them has presented evidence for, or at least has predicated his remarks on the existence of, a particular type of homosexual relation—namely, a relation of structured inequality between males of different ages ("men" and "boys") and/or different social statuses (freeborn men and slaves, citizens and non-citizens). What is more, the hierarchy or asymmetry in age and/or status that defines and structures the social relations between the two male partners correlates, in the case of socially approved relationships at least, with an asymmetry in sexual role: the older or socially superior partner is supposed to be the one who initiates the relationship, who pursues the other, who feels a passionate sexual desire for him (as the Greek term for the senior partner—*erastês*, "lover" or "desirer"—indicates), who seeks to gratify that desire in the sexual act, and who is presumed to penetrate phallically the body of the other, whereas the younger or socially inferior partner is supposed to be the one who is pursued (carried off or seduced or purchased, as the case may be), who is less desiring than desired (as the Greek term for the junior partner—*erômenos*, "beloved" or "desired"—implies, though DeVries argues that scholars may have overstated this point), and whose body is acted on and perhaps even sexually penetrated by the other.

This type of homosexual relation between males, which the Greeks of the classical period designated by the term *paiderastia,* or "paederasty," is conceptually and sociologically distinct from what is referred to nowadays as male "homosexuality":[2] although lots of gay men I know often or even always choose partners who differ from themselves in age or race or nationality or body type or preferred sexual role, reciprocal relations between adults and even persons of similar ages constitutes the norm for gay male relationships in most bourgeois societies today. Although some people may identify themselves as tops or bottoms, sexual roles are not rigidly polarized and it is not considered outlandish for two men to take turns fucking each other—though modern sexual ideology doubtless tends to overplay sexual mutuality and to mute real polarities or asymmetries in sexual roles among gay men.[3] (In this connection, I must say that I find Williams's application of the terms "top" and "bottom" to the insertive and receptive male partners in Roman sexual discourse to be highly misleading, since nowadays those terms signify a sexual preference, personal style, and/or erotic identity, not just a sexual role, and they also delineate different sexual subtypes *within* the more general class of men who supposedly share a common sexual orientation, whereas it is precisely the radical cleavage between the identities attached to "active" and "passive" males that distinguishes the Roman discursive system Williams so eloquently describes.) Of course, not all sexual relations between males in antiquity conformed to this hierarchical, age- or status-differentiated, role-specific pattern, and none of the three speakers claims as much, but all of them do provide documentation for the existence of such a pattern in widely scattered periods and locations in the ancient Mediterranean world.

When, following Kenneth Dover and Michel Foucault, I described this pattern as it informed the classical Greek institution of paederasty in my 1990 book, *One Hundred Years of Homosexuality*, laying special emphasis on its structural specificity and distinctness from modern forms of male homosexuality, I assumed I was dealing with a peculiarly Greek phenomenon, best documented in the case of the classical Athenians and typical of later Greek culture more generally, but not necessarily applicable either to the pre-classical or to the Roman world. Now it looks like the sexual pattern I described extends (with modifications) beyond the horizons of historical Greek culture in at least two directions and turns out to be of greater longevity and wider distribution in the ancient Mediterranean world than either I or previous scholars had imagined.

But before I leave you with that conclusion, I want to raise the possibility that it may be, perhaps in part, something of an optical illusion produced by our reading of the ancient sources. As I mentioned earlier, the argument for pushing back the temporal horizons of paederasty to the Bronze Age stems from the fascinating work of Professor Koehl and, in particular, from his interpretation of the Chieftain Cup. Now that interpretation of the Chieftain Cup depends in turn on the information about the ancient Cretan rules governing male same-sex sexual practices which is provided by Strabo in the first century B.C. on the basis of his reading of a now-lost fourth-century history of Crete by one Ephorus (though Strabo himself knew something about Crete because his maternal ancestors had resided in Cnossus). What we have, then, is a Greek text from the Roman era that purports to convey the substance of another Greek text from the late classical period about even older local customs. Scholars may disagree about what the actual relation is between the sexual rite described by Strabo/Ephorus and prehistoric Minoan practices in the Bronze Age and about the extent to which the passage transmitted to us by Strabo reflects the cultural assumptions of Ephorus's world or of Strabo's own, but there is no disputing the fact that the language of Strabo's text itself is thoroughly contaminated by the terminology—even as Strabo's description is infected by the ethos—of Greek paederasty as it was practiced in the classical and post-classical periods: the prominence of the terms *erastês* and *erômenos* in Strabo's text attests to that.[4] Koehl is of course aware of all this, and he has presented his interpretation as a speculative one. I myself find his reading, and the accumulation of evidence he presents for paederastic relations on Minoan Crete, immensely suggestive and on the whole quite plausible, but I also think it is important to recognize the extent to which our interpretations of the prehistoric material may be colored by the cultural assumptions of literary sources that date from the classical or post-classical period and that determine our approach to artifacts of considerably more ancient origin. Luckily for Koehl's argument, some of his corroborating evidence is archaeological, which is to say independent of the literary sources, and that is what makes his case for the existence of paederastic relations on Bronze Age Crete as compelling as it is.

I am less persuaded, however, that the Cretan rite of passage that Koehl reconstructs is "at the root," as he puts it, "of homosexual expression in the Greek world"; it may be instead a distant and obscure reflection of it. To be sure, Koehl's view is in line with a current fashion in classical scholarship, which has recently witnessed a vigorous revival of turn-of-the-century theories about the supposed connection between the classical institution of Greek paederasty and earlier, more "primitive," initiation rites on Crete and the Peloponnese, in which masculine identity was supposedly transmitted from one generation of men to the next by sexual contact between men and boys.[5] The effect, if not the purpose, of such theories, then as now, was to explain (and, more or less explicitly, to apologize for) the existence of Greek paederasty in the classical period. But our increasing knowledge of the wide distribution of paederastic practices in the ancient Mediterranean, which Koehl himself has helped to document, makes additional explanations for them superfluous, and recent comparative work in ethnography has further contributed to shifting the burden

of explanation by establishing that age-structured and role-specific patterns of same-sex sexual contact are relatively common among males in
pre-industrial cultures. Both Kenneth Dover and I have argued in some
detail against deriving classical Greek paederasty from earlier, shadowy,
prehistoric initiation rites; it is unnecessary to recapitulate those arguments
here.[6] What I would like to do instead is simply to emphasize a couple of
points that often seem to get lost in scholarly discussions of the issue.

Greek paederasty of the sort practiced by the Athenians of the classical
period was often a highly conventional, elaborately formal, and socially
stylized affair, involving lengthy courtship and conspicuous public display (I'm leaving aside, of course, the less respectable versions of man/boy
love in the ancient world, such as male prostitution and the sexual use
of slaves). But it was far removed from an initiation rite, as that term is
understood by anthropologists and employed by Koehl. First of all, there's
a big difference between a social convention and a rite, although students
of ancient or distant cultures often seem to lose sight of the distinction. For
example, it is a social convention for high school students in the United
States to attend a senior prom before they graduate from high school. But
a senior prom is not an initiation rite. Why not? Because, among other
factors, even if most or (for the sake of argument) all high school students
end up going to the senior prom, it is nonetheless possible to graduate from
high school without doing so. There may be intense social pressure to attend the prom, but no one's high school diploma depends on it. Similarly,
the Athenians of the classical period may have practiced paederasty, but
they did not do so universally (to what extent they did is now impossible to
specify precisely), and in any case participation in a paederastic love affair
was not a prerequisite for admission to any rank or group membership in
Athenian society (in fact, it could lead to the forfeiture of certain privileges,
if a boy comported himself disreputably). It was possible for a boy to grow
up in classical Athens and be admitted to the society of adult men without
ever having had an older male lover in his youth. In that sense, at least,
despite what may have taken place on Crete in the Bronze Age, classical
Athenian paederasty itself cannot be described as an initiation rite, and its
relation to the Cretan practice is extremely tenuous.

Moreover, the paradigmatic instances of male initiation rituals among
contemporary tribal peoples in New Guinea and Brazil, the ones featured
in the modern anthropological literature from which Koehl derives his concept and definition of a rite of passage, differ markedly from both the rite
described by Strabo/Ephorus and from Greek paederasty as it was practiced in the classical period (which of course is not to deny that such rituals
provide a rich archive of comparative material for studying Greek social

practices). Among these contemporary peoples, male initiation is universal, collective, and compulsory. In order to become a fully empowered man, a member of the socially recognized group of adult males, a boy has to pass through all the requisite stages of initiation; he is not given a choice, and no exceptions are made. Furthermore, the initiation of boys is often performed by inducting entire age-classes or cohorts: when the men of the village decide that it's time for an initiation, they typically leave the village for a period, then reappear without warning, invade the village with their bodies painted blue, seize all the boys of a certain age and carry them off to the bush for a certain time, and finally return to the village having completed the initiation (or in order to complete it). Compared to such a system, classical Greek paederasty tends rather to resemble a senior prom: it proceeds not by the induction of entire age classes but by elective pair-bonding between individuals—in a word, by *dating*. A boy may have to be elaborately courted by his would-be lover, and in any case he can always say, "No." If he does take part in a paederastic relationship, he does so by personal choice and inclination—which is not to say that taking a male lover is necessarily any more voluntary than going to the senior prom, only that the decision to do so has to be made *by* an individual who has some say in the matter and is not made *for* the individual by another social agent or agency.

Looked at in this light, the account of Cretan customs by Strabo/Ephorus seems like something of a hybrid, an effect of bricolage. As Koehl observes, the Cretan dating game exhibits the tripartite pattern of separation, transition, and incorporation that anthropological observers have discerned in the rites of passage they have studied in tribal cultures. Moreover, the Cretan lover's abduction and instruction of the boy plainly serve an initiatory function: only those boys who have undergone this elaborate ritual in their youth may attain to certain privileges as adult men and receive various marks of special honor in Cretan society. Nonetheless, the Cretan ritual, as Strabo/Ephorus describes it at least, depends on the vagaries of love and personal reputation: unlike marriage, which Cretan custom requires boys to enter upon collectively in groups formed by age classes, paederastic abduction is an individual affair. A man has to develop a crush on one boy in particular, and he has to receive the approval of the boy's family for the actual abduction, while boys are supposed to earn a lover's notice by their bravery, good behavior, and good looks. The account by Strabo/Ephorus sounds to me like an ethnographic potpourri composed of some dimly recollected elements of an archaic initiation ritual blended with more familiar notions about male courtship drawn from the writer's own society and flavored with a series of moral judgments about the proper and improper practice of boy-love. I very much doubt that this much overinterpreted passage is sufficiently accurate or reliable to base an entire theory of Cretan ritual practice on, let alone to derive an etiological account of Greek paederasty from; rather, it is itself a derivative product of the history and practice of male same-sex eroticism in the ancient Greek world. But it may indeed hold the key to interpreting the fascinating artifacts that Koehl has so ably assembled, and so I don't consider that the various objections I have raised do any real damage to the substance of his iconographical interpretation of them.

Professor Williams has performed a signal service to classical scholarship and the history of sexuality by analyzing systematically for the first time the structure of Roman discourse on male eroticism and, thus, identifying the basic coordinates of Roman moral thought as it pertains to sexual behavior among males. I have little to add to his discussion, except for a few quibbles about his concluding remarks on Roman deviations from the earlier paederastic model that tended to govern sexual relations between males in classical Greece. In the body of his paper, Williams does a fine job of contextualizing Roman pronouncements about sex, carefully distinguishing the moral beliefs that routinely and uncontroversially inform statements about sexual misconduct from the controversial and often slanderous content of those statements, as they refer to individual cases. For the individual cases tell us less about the actual person or topic under discussion than they do about the rhetorical situation of the speaker and the moral presumptions shared between the speaker and the audience. Indeed, the strength of Williams's analysis in my view lies in his proper insistence that modern research into sexual life at Rome must confine itself, at least in the first instance, to elucidating the rules of Roman discourse that govern the production of statements about sexual matters, moving on from this world of discourse to the world of social practice only with great care and caution, since so much of our evidence for what people actually did derives from how they spoke and wrote about it. Unlike John Boswell, Eva Cantarella, and Amy Richlin, for example, who have tended to treat the texts they study as transparent windows onto Roman social reality and sexual practice, Williams is alive to the opacity of Roman sexual discourse, to its autonomy as a semiotic system.

It is all the more disappointing, then, to find him lapsing from that methodological habit in the final portion of his paper. To be sure, the goal of distinguishing Roman attitudes from Greek ones, and of describing Roman sexual discourse in all its cultural specificity, is not only an important but a crucial project, if we are ever to bring the distinctive features of Roman culture into sharper focus. But in his zeal to carry out that project, Williams draws some unwarranted conclusions from the evidence he presents. In particular, his argument for the supposedly greater incidence in Rome of sexual relations between adult males fails to take adequate account of the tone of disapproval with which such relations are routinely described by our sources. The fragment of Laberius that refers to a man who has fallen in love with another man so hairy as to be called an "ape" registers the speaker's disgust, as Williams admits in a note; the various biographers who tell us about Roman leaders who had love-affairs with overage boys similarly recapitulate a commonplace of Greek and Roman invective, of a sort well represented by the passage from Seneca's forty-seventh *Epistle,* which Williams quotes, and in any case the lip-smacking, lubricious tone with which our authors single out and convey such piquant information hardly suggests that they expected it to be received by their readership as value-neutral, let alone morally acceptable. When Queen Boudicca makes her jibe about the Romans sleeping with overage boys, she is not paying them a compliment, nor is she making a general observation of an anthropological nature; rather, she is trying to persuade her troops that they will achieve an easy victory over men who are so depraved and so lacking in manly vigor as to keep boyfriends who are of an age to fuck them. I won't continue to pursue all of Williams's examples: suffice it to say that none of them indicates to me an attitude that deviates from the mainstream of Greek moral sentiment about sexual matters. It is quite true, to be sure, as Williams points out in his final note (and as I had observed well before him), that we hear considerably more from Roman sources than from Greek ones about adult men who manifest a liking to be penetrated by other adult men, but once again the tone in which such information is imparted is hardly neutral, let alone approving, and it is difficult at this remove in time to distinguish a social reality from a phobic stereotype.[7] Doubtless such deviant types of men existed, in Rome as in Greece, but it is not to be inferred merely from the somewhat freer mention of them in Roman sources that the sexual system of the Romans offered such deviants greater toleration and acceptance than did the sexual system of the Greeks.

This brings me at last to the fine paper by Professor DeVries. I shall take a little more time discussing this paper, partly because it lies closer to my own area of expertise, and partly because it criticizes a position for which I myself have argued in the past, though DeVries tactfully omits to target my work by name in his own critique. Let me begin by observing that the great virtue of DeVries' approach can be measured by the fact that traditional classical scholarship, which tends to rely for its evidence on literary or documentary texts, rather than on visual or graphic sources, is comparatively inadequate to the task of elucidating classical Greek sexual conventions and practices. As Michel Foucault observed, in a little-noticed review of Kenneth Dover's 1978 monograph *Greek Homosexuality* (the book whose argument for the lack of reciprocity in paederastic relations DeVries is attempting to refute), "The Greeks of the classical period *said* less than they *showed*. The vase paintings are infinitely more explicit than the texts which have come down to us, even the texts of Greek comedy. But many painted scenes would be mute (and have remained so until now) for lack of reference to a text that articulates their erotic meaning. A young man gives a boy a hare: it's a love gift. He caresses the boy's chin: it's a proposition."[8] Foucault's emphasis on the evidentiary value of Greek vase painting for the reconstruction of Greek sexual life may come as something of a surprise to those classicists who faulted Foucault's *History of Sexuality* for its neglect of the ancient visual evidence and who criticized its author for his reliance on prescriptive and philosophical texts, failing to notice that Foucault featured such texts in his account because he was interested not just in the history of sexuality but also in what he called "the history of truth"—in how sexual experience came to be constituted as a morally problematic domain by the ethical discourse of various supposed "experts." In any case, what Foucault says in praise of Dover might equally well be said in praise of the work that DeVries has done and is doing: "The heart of the analysis consists in recovering what the physical acts, the outward expressions of sex and of pleasure say, expressions that we consider universal (what, after all, is more widely shared than the expressive repertory of love?), expressions that when analyzed in their historical specificity tell a quite distinct and peculiar story."[9]

The great value of DeVries' paper, it seems to me, is that it takes us well beyond Dover in decoding the iconographic conventions for representing sex in Greek art. More specifically, I think DeVries succeeds in demonstrating that Dover misinterpreted at least some of the gestures that he took to be indications of the beloved boy's reluctance or resistance to the sexual advances of his male suitors. By means of this survey of the ancient visual evidence, DeVries establishes that sexual relations between men and boys contained more elements of tenderness and emotional intimacy than many readers of Dover had concluded. That is a valuable insight, I believe; it represents a real advance in knowledge. It is therefore well worth emphasizing, and I, for one, am grateful to DeVries for emphasizing it.

I only wish DeVries' analysis had been as rigorously historicist and as culture specific in its treatment of ancient Greek sexual conventions and, particularly, in its treatment of the ancient Greek distinction between *erôs* and *philia* (i.e., between passionate sexual desire and love), as it was in its treatment of iconography. For the distinction between *erôs* and *philia* is also something that is very much worth emphasizing, because it was absolutely crucial to the self-understanding of the Greeks, whereas it is relatively meaningless to us, and so it is constantly at risk of getting lost in the shuffle of modern interpretations and dropping out of the historical picture. In order for us to appreciate the importance of this distinction, it will be necessary to bear in mind some of the ancient cultural background, which I'll summarize as quickly as I can.

The ancient Greeks had no word for love in our general sense; they had, instead, a variety of rather more precise terms, which differentiated among aspects of that conglomerate emotion that we nowadays, in our undifferentiated way, call love. In particular, the Greeks distinguished carefully between *erôs* and *philia*—passionate sexual desire and love, or romantic and non-romantic love. The distinction turns on the difference between desire and love. Greek literary sources consistently ascribe passionate sexual desire only to the senior partner in a paederastic relationship, and ascribe non-passionate love to the junior partner. The point is not at all that Greek boys were conventionally thought, or required, to be "frigid," as DeVries claims, in what I think is a caricature of Dover's reading of both the literary and the visual evidence; the point, rather, is that Greek boys were not thought to be motivated in their erotic relations with their older lovers by a feeling of passionate sexual desire for them.

The reason for this peculiar insistence on the part of our sources is not far to seek. The Greeks understood sex itself to be defined entirely in terms of phallic penetration, regardless of whether the sexual partners were both males, both females, or male and female. The physical act of sex itself presupposed and demanded (in the eyes of Greek males, at least) the assumption by the respective sexual partners of different and asymmetrical sexual roles (the roles of penetrator and penetrated), and those roles in turn were associated with social distinctions of power and gender—differences between dominance and submission as well as between masculinity and femininity. To be sexually penetrated was always therefore potentially shaming for a free male of citizen status. If the penetrated male was, instead, a foreigner at Athens, a slave, or a prostitute, penetration did not diminish his status because that status was already very low to begin with, and what made that status so low was in part the cultural assumption that anyone who occupied the status of foreigner, prostitute, or slave was susceptible by definition to sexual penetration and could not therefore claim to be a serious player in the high-stakes game of male honor that comprised Athenian public and political life.

If the penetrated male was a free boy, however, the situation was much more delicate. The protocols of Athenian paederasty were carefully designed and stylized so as to spare the boy the effeminizing humiliation of bodily penetration and thereby to prevent his future status as an adult man from being compromised in advance. Respectable erotic relations between men and boys preserved the social fiction that the man fucked the boy only between the legs, never in the ass—or, God forbid, in the mouth. It was not a question of what people actually did in bed (the boy was conventionally assumed, I suppose, to be anally receptive to his older lover, although DeVries has plausibly suggested to me that some high-minded lovers may not in fact have required their boyfriends to go through with the act of anal sex); rather, it was a question of how they behaved and talked when they were out of bed. Dover cited in this connection the story that Plutarch tells about Periander, the sixth-century tyrant of Ambracia, who asked his boy, "Aren't you pregnant yet?": the boy, who had apparently raised no objection to being fucked on repeated occasions, was sufficiently outraged by this question when it was put to him aloud—and doubtless in the presence of others—that he responded by killing the tyrant in order to recover his masculine honor (*Amatorius* 768F).

The Greek distinction between the man's erotic passion for the boy and the boy's love and affection for the man fits this whole scenario. Whatever a boy may do in bed, it was crucial that he not seem to be motivated by passionate sexual desire for his lover, for according to the Greek sociosexual system passionate sexual desire for an adult man inescapably implied one of two unacceptable things: either the boy desired to be sexually submissive, to be passive, to be penetrated by his partner, or he desired to penetrate his older lover (which was perverse on his part and, if he got away with it, utterly disreputable and disgraceful on his lover's part). A boy might well choose to "gratify" (*charizesthai*) the desire of his older lover for a variety of personal motives, some of them more respectable than others, but the least respectable motive of all was sexual pleasure. For a boy who took evident pleasure in being anally receptive or submissive identified himself as a *kinaidos,* a pathic, a catamite—there really is no modern English word that can convey the full force of the ancient stigma attached to that abominated identity. *Kinaidos* signified a male possessed of a supposedly feminine love of being sexually penetrated or dominated. It was the most disgraceful, the most stigmatized identity a free male could acquire, and it carried with it a number of devastating social disqualifications.

DeVries' overall interpretation, then, is not wrong, for the most part, although I do think he gets some things wrong, which I'll specify in a moment. In fact, as I said at the outset, I believe that DeVries' emphasis on the possible closeness and intimacy of ancient paederastic relations provides an important corrective to the crude conclusions that some scholars have drawn from their reading of Dover. But I do think his argument often misses the point of the scholarship he is arguing against. First of all, as I have tried to show here, it is misleading to ascribe to Dover and his followers the view that Greek boys were frigid in their relations with men. Although a boy might evince considerable love and affection for his older lover, and can be portrayed on the vases at times as welcoming his lover's advances, even leaping into his arms, a respectable boy studiously avoided giving any indication that he enjoyed playing, much less that he desired to play, a subordinate sexual role. That studied avoidance is something quite different from frigidity. The sexual ethic behind it does explain why boys are so frequently represented on the vases as lacking the erections which their senior partners display, and it also explains why, in those very few cases when boys *are* shown with what Eva Keuls has called "a puerile erection," they nonetheless appear impassive, without betraying any other sign of the passion that animates their older lovers.[10] These exceptional cases, in which boys are shown to be sexually aroused, do give us a precious glimpse of erotic responses that deviate from the strict norm of paederastic protocols, and they may indicate that paederasty was not entirely one-sided in actual erotic practice, that some boys did occasionally get something sexual out of it. The fact remains, however, that the vases seldom represent the boy's penis during intercourse with a male lover, and when they do represent the penises of both partners, either during intercourse or during earlier phases of the courtship, they represent the older man's penis as erect much oftener than they do the younger man's. That asymmetry, which may seem weird to our eyes, is in fact the clue to an important cultural attitude on the part of the Greeks, and we should endeavor not to obscure it (even if the social reality of sexual practice in classical Athens did not always perfectly mirror the social norm).

The specific arguments that DeVries brings forward to support his view that Greek custom licensed some boys to go so far as to exhibit *anterôs*— a passionate sexual desire for their older male lovers, a form of sexual passion that corresponded and responded to their lovers' own desire for them—strike me as very weak indeed. To be sure, there are no lack of sources that testify to the possibility that a boy who was fond of his lover might be expected to return many of his lover's feelings without committing any impropriety. A lover might legitimately wish a boy to reciprocate his "love" (*antiphileisthai*), his "longing" (*antipotheisthai*), and his "desire" for the boy's companionship (*antepithymeisthai:* Xenophon, *Memo-*

rabilia 2.6.28). A decent boy might also "cherish" (*aspazesthai*) his lover and "welcome" (*khairein*) his lover's physical attentions (Plato, *Symposium* 191E—192B).[11] DeVries cites a few texts that vouch for this reciprocal love on the part of a boy, though he does not always choose the best texts to cite (cf., e.g., Xenophon, *Hiero* 1.32–38): the passages he does single out tend to be drawn from particularly controversial moments in the Socratic dialogues, such as *Lysis* 221B, where Socrates is about to force on his youthful interlocutors a conclusion that is at once so logically inescapable and so culturally counterintuitive that it brings the entire conversation to a complete standstill (222A). Nonetheless, reciprocal *love* for a male lover was well within the bounds of proper erotic conduct for a Greek boy. On this point Dover, DeVries, and I all agree. DeVries has in fact compiled a massive archive of literary and epigraphical testimony to this effect, and he has generously shared it with me. It demonstrates beyond a shadow of a doubt that both the language and the culture of male love in all periods of Greek civilization teemed with expressions of reciprocal affection. But expressions of reciprocal affection are one thing, and expressions of reciprocal *erôs,* of mutual desire and sexual passion, are quite another. What was absolutely inadmissible, and what our sources stop abruptly short of suggesting, was the possibility that a decent boy might feel for a man a passionate sexual desire, an *erôs* or *anterôs,* of the same sort that animated the older lover.[12] No extant source from the classical period of Greek civilization assigns the junior partner in a paederastic relationship a share of *erôs* or *anterôs*—with the sole exception of Plato, in a highly tendentious philosophical passage that I'll discuss in a moment. Allusions to reciprocal male *erôs* or *anterôs* are almost entirely missing from DeVries' archive, and when on rare occasions they do occur, the occurrences tend to be quite late historically. That omission is not an accident. Rather, it is the sign of a cultural preoccupation peculiar to the Greeks that we should not attempt to argue out of existence.

Let us look briefly at the sole exception mentioned above. In a famous and daring passage in the *Phaedrus* (255C—E), which DeVries discusses but which I believe he misapplies, Plato does indeed have Socrates argue that in the best sort of erotic relationship a boy comes to feel a genuine *anterôs* for his male lover, a passion whose origin, however, is not the lover himself but the image of the boy's own beauty, which the boy sees reflected back to him in his lover's eyes. This account of the boy's response is acknowledged to be so heterodox and so far-fetched that not even the boy himself would recognize his own emotions in Socrates' description of them; rather, as Socrates freely admits, the boy thinks that he feels for his lover merely what he ought to feel—namely, *philia.* Socrates can maintain his minority opinion about the hypothetical boy's *anterôs* and still manage not to impugn either the boy's decency or his own only because he makes these claims in the course of constructing a highly novel theory of erotic desire according to which (1) desire does not ultimately aim at sexual gratification but at the contemplation of transcendental ideas, (2) all those who take part in an erotic/dialogic relationship—whether as lover and beloved or as teacher and student—become active, desiring lovers, not merely passive objects of desire, and therefore (3) *erôs* does not implicate either its subject or its object in sexual passivity. Far from attempting to capture how his contemporaries understood the internal emotional dynamics of a normal paederastic relationship, Socrates is performing a highly idiosyncratic analysis designed to lay the groundwork for the construction of a unique, elitist, erotic-philosophical community whose members must renounce all attempts to express sexually the desire for the ideas and for truth that draws them to one another. This passage from the *Phaedrus* demonstrates how many common classical Greek assumptions about *erôs* and about paederasty have to be overturned before paederastic *anterôs* can even begin to enter the realms of cultural possibility and moral legitimacy.[13]

The other bits of evidence that DeVries presents in his paper for the contrary view that the Greeks sanctioned and even sometimes prayed for *anterôs* in a boy prove to be equally unreliable witnesses to his case and, if anything, tend to tell strongly against his thesis. Outside the context of love, *anterôs* is a well-attested feature of the male world of ancient Greece, but when that word occurs in a male context its usual meaning is not "mutual love," but "rivalry" or "competition in love," as Dover demonstrated and as my own research has confirmed.[14] In normal Greek, your *anterastês* is not your loving boyfriend but your rival for his affections. DeVries' personal archive of evidence for reciprocity in male erotics is sufficient to persuade me that *anterôs* nonetheless may sometimes have signified reciprocal desire in a male context, but his accumulation of evidence is not sufficient to persuade me that it did signify that often or routinely. Thus, the frieze in the gymnasium at Elis on the Peloponnese that Pausanias (6.23.3, 5) described in the second century A.D. and that DeVries enlists to support his case actually testifies eloquently against it.[15] For even DeVries concedes that the frieze depicts a scene of rivalry: Anteros struggles to wrest from Eros a palm branch, signifying victory. DeVries interprets the iconography to mean that "responsive eros can rival [*sic*] in power primary eros." But what, in the all-male context of a gymnasium, this contest between rival competitors surely signifies is not erotic mutuality but rather the competitive "love" of victory, the competitive zeal to surpass one's opponent that supposedly animates the most accomplished athletes. Eros and Anteros personify the spirit of mutual emulation that drives athletes who compete against one another to push one another to higher levels of achievement in their individual passion for victory. Here it is rivalry, as one would expect, that turns out to be the dominant meaning of *anterôs*.

The altar to Anteros on the Athenian Acropolis that Pausanias describes elsewhere (1.30.1) is a somewhat more ambiguous case, but here too the evidence hardly supports DeVries' sentimental reading. First of all, the worship of Eros and Aphrodite on the Athenian Acropolis was very ancient, and the original meaning of the altar to Anteros may be lost; we have no assurance that the story Pausanias tells in order to explain its origin accurately represents what Anteros signified to those who established the altar to him. Second, the story itself is not one of mutual felicity but of tragedy and revenge. DeVries says that the Athenian cult of Anteros "was founded in the aftermath of a failed homosexual courtship." In fact, Pausanias recounts that the altar was dedicated by resident aliens at Athens who wished to commemorate the suicide of an Athenian youth who belatedly appreciated the nobility of the foreign lover he had rejected when the latter leapt to his death from the Acropolis in obedience to the youth's contemptuous command. In Pausanias's telling of the story, the boy's suicide is motivated most immediately not by *anterôs* but by *metanoia,* a change of heart, and in any case the boy only returned his lover's *erôs* after the latter was safely dead. *Anterôs* is the vindictive construction placed on the boy's motives by the resident aliens, who conceive of *Anterôs* not as a reciprocated desire but as an *alastôr,* an avenging deity. No doubt the Athenian altar to Anteros witnessed the fervent prayers of many a disappointed lover in later days, just as DeVries imagines, but on the evidence that Pausanias presents what such lovers most likely prayed for was not that their frigid boyfriends might become more sexually responsive to their physical embraces but rather that the boys who had rejected them would be punished for their cruelty by being struck down by an equally tormenting and unrequited desire (either for them or for other unattainable objects). That, after all, is exactly what spurned Greek lovers had been accustomed to pray for at least since the time of Sappho, to judge from her only complete preserved poem (the famous ode to Aphrodite), and that is what many rejected lovers throughout antiquity continued to ask the gods to grant them, if the erotic spells in the surviving corpus of Greek magical papyri are any indication.[16] Understood in such a way, the altar to Anteros at Athens offers little support for DeVries' thesis about the reciprocal nature of sexual passion in Greek paederasty.

One more point. Even if DeVries is right in his interpretation of the wrist-grasping gesture, and even if Dover was wrong to suppose that it indicated a boy's attempt to repel a would-be lover, DeVries' important correction of Dover on this particular question hardly carries with it the dire consequences for Dover's larger picture of classical Athenian paederasty that DeVries appears to think it does. For Greek convention did not make it incumbent on a decent boy to resist his suitors physically, unless they were attempting to use force against him (which was not only considered outrageous but was reckoned an act of *hybris*, a serious crime at Athens). There remains plenty of literary and visual material to sustain Dover's basic claim that the Greeks set a very high value on a boy's modesty, on his playing hard to get.

All this leads to my final and most serious reflection on DeVries' paper. Again and again, DeVries insists that paederastic relations between classical Athenian men and boys were, to quote his favorite adjectives, "warm," "loving," "affectionate," and "tender"; he emphasizes the "closeness," "intimacy," "love," "affection," "warm feelings," and even "responsiveness" that could characterize such relations. In all of this he is surely right. But what exactly does it prove? What kind of objection is it to say, against the view that paederastic relations were asymmetrical, hierarchical, and generally non-reciprocal in their distribution of sexual pleasure, that men and boys really loved each other? I am reminded in this context of earlier disputes about the position of women in society. In the past, when research into the social position of classical Greek women, or Victorian women, disclosed striking inequities between their social status and that of men, numbers of chivalrous gentlemen would typically come forward to assure us that the Greeks, or the Victorians, really loved their wives.

But the point at issue here is not the emotional temperature of personal relationships but the social structuration of erotic life. It is not a question of choosing between personal affection and social subordination as alternate and rival interpretations of the same phenomena. Rather, they are two sides of the same coin. As two generations of feminist research has shown, the personal *is* political, and social domination is not opposed to, but in fact may well be an essential condition of, "true love." (Perhaps, to reverse Oscar Wilde, all men love the things they hurt.) In any case, while I don't dispute DeVries' claim that the gesture of grasping someone by the wrist in ancient Greece may have been the equivalent to taking hold of someone's hand nowadays, I don't see anything in either gesture, then or now, that I would consider innocent of social meaning or exempt from elements of social power. As anyone who has ever gone on a date and wondered when or whether to take hold of his boyfriend's hand for the first time can surely testify, there enters into such a decision a whole battery of doubts and calculations about the significance of the gesture. Should I wait for him to take my hand, or should I take his first? Should I do so in private or in public? Or should I rather let him take the lead? If I act first, will he think I am being aggressive, coming on to him, or just being affectionate? The point about love's lack of externality to power is well made by a fictional character in Pat Barker's *The Regeneration Trilogy:* "One of the things I like sexually, one of the things I fantasise about, is simply being fully dressed with a naked lover, holding him or her from behind. And what I feel (apart from the obvious) is great tenderness—the sort of tenderness that depends on being more powerful, and that is really, I suppose, just the acceptable face of sadism." [17] It should be possible to put the same point in less self-accusing terms.

"Of course," Foucault wrote in his 1982 review of Dover,

> there will still be some folks disposed to think that, in the final analysis, homosexuality has always existed. . . . To such naive souls Dover gives a good lesson in historical nominalism. [Sexual] relations between two persons of the same sex is one thing. But to love the same sex as oneself, to take one's pleasure in that sex, is quite another thing, it's a whole experience, with its own objects and their meanings, with a specific way of life and a consciousness on the lover's part. That experience is complex, it is diverse, it takes different forms, it changes. [18]

I believe that if classical scholarship is ever to challenge heterosexuality's claims to normality and universality—its claims to be the sexuality of the majority of the population in all times and all places—it will have to do what it can to hang on to Foucault's fundamental insight.

Notes

INTRODUCTION

1. David M. Halperin, *One Hundred Years of Homosexuality and Other Essays on Greek Love* (New York: Routledge, 1990).

2. David M. Halperin, *Before Pastoral: Theocritus and the Ancient Tradition of Bucolic Poetry* (New Haven, Conn.: Yale University Press, 1983), "The Forebears of Daphnis," *Transactions of the American Philological Association* 113 (1983): 183–200, "All Dressed Up and No Place to Go," *Yale Review* 74 (1984/85): 587–96, "Bucolic Poetry," in *Civilization of the Ancient Mediterranean: Greece and Rome,* ed. Michael Grant and Rachel Kitzinger (New York: Scribner's, 1988), 1467–75.

3. David M. Halperin, "Plato and Erotic Reciprocity," *Classical Antiquity* 5 (1986): 60–80, "Platonic *Erôs* and What Men Call Love," *Ancient Philosophy* 5 (1985): 161–204, "Plato and the Metaphysics of Desire," in *Proceedings of the Boston Area Colloquium in Ancient Philosophy,* vol. 5, *1989,* ed. John J. Cleary and Daniel C. Shartin (Lanham, Md.: University Press of America, 1991), 27–52, "Plato and the Erotics of Narrativity," in *Methods of Interpreting Plato and His Dialogues,* ed. James C. Klagge and Nicholas D. Smith, Oxford Studies in Ancient Philosophy, suppl. vol. 2 (Oxford: Clarendon, 1992), 93–129 (reprinted in *Innovations of Antiquity,* ed. Daniel Selden and Ralph Hexter [New York: Routledge, 1992], 95–126, and in *Plato and Postmodernism,* ed. Steven Shankman [Glenside, Pa.: Aldine, 1994], 43–75).

4. See George Chauncey, Jr., "From Sexual Inversion to Homosexuality: The Changing Medical Conceptualization of Female Deviance," *Salmagundi* (Special Issue: "Homosexuality: Sacrilege, Vision, Politics," ed. Robert Boyers and George Steiner), vols. 58–59 (1982–83), 114–46, "Christian Brotherhood or Sexual Perversion? Homosexual

Identities and the Construction of Sexual Boundaries in the World War One Era," *Journal of Social History* 19 (1985/86): 189–211, *Gay New York: Gender, Urban Culture, and the Making of the Gay Male World, 1890–1940* (New York: Basic Books, 1994). Also important to me at the time were the following works: Randolph Trumbach, "London's Sodomites: Homosexual Behavior and Western Culture in the Eighteenth Century," *Journal of Social History* 11 (1977): 1–33; Barry D. Adam, "Structural Foundations of the Gay World," *Comparative Studies in Society and History* 27 (1985): 658–71; and Arnold I. Davidson, "Sex and the Emergence of Sexuality," *Critical Inquiry* 14, no. 1 (1987): 16–48.

5. K. J. Dover, *Greek Homosexuality* (Cambridge, Mass.: Harvard University Press, 1978).

6. David M. Halperin, John J. Winkler, and Froma I. Zeitlin, eds., *Before Sexuality: The Construction of Erotic Experience in the Ancient Greek World* (Princeton, N.J.: Princeton University Press, 1990).

7. Maud W. Gleason, *Making Men: Sophists and Self-Presentation in Ancient Rome* (Princeton, N.J.: Princeton University Press, 1995); Craig A. Williams, *Roman Homosexuality: Ideologies of Masculinity in Classical Antiquity* (New York: Oxford University Press, 1999).

8. Eva Cantarella, *Bisexuality in the Ancient World,* trans. Cormac Ó Cuilleanáin (New Haven, Conn.: Yale University Press, 1992); Bernadette J. Brooten, *Love between Women: Early Christian Responses to Female Homoeroticism* (Chicago: University of Chicago Press, 1996); William Armstrong Percy III, *Pederasty and Pedagogy in Archaic Greece* (Urbana: University of Illinois Press, 1996); Bruce S. Thornton, *Eros: The Myth of Ancient Greek Sexuality* (Boulder, Colo.: Westview, 1997); James Davidson, *Courtesans and Fishcakes: The Consuming Passions of Classical Athens* (London: HarperCollins, 1997).

9. Henry Abelove, Michèle Aina Barale, and David M. Halperin, eds., *The Lesbian and Gay Studies Reader* (New York: Routledge, 1993).

10. For example, Amy Richlin, "Zeus and Metis: Foucault, Feminism, Classics," *Helios* 18, no. 2 (autumn 1991): 160–80, makes the following outraged claim: "Judith Hallett's 1989 article on lesbians in Roman sources appears nowhere in this book, despite the fact that David Halperin . . . [was] on the same panel when she presented this material in 1988 as a paper at the second Yale conference on gay and lesbian studies" (176). In fact, a reference to Hallett's article, which was still unpublished at the time *One Hundred Years of Homosexuality* was written, appears in my book on p. 166, at the end of n. 83. Hallett had herself provided me with the publication information, and she knew very well how eager I was to include a reference to her forthcoming article in my book, but she never corrected Richlin's misinformation. Richlin similarly complained that "the word 'lesbian' does not appear in Halperin's Index" (176). Quite so: it is after all an index of names, which is why neither "homosexuality" nor "paederasty" appears in it either. I should have liked at some point to respond to Richlin's attack, but I felt the task was better left to others.

11. The New Historicism was a scholarly movement that began in the early 1980s and was based at universities in California—principally at the University of California, Berkeley—where it was associated with the journal *Representations*. Inspired, on the one hand, by the cultural anthropologist Clifford Geertz (who had been inspired in turn by Paul Ricoeur) and, on the other hand, by Peter Brown and Michel Foucault, New Historicists such as Stephen Greenblatt, Louis Montrose, and Steven Mullaney produced

coordinate readings of early modern texts and early modern social practices and used their readings to generate a series of X-rays of the political and epistemic structures of early modern cultures.

12. David M. Halperin, "Sexual Ethics and Technologies of the Self in Classical Greece," *American Journal of Philology* 107 (1986): 274–86.

13. My review of *L'usage des plaisirs* was included in the chapter titled "Two Views of Greek Love," esp. 62–69.

14. See, for example, Camille Paglia, "Junk Bonds and Corporate Raiders: Academe in the Hour of the Wolf," *Arion,* 3d ser., 1, no. 2 (spring 1991): 139–212, reprinted in Paglia, *Sex, Art, and American Culture* (New York: Vintage, 1992), 170–248; Richard D. Mohr, "The Thing of It Is: Some Problems with Models for the Social Construction of Homosexuality," in *Gay Ideas: Outing and Other Controversies* (Boston: Beacon, 1992), 221–42, 285–97; Bruce Bawer, *A Place at the Table: The Gay Individual in American Society* (New York: Poseidon, 1993), 211; Bruce Thornton, "Constructionism and Ancient Greek Sex," *Helios* 18, no. 2 (autumn 1991): 181–93, and "Idolon Theatri: Foucault and the Classicists," *Classical and Modern Literature* 12, no. 1 (fall 1991): 81–100; Micaela Janan, review of *One Hundred Years of Homosexuality,* by David M. Halperin, *Women's Classical Caucus Newsletter* 17 (1991): 40–43; Amy Richlin, review of *One Hundred Years of Homosexuality,* by David M. Halperin, *Bryn Mawr Classical Review* 2, no. 1 (1991): 17–18, and "Not before Homosexuality: The Materiality of the *Cinaedus* and the Roman Law against Love between Men," *Journal of the History of Sexuality* 3, no. 4 (April 1993): 523–73; Judith P. Hallett, "Ancient Greek and Roman Constructions of Sexuality: The State of the Debate," paper presented at "Sexualities, Dissidence, and Cultural Change: A Symposium," University of Maryland at College Park, April 10, 1992.

15. David M. Halperin, *Saint Foucault: Towards a Gay Hagiography* (New York: Oxford University Press, 1995).

16. Eve Kosofsky Sedgwick, *Epistemology of the Closet* (Berkeley: University of California Press, 1990), esp. 44–48. Subsequent citations to this book appear in parentheses in the text.

17. Ross Chambers, "Strategic Constructivism? Sedgwick's Ethics of Inversion," in *Regarding Sedgwick: Essays on Queer Culture and Critical Theory,* ed. Stephen M. Barber and David L. Clark (New York: Routledge, 2002), 165–80 (quotation on p. 166).

18. Michel Foucault, *Discipline and Punish: The Birth of the Prison,* trans. Alan Sheridan (New York: Pantheon, 1978), 31.

19. See Elizabeth A. Povinelli and George Chauncey, eds., *Thinking Sexuality Transnationally* (Durham, N.C.: Duke University Press, 1999), published as *GLQ: A Journal of Lesbian and Gay Studies,* vol. 5, no. 4 (1999).

20. See Halperin, *Saint Foucault,* 104–6.

21. For a particularly powerful, eloquent, and politically constructive articulation of this point, see Douglas Crimp, "Right On, Girlfriend!" in *Fear of a Queer Planet: Queer Politics and Social Theory,* ed. Michael Warner (Minneapolis: University of Minnesota Press, 1993), 300–320.

22. The pamphlet has been conveniently reprinted by Mark Blasius and Shane Phelan, eds., *We Are Everywhere: A Historical Sourcebook of Gay and Lesbian Politics* (New York: Routledge, 1997), 773–780 (quotation on 774).

23. Larry Kramer, *"The Normal Heart" and "The Destiny of Me": Two Plays by Larry Kramer* (New York: Grove Press, 2000), 109.

24. For the most careful, responsible, and socially sensitive example of such an effort, see Carolyn Dinshaw, *Getting Medieval: Sexualities and Communities, Pre- and Postmodern* (Durham, N.C.: Duke University Press, 1999), from whose example I have learned a great deal.

25. My invocation of "historicism" here is therefore poles apart from Dipesh Chakrabarty's in *Provincializing Europe: Postcolonial Thought and Historical Difference* (Princeton, N.J.: Princeton University Press, 2000), 6–8 ff. Chakrabarty understands "historicism" as part of a nineteenth-century Western European ideology of progress, according to which less developed nations must follow a linear path of historical evolution that will lead them to resemble, in time, the currently more developed ones. Chakrabarty explicitly contrasts what he calls "historicism" with the approach represented by Foucault, who indeed enables us to think historical change beyond ideas of progress. Elsewhere in *Provincializing Europe* Chakrabarty speaks more aptly of "historicization" (101) or "historicizing" (112), rather than historicism. It is precisely a non-colonial relation to the past that historicism, as I understand it, is dedicated to instantiating.

26. See, esp., Chakrabarty's essay, "Minority Histories, Subaltern Pasts," in *Provincializing Europe,* 97–113 (quotations on 109).

27. Jean Le Bitoux, "Le Gai Savoir: Entretien avec Michel Foucault," *La revue h,* 2 (autumn 1996): 42–54, esp. 50.

28. Dr. Charles Silverstein and Edmund White, *The Joy of Gay Sex: An Intimate Guide for Gay Men to the Pleasures of a Gay Lifestyle* (New York: Crown, 1977), 10–11. See also 185–87: "Since the advent of feminism and gay liberation, 'role-playing' has taken on a decidedly negative aura. . . . To the gay liberationist role-playing conjures up a picture of two men living out a grotesque parody of heterosexual married life. . . . The disadvantages of role-playing are manifold and increasingly obvious. . . . In the late sixties, the birth of modern feminism and gay liberation called for the abolition of all role-playing."

29. Reinaldo Arenas, *Before Night Falls,* trans. Dolores M. Koch (New York: Viking, 1993), 106.

30. W. Thomas MacCary, *Childlike Achilles: Ontogeny and Phylogeny in the "Iliad"* (New York: Columbia University Press, 1982), x.

31. Some of my readers may scoff at this example of historiographical aspiration, thinking that no one today would formulate the aim of historical research in such terms. But the goal of classical scholarship has remained largely unchanged since it was articulated by the great German classicists of the late nineteenth century: it is to arrive, through a strenuous, conscious, and systematic bracketing of modern assumptions and preconceptions, at something approximating the original experience of the ancient peoples themselves. The rigors of training in classical scholarship are ideologically justified by that goal, inasmuch as nothing short of immense linguistic and historical erudition can enable people living thousands of years afterward to reconstruct, to the maximum extent possible, what was actually going on in the minds of the ancient Greeks and Romans. Anyone who doubts that classical philology continues to formulate its aims and purpose in these terms should consider the following statement: "When reading a text, most of all a work of prosaic or poetic art, it is the duty of the interpreter to find out with all tools available to him [*sic*] the intention with which the author wrote his [*sic*] work. At least I hope what Virgil had in mind composing his *Aeneid* will by most interpreters be ascribed to the will of the poet and not to the performance of social agents.

Exploring this intention by the ways just described, and nothing else, is philology." That statement was not made in the nineteenth century but on July 23, 2001, by Christoph Kugelmeier of the Universität des Saarlandes, Saarbrücken, in the *Bryn Mawr Classical Review*, 01.07.23 (http://ccat.sas.upenn.edu/bmcr/). I have added my own italics.

32. See Stephen O. Murray, *Homosexualities* (Chicago: University of Chicago Press, 2000), 2–3: "While relationships structured by age, gender, profession, and comradeship may coexist in a society, one of them tends to be more visible 'on the ground,' both among those who are native to the society and in explanation to aliens who ask about same-sex sexual relations."

33. On global differences in patterns of same-sex sexual practice, see, for example, Gary Smith, "Heterosexual and Homosexual Anal Intercourse: An International Perspective," *Venereology* 14, no. 1 (2001): 28–37.

34. For a recent elegant and persuasive demonstration of the historical difference made by the emergence of sexuality, see Alan Bray and Michel Rey, "The Body of the Friend: Continuity and Change in Masculine Friendship in the Seventeenth Century," in *English Masculinities, 1660–1800,* ed. Tim Hitchcock and Michèle Cohen (London: Addison Wesley Longman, 1999), 65–84.

35. Alan Sinfield, *Gay and After* (London: Serpent's Tail, 1988), 44. See, also, Alan Sinfield, "The Production of Gay and the Return of Power," in *De-Centring Sexualities: Politics and Representations beyond the Metropolis,* ed. Richard Phillips, Diane Watt, and David Shuttleton (London: Routledge, 2000), 21–36, esp. 22: "Metropolitan gay and lesbian concepts should be regarded, therefore, not as denoting the ultimate achievement of human sexuality, but as something we have been producing— we homosexuals and we heterosexuals—in determinate economic and social conditions."

CHAPTER ONE

1. For all of the information and the quotations in this paragraph, I am indebted to David Macey, *The Lives of Michel Foucault* (London: Hutchinson, 1993), esp. 358–60. See, further, Jean Baudrillard, *Cool Memories, I et II: 1980–1990* (1987, 1990; reprinted, Paris: Le Livre de Poche, 1993), 139–42, esp. 140 ("L'oublier était lui rendre service, l'aduler était le desservir"), and 139 ("Mort de Foucault. Perte de confiance en son propre génie. . . . La perte des systèmes immunitaires, en dehors de tout aspect sexuel, n'est que la transcription biologique de l'autre processus").

For some resumptions of the "forget Foucault" theme, see E. Greblo, "Dimenticare Foucault?" *Aut-Aut* 242 (March—April 1991): 79–90; Kate Soper, "Forget Foucault?" *New Formations* 25 (summer 1995): 21–27.

2. Baudrillard delivers himself of this enlightened opinion in the course of an interview with F. Rötzer, "Virtuelle Katastrophen," *Kunstforum* (January—February 1990), 266; I reproduce here the quotation and citation provided by Douglas Crimp, "Portraits of People with AIDS," in *Cultural Studies,* ed Lawrence Grossberg, Cary Nelson, and Paula A. Treichler (New York: Routledge, 1992), 117–33 (quotation on 130).

3. Michel Foucault, *The History of Sexuality*, vol. 1, *An Introduction*, trans. Robert Hurley (New York: Vintage, 1980), 159; cf. Michel Foucault, *La volonté de savoir*, vol. 1 of *Histoire de la sexualité* (1976; reprinted, Paris: Gallimard, 1984), 211. Wherever possible, I quote the English text of Foucault's *History of Sexuality*, because it is that text that has influenced Foucault's Anglophone disciples, with whom I am concerned

in this essay, but I have altered the published translation whenever necessary to restore Foucault's original emphasis or meaning.

4. For example, in an interview published in *La Quinzaine littéraire* in early January 1977, to promote *The History of Sexuality,* vol. 1, Foucault described as the book's point of departure the premise that "the idea of sex is internal to the apparatus of sexuality, and that what is to be found at the root of the latter is not the rejection of sex but a quite definite, specific economy of bodies and of pleasure" [l'idée de sexe était intérieure au dispositif de la sexualité et que par conséquent ce qu'on doit retrouver à sa racine, ce n'est pas le sexe refusé, c'est une économie positive des corps et du plaisir] (Michel Foucault, "Les rapports de pouvoir passent à l'intérieur des corps," in *Dits et écrits, 1954–1988,* ed. Daniel Defert and François Ewald [Paris: Gallimard, 1994], 3:228–36 [quotation on 234]). English translations of this text have appeared, under the title "The History of Sexuality" in Michel Foucault, *Power/Knowledge: Selected Interviews and Other Writings, 1972–77,* ed. Colin Gordon, trans. Colin Gordon, Leo Marshall, John Mepham, and Kate Soper (Brighton, Sussex: Harvester, 1980), 183–93, and under the title "Power Affects the Body" in *Foucault Live (Interviews, 1961–1984),* ed. Sylvère Lotringer (New York: Semiotext(e), 1989), 207–13.

5. Similarly, in "Les rapports de pouvoir passent à l'intérieur des corps," 235, Foucault goes on to call not for "liberation" but "desexualization," that is, "a general economy of pleasure which would not be sexually normed" [une économie générale du plaisir qui ne soit pas sexuellement normée].

6. Foucault, *The History of Sexuality,* 1:157. See, further, David M. Halperin, *Saint Foucault: Towards a Gay Hagiography* (New York: Oxford University Press, 1995), 92–97.

7. Foucault, *The History of Sexuality,* 1:157 (emended), and *La volonté de savoir,* 208.

8. Stephen O. Murray, *Homosexualities* (Chicago: University of Chicago Press, 2000), 11n, claims that I have "slipped 'sodomite' into the opposition Foucault made (in French, not just in translation into English) between 'sodomy' (an act) and 'the homosexual' (a kind of person)." Murray evidently did not read to the end of the famous paragraph by Foucault quoted below.

9. Foucault, *The History of Sexuality,* 1:43 (translation considerably modified); *La volonté de savoir,* 59.

10. This view has been contested by Mark D. Jordan, *The Invention of Sodomy in Christian Theology* (Chicago: University of Chicago Press, 1997), esp. 42, 44, 163.

11. In a passage that provides the closest textual and historical parallel in Foucault's writings to the famous passage in *The History of Sexuality,* vol. 1, Foucault seems to distinguish between sodomy and homosexuality in much the same terms as do those historians of sexuality whose views I am criticizing here. The passage occurs in a book-length transcript of six taped interviews with a young gay man named Thierry Voeltzel that Foucault recorded during the summer of 1976, just as he was completing *The History of Sexuality,* vol. 1, and that he arranged to have published under Voeltzel's name. At one point in the conversation the anonymous interviewer (i.e., Foucault) makes the following observation: "The category of the homosexual was invented lately. It didn't use to exist; what existed was sodomy, that is to say a certain number of sexual practices which, in themselves, were condemned, but the homosexual individual did not exist" [La catégorie de l'homosexuel a été inventée tardivement. Ça n'existait pas, ce qui existait, c'était la sodomie, c'est-à-dire un certain nombre de pratiques sexuelles qui, elles, étaient

condamnées, mais l'individu homosexuel n'existait pas]. See Thierry Voeltzel, *Vingt ans et après* (Paris: Grasset, 1978), 33.

In this conversation with Voeltzel, Foucault may sound as if he's saying that once upon a time there were only sexual acts, not sexual actors. (That is how Didier Eribon interprets the passage: see Eribon, *Réflexions sur la question gay* [Paris: Fayard, 1999], 372–442, trans. Michael Lucey as "Michel Foucault's Histories of Sexuality," *GLQ: A Journal of Lesbian and Gay Studies* 7, no. 1 [2001]: 31–86.) Note, however, that Foucault is simplifying matters for the benefit of his decidedly unacademic interlocutor; that, even so, he stops short of making a formal distinction between acts and identities; and that he never says that before the nineteenth century there were no sexual identities, only sexual acts. What preoccupies him in his exchange with Voeltzel, just as in *The History of Sexuality,* vol. 1, is the relatively recent invention of the normalizing "category" of the homosexual, the discursive constitution of a class of deviant individuals as opposed to the mere enumeration of a set of forbidden practices; when he refers to "the homosexual individual," he is referring to the entity constructed by the modern discourses of psychiatry and sexology. It is only lately, Foucault emphasizes in his interview with Voeltzel, that it has become almost impossible simply to pursue the pleasures of homosexual contact, as Voeltzel appears to have done, "just so, when you felt like it, every once in a while, or in phases" [comme ca, quand tu en avais envie, par moments, ou par phases], without being forced to deduce from one's own behavior that one *is* homosexual, without being interpellated by the culpabilizing category of "the homosexual." Voeltzel's narrative therefore reminds Foucault of an earlier historical period when it was possible to *practice* homosexuality without *being* homosexual.

As time went by, and Foucault's thinking about the history of sexuality evolved, he abandoned the contrast between sodomy and homosexuality along with the implicit opposition between practices and persons and came up with new ways of representing the differences between modern and pre-modern forms of same-sex sexual experience. In 1982, for example, in a review of the French translation of K. J. Dover's 1978 monograph, *Greek Homosexuality,* Foucault wrote:

> Of course, there will still be some folks disposed to think that, in the final analysis, homosexuality has always existed. . . . To such naive souls Dover gives a good lesson in historical nominalism. [Sexual] relations between two persons of the same sex are one thing. But to love the same sex as oneself, to take one's pleasure in that sex, is quite another thing, it's a whole experience, with its own objects and their meanings, with a specific way of being on the part of the subject and a consciousness which he has of himself. That experience is complex, it is diverse, it takes different forms, it changes.

> [Bien sûr, on trouvera encore des esprits aimables pour penser qu'en somme l'homosexualité a toujours existé. . . . A de tels naïfs, Dover donne une bonne leçon de nominalisme historique. Le rapport entre deux individus du même sexe est une chose. Mais aimer le même sexe que soi, prendre avec lui un plaisir, c'est autre chose, c'est toute une expérience, avec ses objets et leurs valeurs, avec la manière d'être du sujet et la conscience qu'il a de lui-même. Cette expérience est complexe, elle est diverse, elle change de formes.]

(Michel Foucault, "Des caresses d'hommes considérées comme un art," *Libération,* 1 June 1982, 27, reprinted in *Dits et écrits,* 4:315–17 [quotation on 315–16])

Here Foucault inveighs against applying to the Greeks an undifferentiated, ahistorical, and transcendental notion of homosexuality defined purely behaviorally, in terms of sexual practice ("sexual relations between two persons of the same sex"), in favor of a more nuanced, contextualized understanding that foregrounds specific, conscious "ways of being" on the part of different historical and sexual subjects. That is very much in keeping with Foucault's emphasis in his famous 1981 interview in *Le gai pied* on homosexuality as a "way of life" (*mode de vie*): Michel Foucault, "De l'amitié comme mode de vie," *Le gai pied* 25 (April 1981): 38–39, trans. John Johnston in *Foucault Live,* 308–12. But now it is not so much a question of opposing "sexual practices" to categories of individuals, as Foucault was inclined to do in 1976; rather, it is a question of systematically defining different historical forms of sexual experience—different ways of being, different sets of relations to others and to oneself, different articulations of pleasure and meaning, different forms of consciousness. The exact terms in which such historical discriminations are to be made, however, remain unspecified. Foucault leaves that practical question of historical analysis and methodology to the individual historian. He is content simply to offer a model of how to proceed in the second and third volumes of his own unfinished *History of Sexuality.*

12. For example, Murray, in *Homosexualities,* 8n, appears to ascribe to me the absurd view that "no one before 1869 or non-'Western' has noticed and been interested in who has sex with what kinds of persons." Giulia Sissa, also summarizing what she takes to be my position, writes, "before sexuality one does not find homosexuality but only a variety of sexual acts; not an identity, only a freedom of choice"; she bizarrely takes this view to be equivalent to claiming that there is no difference between classical Athens and contemporary San Francisco. See Sissa, "Sexual Bodybuilding: Aeschines against Timarchus," in *Constructions of the Classical Body,* ed. James I. Porter (Ann Arbor: University of Michigan Press, 1999), 147–68 (esp. 147 and 164). My own view is rather more nuanced than the one Sissa attributes to me, and I have tried to be precise in articulating it: "Before the scientific construction of 'sexuality' as a supposedly positive, distinct, and constitutive feature of individual human beings—an autonomous system within the physiological and psychological economy of the human organism—certain kinds of sexual *acts* could be individually evaluated and characterized, **and so could certain sexual tastes or inclinations,** but there was no conceptual apparatus available for identifying a person's fixed and determinate sexual *orientation,* much less for assessing and classifying it" (David M. Halperin, *One Hundred Years of Homosexuality and Other Essays on Greek Love* [New York: Routledge, 1990], 26, boldface added). The contrast here is between acts, tastes, and inclinations, on the one hand, and the modern sexological concept of sexual orientation, on the other. For a further refinement of this view, see my essay, "How to Do the History of Male Homosexuality," in this volume.

13. See, for example, Mary McIntosh, "The Homosexual Role," *Social Problems* 16 (1968/69): 182–92; Randolph Trumbach, "London's Sodomites: Homosexual Behavior and Western Culture in the Eighteenth Century," *Journal of Social History* 11 (1977): 1–33; Richard Sennett, *The Fall of Public Man: On the Social Psychology of Capitalism* (New York: Vintage, 1978); Jeffrey Weeks, *Sex, Politics and Society: The*

Regulation of Sexuality since 1800 (London: Longmans, 1981); Arnold I. Davidson, "Sex and the Emergence of Sexuality," *Critical Inquiry* 14, no. 1 (1987): 16–48; John D'Emilio and Estelle D. Freedman, *Intimate Matters: A History of Sexuality in America* (New York: Harper & Row, 1988); Thomas Laqueur, *Making Sex: Body and Gender from the Greeks to Freud* (Cambridge, Mass.: Harvard University Press, 1990); George Chauncey, *Gay New York: Gender, Urban Culture, and the Making of the Gay Male World, 1890–1940* (New York: Basic Books, 1994); Jonathan Ned Katz, *The Invention of Heterosexuality* (New York: Dutton, 1995); Carolyn J. Dean, *Sexuality and Modern Western Culture* (New York: Twayne, 1996).

14. See the very careful demonstration of this point by Arnold I. Davidson, "Closing up the Corpses: Diseases of Sexuality and the Emergence of the Psychiatric Style of Reasoning," in *Meaning and Method: Essays in Honor of Hilary Putnam,* ed. George Boolos (Cambridge: Cambridge University Press, 1990), 295–325.

15. For a similar argument to the same effect, see Ruth Mazo Karras, "Prostitution and the Question of Sexual Identity in Medieval Europe," *Journal of Women's History* 11, no. 2 (1999): 159–77. Karras's article appeared after the original version of "Forgetting Foucault" was published, but Karras arrived at her conclusions independently. Karras's and my approaches have been helpfully compared and assessed by Carla Freccero, "Acts, Identities, and Sexuality's (Pre)Modern Regimes," *Journal of Women's History* 11, no. 2 (1999): 186–92. Karras freely speaks of "sexuality" and "sexual identity" in pre-modern Europe; "I expect Halperin would disagree with much of what I have said here," she remarks in a rejoinder to Freccero's critique, "but I find his formulations useful nonetheless" (see Ruth Mazo Karras, "Response: Identity, Sexuality, and History," *Journal of Women's History* 11, no. 2 [1999]: 193–198 [quotation on 198n. 19]). I admit that I find Karras's treatment of the theoretical issues lacking in precision, care, and nuance, and I would not be likely to speak so incautiously about "sexuality" or "sexual identity" in reference to Karras's material, but I welcome her important and persuasive historical argument for the existence of identity categories in European discourses of sex in the medieval period. In that respect, her work is very much in line with the thesis of this essay.

See, also, Jeffrey Merrick, "Sodomitical Inclinations in Early Eighteenth-Century Paris," *Eighteenth-Century Studies* 30, no. 3 (1997): 289–94, who insists that "the more we learn about early modern sexual subcultures, the more reason we have to question, or at least to qualify, Michel Foucault's celebrated assertion that sodomites were nothing more than the 'juridical subjects' of sodomy before the nineteenth century" (quotation on 293). I wish to thank Norman Jones for calling my attention to this passage. Foucault, I shall argue, was not making an assertion about actual sexual practices, and so it is not *his* assertion that will need to be qualified.

16. Foucault's French text, ironically, allows more scope for misinterpretation than the English-language version, which explicitly emphasizes that the relevant sense of the term "sodomy" in this passage is determined by the formal discursive context of medieval civil and canon law. In Foucault's original formulation, the unambiguous initial phrase "as defined by" does not occur; instead, we find a more offhand reference to "the sodomy of the old civil and canonical codes." Foucault, it seems, didn't feel the need to be so careful about instructing his French readers to understand "sodomy" here as a strictly discursive category rather than as a sexual practice or as a cultural representation; instead, it is Foucault's translator who has expanded the original formulation in order to make its meaning clear. As I am concerned with the misreadings of Foucault by

scholars who work largely from the published translation of *The History of Sexuality,* vol. 1, and as my exegesis of Foucault is facilitated by (without at all depending on) the greater explicitness of the English-language version, I have not hesitated to cite it in my text for the sake of clarity, jettisoning it later once the interpretative point has been established.

17. Foucault, *The History of Sexuality,* 1:42–43; *La volonté de savoir,* 58–59. Emphasis in original.

18. Foucault, *The History of Sexuality,* 1:37 (translation modified); *La volonté de savoir,* 51. Emphasis added.

19. Foucault, *The History of Sexuality,* 1:38 (translation modified); *La volonté de savoir,* 52–53. Foucault explains, in a sentence that follows the conclusion of the passage quoted here, that "the 'nature' on which [sexual prohibitions] were based was still a kind of law."

20. Foucault, *The History of Sexuality,* 1:48; *La volonté de savoir,* 66.

21. A complete and systematic definition of the Latin form of this ancient term has now been provided by Craig A. Williams, *Roman Homosexuality: Ideologies of Masculinity in Classical Antiquity* (New York: Oxford University Press, 1999), 175–78, esp. 175–76:

> The word most often used to describe a man who had been anally penetrated was the noun *cinaedus.* But . . . *cinaedus* is not actually anchored in that specific sexual practice. . . . It refers instead to a man who has an identity as gender deviant. In other words, a *cinaedus* is a man who fails to live up to traditional standards of masculine comportment, and one way in which he may do so is by seeking to be penetrated; but that is merely a symptom of a deeper disorder, his gender deviance. Indeed, the word's etymology suggests no direct connection to any sexual practice. Rather, borrowed from Greek *kinaidos* (which may itself have been a borrowing from a language of Asia Minor), it primarily signifies an effeminate dancer who entertained his audiences with a *tympanum* or tambourine in his hand, and adopted a lascivious style, often suggestively wiggling his buttocks in such a way as to suggest anal intercourse. . . . The primary meaning of *cinaedus* never died out; the term never became a dead metaphor.

And Williams concludes, "In sum, the word *cinaedus* originally referred to men who were professional dancers of a type associated with the East, dancing with a *tympanum* and seductively wiggling their buttocks in such a way as to suggest anal intercourse. In a transferred sense it came to describe a man who was not a dancer but who displayed the salient characteristics of a *cinaedus* in the strict sense: he was a gender-deviant, a 'non-man' who broke the rules of masculine comportment and whose effeminate disorder might be embodied in the particular symptom of seeking to be penetrated" (178).

22. John J. Winkler, *The Constraints of Desire: The Anthropology of Sex and Gender in Ancient Greece* (New York: Routledge, 1990), 45–46. The formulation is repeated, somewhat less emphatically, by Winkler in "Laying Down the Law: The Oversight of Men's Sexual Behavior in Classical Athens," in *Before Sexuality: The Construction of Erotic Experience in the Ancient Greek World,* ed. David M. Halperin, John J.

Winkler, and Froma I. Zeitlin (Princeton, N.J.: Princeton University Press, 1990), 171–209, esp. 176–77.

23. I borrow the distinction between universalizing and minoritizing concepts of (homo)sexual identity from Eve Kosofsky Sedgwick, *Epistemology of the Closet* (Berkeley: University of California Press, 1990), 1, 9, 85–86.

24. Winkler, *The Constraints of Desire,* 50, and "Laying Down the Law," 182.

25. See, for example, Plato, *Gorgias* 494C—E (quoted and discussed by Winkler, *The Constraints of Desire,* 53).

26. For ancient physiological explanations, see pseudo-Aristotle, *Problems* 4.26; Phaedrus, 4.15 (16). For imputations of mental disease, see Aristotle, *Nicomachean Ethics* 7.5.3–4 (1148b26–35); *Priapea* 46.2; Seneca, *Natural Questions* 1.16.1–3; Dio Cassius 80.16.1–5; Caelius Aurelianus, *On Chronic Diseases* 4.9. Williams, *Roman Homosexuality,* to whom I owe the foregoing citation from the *Priapea,* also provides additional parallels (Seneca, *Letters* 83.20; Juvenal, *Satires* 2.17 and 2.50), noting, however, that "a predilection for various kinds of excessive or disgraceful behavior was capable of being called a disease" by the Romans (he cites a number of compelling instances of such a usage) and therefore "*cinaedi* were not said to be *morbosi* in the way that twentieth-century homosexuals have been pitied or scorned as 'sick' " (181). The medicalizing language, in other words, does not operate in the two cultures in the same way, nor does it give rise to the same kind of disqualification. The point is an important one: the ancient usage is disapproving, but it is not wholly pathologizing.

27. Maud W. Gleason, "The Semiotics of Gender: Physiognomy and Self-Fashioning in the Second Century C.E.," in *Before Sexuality,* ed. Halperin, Winkler, and Zeitlin, 389–415 (quotation on 390), *Making Men: Sophists and Self-Presentation in Ancient Rome* (Princeton, N.J.: Princeton University Press, 1995), 58.

28. Gleason, *Making Men,* 64; Gleason, "The Semiotics of Gender," 396.

29. Gleason, "The Semiotics of Gender," 411–12. Cf. Halperin, *One Hundred Years of Homosexuality,* 22–24.

30. Williams, *Roman Homosexuality,* 178.

31. Ibid., 210–11.

32. For an expansion of this argument, see the quotation from Williams, *Roman Homosexuality,* in n. 21, above. Of course, the distinction between gender and sexuality, or between gender identity and sexual object-choice, is artificial, to say the least. Gender identity often is loaded with sexual identity and erotic subjectivity, and in any particular cultural context gender is bound to be quite specifically "subjectified" or "subjectivated." Thus, Williams, *Roman Homosexuality,* 215–18, inquires into the *cinaedus* as a desiring subject. Don Kulick has also warned us against tightly compartmentalizing transgender identity (which is what the *cinaedus* may, in part, embody) as a purely gendered identity, totally independent from matters of erotic desire (see his *Travesti: Sex, Gender, and Culture among Brazilian Transgendered Prostitutes* [Chicago: University of Chicago Press, 1998]; see also his "Problematic Childhood Sexuality" [paper presented at the annual meeting of the American Anthropological Association, Philadelphia, 2–6 December 1999]).

33. In an extended series of essays, much discussed and generally well received by professional classicists in the United States and the United Kingdom, Amy Richlin has assailed the historical work of Winkler, myself, and our collaborators (such as Gleason), all of whom she lumps together under the uncomplimentary (not to say phobic) title of "Foucaultians." (See Amy Richlin, review of *One Hundred Years of Homosexuality,* by

David M. Halperin, *Bryn Mawr Classical Review* 2, no. 1 [1991]: 16–18, "Zeus and Metis: Foucault, Feminism, Classics," *Helios* 18, no. 2 [autumn 1991]: 160–80, introduction to *The Garden of Priapus: Sexuality and Aggression in Roman Humor,* rev. ed. [New York: Oxford University Press, 1992], xiii–xxxiii, introduction to *Pornography and Representation in Greece and Rome* [New York: Oxford University Press, 1992], xi–xxiii, "Not before Homosexuality: The Materiality of the *Cinaedus* and the Roman Law against Love between Men," *Journal of the History of Sexuality* 3, no. 4 [April 1993]: 523–73, "The Ethnographer's Dilemma and the Dream of a Lost Golden Age," in *Feminist Theory and the Classics,* ed. Nancy Sorkin Rabinowitz and Amy Richlin [New York: Routledge, 1993], 272–303, "Towards a History of Body History," in *Inventing Ancient Culture: Historicism, Periodization. and the Ancient World,* ed. Mark Golden and Peter Toohey [London: Routledge, 1997], 16–35, and "Foucault's *History of Sexuality:* A Useful Theory for Women?" in *Rethinking Sexuality: Foucault and Classical Antiquity,* ed. David H. J. Larmour, Paul Allen Miller, and Charles Platter [Princeton, N.J.: Princeton University Press, 1998], 138–70.)

Richlin faults us in particular for approaching the figure of the *kinaidos* from the standpoint of ancient sexual discourses. She prefers to see in that figure a material embodiment of "homosexuality," which she regards as a useful category for analyzing ancient societies—although she concedes that "there was no ancient word for 'homosexual' " ("Not before Homosexuality," 530; also, 571, where Richlin describes her work as employing "a model that uses 'homosexuality' as a category for analyzing ancient societies" [and in the revised introduction to *The Garden of Priapus,* Richlin insists that her approach is distinguished by its "essentialism" and "materialism" (xx)]). For a lucid survey of Richlin's equivocations on the issue of whether or not *cinaedi* should be described as "homosexuals," see Williams, *Roman Homosexuality,* 355, n. 319.

Much could be said about the gaps in Richlin's argument, about its simplistic treatment of the interpretative issues, or about its unappetizing but evidently highly palatable combination of an old-fashioned positivism with a more fashionable blend of political and professional opportunism. (Compare, for example, the following two statements by Richlin, both of them made in the revised introduction to *The Garden of Priapus:* "I suggest that Foucault's work on antiquity is so ill-informed that it is not really worth reading" [xxix, n. 2], and "Thus *The Garden of Priapus,* though it originated in a different critical space from Foucauldian work, exhibits some similar traits, a true Foucauldian child of its time. . . . I accept wholeheartedly the approach that melds anthropology with history; I define humor as a discourse of power; I view texts as artifacts; I am seeking to piece together social norms by juxtaposing different kinds of evidence that seem to describe different realities, and I am examining what produces those disparities" [xxvii]. In other words: "Everything Foucault said was wrong, and besides I said it first.") Indeed, the ferocity and tenacity of Richlin's polemics have largely succeeded in intimidating and silencing public expressions of disagreement with her. For two exceptions, see the review of *Pornography and Representation in Greece and Rome* by Earl Jackson Jr., *Bryn Mawr Classical Review* 3 (1992): 387–96; and Marilyn B. Skinner, "Zeus and Leda: The Sexuality Wars in Contemporary Classical Scholarship," *Thamyris* 3, no. 1 (spring 1996): 103–23.

The point I need to make here about Richlin's critique is that it is doubly ignorant and misinformed—wrong, that is, both about Foucault and about so-called Foucaultians. In the first case, Richlin claims that in the famous passage from *The History of Sexuality,* vol. 1, "Foucault is distinguishing . . . between behavior and essence"; in the second case, she maintains that accounts of sex in antiquity by "Foucaultians" such as Winkler and myself "start from this axiom" ("Not before Homosexuality," 525). In fact, as I have tried to show here, Foucault was not distinguishing between anything so metaphysical as behavior and essence but simply between two different discursive strategies for disqualifying male love. Winkler and Gleason, moreover, far from adhering uncritically to the erroneous reading of Foucault that Richlin herself propounds, explicitly challenged the misapplication of such a pseudo-Foucauldian "axiom" to the interpretation of the figure of the *kinaidos*. And in *One Hundred Years of Homosexuality* I made a rigorous distinction between a sexual orientation in the modern sense and the kinds of sexual identity current in the ancient Greek world; the latter, I argued, tended to be determined by a person's gender and social status rather than by a personal psychology. And I was careful to emphasize in a number of passages that it was possible for sexual acts to be linked in various ways with a sexual disposition or sexual subjectivity well before the nineteenth century. (See the passage quoted in n. 12 above. For other examples, see *One Hundred Years of Homosexuality,* 8: "A certain identification of the self with the sexual self began in late antiquity; it was strengthened by the Christian confessional. Only in the high middle ages did certain kinds of sexual acts start to get identified with certain specifically sexual types of person: a 'sodomite' begins to name not merely the person who commits an act of sodomy but one distinguished by a certain type of specifically sexual subjectivity"; 48: the *kinaidos* is a "life-form.") Richlin's "Foucaultians," no less than her Foucault, are the product and projection of her own misreadings. Why her misreadings have been so widely, and so uncritically, acclaimed is another question, an interesting one in its own right, but this is not the place to pursue it.

34. Jonathan Walters, " 'No More Than a Boy': The Shifting Construction of Masculinity from Ancient Greece to the Middle Ages," *Gender and History* 5, no. 1 (spring 1993): 20–33.

35. Ibid., 22–23, quoting Apuleius, *The Golden Ass* 9.14.

36. See Walters, " 'No More Than a Boy,' " 22. On April 13, 2001, Professor Carla Freccero of the University of California, Santa Cruz, presented a critique of my argument in a paper delivered at the University of Michigan, entitled "Were Fourteenth Century Perugini Homophobic? Foucault, Halperin, and Early Modern Sexual Subjectivities." I did not hear the paper myself, and Freccero has not shared it with me, and so I have been unable to take advantage of her remarks in reformulating my argument here.

37. Walters, " 'No More Than a Boy,' " 24.

38. Ibid., 26: "In Boccaccio's version . . . we find the husband defined wholly in terms of his sexual desire, which marks him as abnormal from the start and indeed sets the plot in motion."

39. Compare ibid., 24–25. For the common view in Florentine texts of the period that sodomites "had little erotic interest in women," see Michael Rocke, *Forbidden Friendships: Homosexuality and Male Culture in Renaissance Florence* (New York: Oxford University Press, 1996), 40–41, 123 ff., who also provides a useful survey of other literary portraits of sodomites in contemporary Italian *novelle,* many of which correspond in a number of respects to Boccaccio's portrait of Pietro di Vinciolo (123 ff. and 295, n. 79). Rocke also points out, however, that many Florentine sources, both literary and judicial, presume that a man with sodomitical desires for boys might equally desire insertive sex with women (124–27).

40. Walters, " 'No More Than a Boy,' " 27, also emphasizes this point.

41. See, further, ibid., 27–28. Whereas the ancient conception of the *kinaidos* foregrounded his effeminacy and passivity, the fourteenth- and fifteenth-century Florentine definitions of "sodomy" and "sodomite" referred only to the "active" or insertive partner in anal intercourse: see Rocke, *Forbidden Friendships,* 14, 110. Cesare Segre, the editor of my text of Boccaccio, gets this point exactly wrong when he says, in a note, that the Perugians regarded Pietro as *un invertito* (Giovanni Boccaccio, *Opere,* ed. Cesare Segre [Milan: Mursia, 1966], 1280). Pietro is a sodomite but, unlike the *kinaidos,* he is not transgendered, or an invert.

42. An erotic temperament midway between that of Apuleius's baker and Boccaccio's Pietro is represented a century before Apuleius in a two-line poem by the Roman poet Martial, *Epigrams* 2.49.

> Uxorem nolo Telesinam ducere: quare?
> moecha est. sed pueris dat Telesina. volo.

> [I don't want to take Telesina for my wife. —Why not?
> She's an adulteress. —But Telesina puts out for boys. —I'll take her!]

As Williams, *Roman Homosexuality,* 27, to whom I owe this reference, explains, Martial's joke depends on the background knowledge that a longstanding traditional punishment for adultery in the classical world was anal rape of the male offender. The man imagined in the epigram overcomes his initial reluctance to marry Telesina when it is pointed out to him that her bad character will procure him endless opportunities for enacting a sweet revenge on her youthful partners. Martial's satirical epigram constructs an outlandish scenario in which a man is so fond of insertive anal sex with boys that he is willing to enter into a disgraceful and corrupt marriage merely in order to expand his possibilities for enjoying it. Exaggeration is part of the joke; nonetheless, as Williams—who also cites the passage from Apuleius in this connection—demonstrates with abundant argumentation and evidence, the imaginary husband's preference falls well within the range of acceptable male sexual tastes in Roman culture.

43. Walters, " 'No More Than a Boy,' " 26–27, overstates the case, I believe, when he writes, "What we see in Boccaccio's version of the story is one of the earliest portrayals in Western culture of a man defined by his sexuality, which is somehow his most deeply defining characteristic, and which tells 'the truth' about him. We witness here an early form of the constitution and demarcation of the field of sexuality." Compare Glenn W. Olsen, "St. Anselm and Homosexuality," *Anselm Studies: An Occasional Journal* (Special issue: "Proceedings of the Fifth International Saint Anselm Conference: St. Anselm and St. Augustine—Episcopi ad Saecula," ed. Joseph C. Schnaubelt et al.), vol. 2 (1988), 93–141, esp. 102–3:

> If one were to eliminate from Boswell's book [*Christianity, Social Tolerance, and Homosexuality*] all the materials which do not satisfy his definition of "gay," one might arguably be left with the truly novel and important observation that, as far as the Middle Ages are concerned, it was about 1100 in certain poems of Marbod of Rennes, and then later in the century in writers like Bernard of Cluny and Walter of Chatillon, and above all in the late twelfth century "A Debate between Ganymede

and Helen," that we might see the appearance of a clear erotic preference for one's own sex that, by still being called "sodomy," began the
expansion of that term into the modern "homosexuality."

(See also 129–30, n. 61, and 133, n. 87.) Olsen puts the point very clearly, and in fact he
might have been speaking of Boccaccio's Pietro di Vinciolo, although Boccaccio never
uses the term "sodomy" in reference to Pietro.

Nonetheless, I would still want to insist that mere sexual object-choice, even the
settled and habitual preference for sexual relations with persons of the same sex as oneself, falls short of the definitional requirements of "(homo)sexuality" or "sexual orientation." After all, such exclusive sexual preferences were not unknown in the ancient
world: see my partial list of citations in *One Hundred Years of Homosexuality,* 163, n.
53. A "sexuality" in the modern sense would seem to require considerably more than
merely same-sex sexual object-choice, more even than conscious erotic preference. In
particular, "homosexuality" requires, first of all, that homosexual object-choice itself
function as a marker of difference, of social and sexual deviance, independent of the
gender identification or sexual role (active or passive) performed or preferred by the
individual; second, it requires that homosexual object-choice be connected with a psychology, an inner orientation of the individual, not just an aesthetics or a form of erotic
connoisseurship. See *One Hundred Years of Homosexuality,* 24–29, esp. 26–27 with
notes; for more recent expansions of that argument, see my essays, "Historicizing the
Subject of Desire," in this volume, which documents several instances of same-sex sexual
object-choice, and even of conscious erotic preferences for persons of the same sex as
oneself, that nonetheless do not satisfy the criteria for homosexuality, and "How to Do
the History of Male Homosexuality," which makes the conceptual distinctions in more
detail. In the absence of the distinctively modern set of connections linking sexual object-
choice, inner orientation, and deviant personality with notions of identity and difference,
the substantive category of "homosexuality" dissolves into the descriptive category of
"men who have sex with men" (an artifact of AIDS epidemiology, not a sexuality per
se), and homosexually active but otherwise non-gay-identified men escape interpellation
by the category of "homosexuality."

44. I have chosen to dwell on the figure of Boccaccio's Pietro di Vinciolo not because
I believe he is somehow typical or representative of medieval sodomites in general but
because he provides the starkest possible contrast with the ancient figure of the *kinaidos:*
the latter represents an instance of sexual morphology without sexual subjectivity, or so
at least I am contending for the purposes of this argument, whereas Pietro represents an
instance of sexual subjectivity without sexual morphology. I do not mean to imply that
constructions of the sodomite in pre-modern Europe mostly or even typically emphasized
sexual subjectivity at the expense of sexual morphology, or that the sodomite was never
thought to have a peculiar sensibility or style of gender presentation or appearance (on
the gradual expansion of the term "sodomy," see Olsen, "St. Anselm and Homosexuality," 102–3). It is precisely the aim of this essay to open up such questions for further
research.

45. This is not to deny that some lesbians can be conventionally feminine or that
some gay men can be conventionally masculine and that both can pass for straight—
some can and some do—but rather to insist that modern concepts and images of homosexuality have never been able to escape being haunted by the specter of gender inversion, gender deviance, or at least some kind of visibly legible difference. For a systematic

and brilliant exploration of this issue, see Lee Edelman, *Homographesis: Essays in Gay Literary and Cultural Theory* (New York: Routledge, 1994). See, also, Sedgwick, *Epistemology of the Closet.*

46. For a further elaboration of this point, see "How to Do the History of Male Homosexuality," 128–34, esp. 131.

47. I wish to thank Carolyn Dinshaw for pointing out to me that the term "identity" is absent from Foucault's text.

48. Compare Alan Sinfield, *Cultural Politics—Queer Reading* (Philadelphia: University of Pennsylvania Press, 1994), 14, noting that pre-modern histories of homosexuality by social-constructionist historians "tend to discover ambivalent or partial signs of subjectivity; they catch not the absence of the modern subject, but its emergence." He adds, "I suspect that what we call gay identity has, for a long time, been always in the process of getting constituted." This last remark closes off, rather too glibly, the historiographic and conceptual issues before us.

49. I elaborate further on this point in "The Art of Not Being Governed: Michel Foucault on Critique and Transgression," to be published in *boundary 2.*

50. Foucault, *The History of Sexuality,* 1:68.

51. I wish to thank Lee Edelman for discussing the issues in this paragraph with me, for his persistent critiques of this section of my essay, and for supplying me with a number of the formulations now contained in it.

A notable exception to this hankering on the part of "queer theorists" for a correct theory of sexuality is Eve Kosofsky Sedgwick, "Queer Performativity: Henry James's *The Art of the Novel,*" *GLQ: A Journal of Lesbian and Gay Studies* 1, no. 1 (1993): 1–16, esp. 11: "The thing I *least* want to be heard as offering here is a 'theory of homosexuality.' I have none and I want none." See, also, Jordan, *The Invention of Sodomy,* 5: "I myself tend to think that we have barely begun to gather [historical] evidence of same-sex desire. We are thus very far from being able to imagine having a finished theory." Statements to this effect in works of so-called queer theory are rather less frequent than one might imagine.

52. For the notion that theory is ultimately "the universal theory of the impossibility of theory" and therefore that "nothing can overcome the resistance to theory since theory is itself this resistance," see Paul de Man, "The Resistance to Theory," in *The Resistance to Theory* (Minneapolis: University of Minnesota Press, 1986), 3–20 (quotations on 19). For a further exploration of these paradoxes, see the scathing remarks of Paul Morrison, "Paul de Man: Resistance and Collaboration," *Representations* 32 (fall 1990): 50–74.

53. Michel Foucault, "Fantasia of the Library," in *Language, Counter-Memory, Practice: Selected Essays and Interviews,* ed. and trans. Donald F. Bouchard (Ithaca, N.Y.: Cornell University Press, 1977), 87–109 (quotation on 90). This passage was originally brought to my attention by James W. Bernauer, *Michel Foucault's Force of Flight: Toward an Ethics for Thought* (Atlantic Highlands, N.J.: Humanities Press International, 1990), 183.

CHAPTER TWO

Previous versions or sections of this argument have appeared, in somewhat more specialized form, as "Response: Halperin on Brennan on Brooten," *Bryn Mawr Classical Review* (http://ccat.sas.upenn.edu/bmcr/), 97.12.3 (5 December 1997), "Lesbian

Historiography before the Name? Commentary," *GLQ: A Journal of Lesbian and Gay Studies* 4, no. 4 (1998): 559–78, and "Sex, Sexuality, and Sexual Classification," in *Critical Terms for Gender Studies,* ed. Gilbert Herdt and Catharine R. Stimpson (Chicago: University of Chicago Press, 2003), in press.

1. For recent examples of contrasting approaches to the problem of how to balance continuities and discontinuities in feminist and gay male historiography, see Judith M. Bennett, "Confronting Continuity," *Journal of Women's History* 9, no. 3 (autumn 1997): 73–94; and David M. Halperin, "How to Do the History of Male Homosexuality," in this volume.

2. See D. Graham J. Shipley's entry on Lesbos in *The Oxford Classical Dictionary,* 3d ed. (Oxford: Oxford University Press, 1996), 845.

3. Chapter 21 of Aldous Huxley's *Antic Hay* (London: Flamingo, 1994), 226.

4. For a detailed survey of the evidence, on which my summary is based, see Peter F. Dorcey, "Before Lesbianism" (unpublished manuscript, in the possession of Professor John Rundin of the University of Texas at San Antonio).

5. Bernadette J. Brooten translates the phrase "unwilling to let men do it to them," more literally but less idiomatically, as "who are unwilling to suffer 'it' from men": see her "Lesbian Historiography before the Name? Response," *GLQ: A Journal of Lesbian and Gay Studies* 4, no. 4 (1998): 606–30 (quotation on 619).

6. Alan Cameron, "Love (and Marriage) between Women," *Greek, Roman, and Byzantine Studies* 39 (1998): 137–56 (quotation on 149n. 36 [emphasis mine]).

7. That what Lucian is describing is tribadism and not lesbianism is even clearer in Lucian's Greek, where "women like that" (which is a translation of the single word *toiautas*) refers back to the noun *hetairistria:* "I don't know what you mean, unless she's a *hetairistria*—they say there are women like that [or "such women"] in Lesbos," etc. In other words, "they say there are *hetairistriai* in Lesbos," etc. Since there is considerable evidence (discussed in my text, below) that *hetairistria* is a synonym of "tribade," the reference to "women like that in Lesbos" is, in context, mostly likely an allusion specifically to tribadism.

8. On this text, see Bernadette J. Brooten, *Love between Women: Early Christian Responses to Female Homoeroticism* (Chicago: University of Chicago Press, 1996), 5, and the detailed, convincing critique of her interpretation of Arethas's usage by Cameron, "Love (and Marriage) between Women," 144–49.

9. Two authoritative French dictionaries, Frédéric Godefroy's ten-volume *Dictionnaire de l'ancienne langue française* (1880) and *Le Grand Robert de la langue française,* agree in dating the earliest occurrence of "tribade" in French to bk. 1, chap. 13 of Henri Estienne's treatise, *Introduction au traité de la conformité des merveilles anciennes avec les modernes ou Traité préparatif à l'apologie pour Hérodote,* published in Geneva in 1566 (see Elizabeth Susan Wahl, *Invisible Relations: Representations of Female Intimacy in the Age of Enlightenment* [Stanford, Calif.: Stanford University Press, 1999], 23, and 258n. 3).

10. See Valerie Traub, "The Renaissance of Lesbianism in Early Modern England," *GLQ: A Journal of Lesbian and Gay Studies* 7, no. 2 (2001): 245–63, esp. 249: "Representations of female-female desire during this period depend heavily on classical antecedents for their modes of comprehension. It is through, quite literally, a rebirth of classical idioms, rhetorics, tropes, and illustrative examples that female homoeroticism gained intelligibility in early modern England. By renovating the discourses of the ancients, writers in the sixteenth and seventeenth centuries attempted to legitimize

their own formulations, drawing on authoritative precedents . . . for risqué or troubling ideas."

11. See Brantôme, *Recueil des Dames, poésies et tombeaux,* ed. Etienne Vaucheret, Bibliothèque de la Pléiade (Paris: Gallimard, 1991), 361–71 (quotation on 367).

12. Ibid., 364 and 365.

13. I owe this formulation, as well as the information in the following sentence, to Elizabeth S. Wahl (e-mail to me, May 1999, and her book, *Invisible Relations,* 61 and 277–78n).

14. Emma Donoghue, *Passions between Women: British Lesbian Culture, 1668–1801* (1993; reprinted, New York: HarperCollins, 1995), 3, 258–59.

15. See n. 8 above for the full bibliographic citation. All further pages references to this book will be included in the text. The study of lesbianism in classical antiquity has accelerated since the publication of Brooten's book. I confess that I have not seen Juan Francisco Martos Montiel, *Desde Lesbos con amor: Homosexualidad femenina en la Antigüedad* (Madrid: Ediciones Clásicas, 1996) or the new collection of papers edited by Nancy Rabinowitz and Lisa Auanger, *From the Homosocial to the Homo-erotic: Women's Relations to Women in Antiquity* (Austin: University of Texas Press, 2001).

16. A number of sources omitted by Brooten are helpfully assembled by T. Corey Brennan in a dazzling review of Brooten's book in the *Bryn Mawr Classical Review* (http://ccat.sas.upenn.edu/bmcr/), 97.5.7 (15 May 1997).

17. See my entry on "Homosexuality" in *The Oxford Classical Dictionary,* 3d ed., 720–23, and my earlier remarks in *One Hundred Years of Homosexuality and Other Essays on Greek Love* (New York: Routledge, 1990), 33–35.

18. In "Lesbian Historiography before the Name? Response," 623–25, Brooten passionately declares her "skepticism about contemporary genetic and neuroscientific research on sexual orientation," asserts that "the current dimorphic model" of sexual orientation is "culturally limited," and concludes that the "ancient etiological attempts to make sense of erotic inclination . . . do not resemble twentieth-century conceptualizations."

19. See Halperin, "How to Do the History of Male Homosexuality," in this volume, 131.

20. A similar point is convincingly made about the history of male homosexuality by George Haggerty, *Men in Love: Masculinity and Sexuality in the Eighteenth Century* (New York: Columbia University Press, 1999).

21. In the course of a very favorable assessment of Brooten's book, Natalie Boymel Kampen, "Lesbian Historiography before the Name? Commentary," *GLQ: A Journal of Lesbian and Gay Studies* 4, no. 4 (1998): 595–601, cites Mark Jordan's apt comments about Boswell's "commitment to the ideal of historiography of sex as a positive science," his presumption that "human sexuality . . . is just another hard-edged object in an external world, there to be observed and subsumed under generalizations" (596; see Mark D. Jordan, "A Romance of the Gay Couple," *GLQ: A Journal of Lesbian and Gay Studies* 3, nos. 2–3 [1996]: 301–10, quotation on 302). This characterization captures better than I can the principles implicitly guiding Brooten's own approach to the history of sexuality.

22. In a commentary on my critique of her work, Brooten claims that I, too, employ the terms "slavery," "marriage," and "family" without historical qualification in *One Hundred Years of Homosexuality:* see Brooten, "Lesbian Historiography before

the Name? Response," 619–20. And perhaps I do: it is hard to suspend all modern categories all the time in the course of historical analysis. But my lapses, however serious or regrettable, do not justify Brooten's. Nor does my failure to apply consistently my own historicist principles provide other historians of sexuality with a license to be anachronistic. Brooten's riposte may score a point against me, personally or intellectually, but it hardly invalidates the point of my own critique of her methods.

23. See Halperin, *One Hundred Years of Homosexuality,* 46.

24. See John Boswell, "Categories, Experience and Sexuality," in *Forms of Desire: Sexual Orientation and the Social Constructionist Controversy,* ed. Edward Stein, Garland Gay and Lesbian Studies, 1 (New York: Garland, 1990), 133–73.

25. See, for example, Ramsay MacMullen, "Roman Attitudes to Greek Love," *Historia* 31 (1982): 484–502; more recently, Amy Richlin, "Not before Homosexuality: The Materiality of the *Cinaedus* and the Roman Law against Love between Men," *Journal of the History of Sexuality* 3, no. 4 (April 1993): 523–73; and Thomas K. Hubbard, "Popular Perceptions of Elite Homosexuality in Classical Athens," *Arion* 6, no. 1 (1998): 48–78. In a much more unusual move, Giulia Sissa attempts to rehabilitate "homosexuality," "homophobia," and even "gay" as authentically classical Greek categories of thought and experience while carefully avoiding the mistake of confusing acts with identities; instead, she substitutes a highly tendentious and misleading paraphrase of Aeschines' *Against Timarchus* for a close reading of it, and then advances her argument on the basis of her own paraphrase ("Sexual Bodybuilding: Aeschines against Timarchus," in *Constructions of the Classical Body,* ed. James I. Porter [Ann Arbor: University of Michigan Press, 1999], 147–68).

26. Craig A. Williams, "Greek Love at Rome," *Classical Quarterly* 45 (1995): 517–39, revised and expanded in his *Roman Homosexuality: Ideologies of Masculinity in Classical Antiquity* (New York: Oxford University Press, 1999), esp. 62–72.

27. Mario DiGangi, *The Homoerotics of Early Modern Drama* (Cambridge: Cambridge University Press, 1997), 16.

28. Ibid., 16. (The entire passage is quoted by Valerie Traub, "The Rewards of Lesbian History," *Feminist Studies* 25, no. 2 [summer 1999]: 363–94 [quotation on 376]. Traub's magisterial review essay also includes an appreciation and critique of Brooten's book.) Compare Williams, *Roman Homosexuality,* 217: "To describe ancient bias against *cinaedi* as 'homophobic' or as constituting a problematization of male homosexuality is, I suggest, comparable to suggesting that Roman biases against female prostitutes or adulteresses were 'heterophobic' or in some way problematized heterosexuality."

29. Compare Halperin, *One Hundred Years of Homosexuality,* 28–29, 40.

30. See Michel Foucault, *The Use of Pleasure,* trans. Robert Hurley, vol. 2 of *The History of Sexuality* (New York: Random House, 1985); Arnold I. Davidson, "Sex and the Emergence of Sexuality," *Critical Inquiry* 14, no. 1 (1987): 16–48, and "Closing Up the Corpses: Diseases of Sexuality and the Emergence of the Psychiatric Style of Reasoning," in *Meaning and Method: Essays in Honor of Hilary Putnam,* ed. George Boolos (Cambridge: Cambridge University Press, 1990), 295–325; John J. Winkler, *The Constraints of Desire: The Anthropology of Sex and Gender in Ancient Greece* (New York: Routledge, 1990); Halperin, *One Hundred Years of Homosexuality;* Williams, *Roman Homosexuality.*

31. In "Lesbian Historiography before the Name? Response," 620, Brooten expresses a certain indignation that I should characterize female prostitution in the Ro-

man world as a "career choice," as if it were merely one profession among many open to socially empowered "career women," when in fact, as she observes, many ancient prostitutes were slaves. To the extent that this objection is anything more than pure grandstanding (after all, I had intended the turn of phrase to be heard as a deliberate anachronism), Brooten's objection is of course entirely just—though its effect in this context is to undermine still further her interpretation of the astrological texts. For if *meretrix* describes the unwilling fate to which an unfree person was consigned by her master or mistress, then it is even less plausibly conceptualized as a lifelong erotic orientation, and "prostitute" becomes even more disanalogous with "tribade" and "virago," if the meaning of those terms in the writings of the ancient astrologers is understood the way Brooten seems to understand it, as a personal, erotic identity rather than as a public, socially stigmatized behavior (Brooten, "Lesbian Historiography before the Name? Response," 624–25, denies however that she intends any such opposition between public and personal identity). So that consideration does more, not less, damage to the logic of Brooten's overall argument.

32. See, for example, the following works: Ruth Mazo Karras, "Holy Harlots: Prostitute Saints in Medieval Legend," *Journal of the History of Sexuality* 1, no. 1 (1990): 3–32; David Lorenzo Boyd and Ruth Mazo Karras, "The Interrogation of a Male Transvestite Prostitute in Fourteenth-Century London," *GLQ: A Journal of Lesbian and Gay Studies* 1, no. 4 (1994): 459–65; Ruth Mazo Karras and David Lorenzo Boyd, "*Ut cum muliere:* A Male Transvestite Prostitute in Fourteenth-Century London," in *Premodern Sexualities,* ed. Louise Fradenburg and Carla Freccero (New York: Routledge, 1996), 101–16; Ruth Mazo Karras, *Common Women: Prostitution and Sexuality in Medieval England* (New York: Oxford University Press, 1996), "Prostitution and the Question of Sexual Identity in Medieval Europe," *Journal of Women's History* 11, no. 2 (1999): 159–77, and "Response: Identity, Sexuality, and History," *Journal of Women's History* 11, no. 2 (1999): 193–98.

33. Karras, "Prostitution and the Question of Sexual Identity in Medieval Europe," 171; more generally, 161–63.

34. Karras fully anticipates this objection: "I expect Halperin would disagree with much of what I have said here," she remarks in "Response: Identity, Sexuality, and History," 198n. 19.

35. Carla Freccero, "Acts, Identities, and Sexuality's (Pre)Modern Regimes," *Journal of Women's History* 11, no. 2 (1999): 186–92 (quotation on 188), citing Karras, "Prostitution and the Question of Sexual Identity in Medieval Europe," 173n. 14.

36. Traub, "The Rewards of Lesbian History," 369.

37. On the relevant passages in the *Laws,* see Nathalie Ernoult, "L'homosexualité féminine chez Platon," *Revue française de Psychanalyse* 58, no. 1 (1994): 207–18.

38. See the learned discussion by Cameron, "Love (and Marriage) between Women," 145–49. Brooten is well aware of these two scholia (see *Love between Women,* 5 and 55n. 119).

39. In her objection to this critique ("Lesbian Historiography before the Name? Response," 619), Brooten correctly observes that both Megilla and her girlfriend Demonassa are involved in the seduction of Leaena. It might also be possible to argue that the role played by Demonassa in the whole affair does not conform to a strict division between conventionally defined masculine and feminine sex roles, since she is the "wife" of Megilla but an aggressor in lovemaking with Leaena.

40. Moeris (p. 196.24 Bekker): *hetairistriai Attikoi, tribades Hellênes.* For Brennan,

see n. 16 above. See, also, Cameron, "Love (and Marriage) between Women," 148–49, who provides the citation from Moeris quoted here (149n. 34).

41. Cameron, "Love (and Marriage) between Women," 149, noting that Timaeus glosses *hetairistriai* as *hai kaloumenai tribades*.

42. The point about victims of male sexual assault is made by Williams, *Roman Homosexuality,* 178.

43. The difference seems to have been a matter of reputation and social standing rather than one of actual conduct. As Williams points out, "[respectable] boys could get away with things that *cinaedi* could not" (ibid., 183).

44. See my entry on "Homosexuality" in the *Oxford Classical Dictionary,* 3d ed., 720–23, as well as my subsequent clarification of these points in "Questions of Evidence: Commentary on Koehl, DeVries, and Williams," in *Queer Representations: Reading Lives, Reading Cultures,* ed. Martin Duberman (New York: New York University Press, 1997), 39–54, and also in this volume.

45. Williams, *Roman Homosexuality,* 175–76. Williams recapitulates his definition on p. 178 as follows: "In sum, the word *cinaedus* originally referred to men who were professional dancers of a type associated with the East, dancing with a *tympanum* and seductively wiggling their buttocks in such a way as to suggest anal intercourse. In a transferred sense it came to describe a man who was not a dancer but who displayed the salient characteristics of a *cinaedus* in the strict sense: he was a gender-deviant, a 'non-man' who broke the rules of masculine comportment and whose effeminate disorder might be embodied in the particular symptom of seeking to be penetrated."

46. See also Brooten, *Love between Women,* 7, on "the existence of 'man-boy love' sections in gay bookstores." Traces of these polemics can be discerned (to cite two distinguished examples) in Adrienne Rich's opprobrious remarks about "the patterns of anonymous sex among male homosexuals, and the pronounced ageism in male homosexual standards of sexual attractiveness" ("Compulsory Heterosexuality and Lesbian Existence" [1980], reprinted in *The Lesbian and Gay Studies Reader,* ed. Henry Abelove, Michèle Aina Barale, and David M. Halperin [New York: Routledge, 1993], 227–54 [quotation on 239]) and in Marilyn Frye's treatment of male homosexuality as an expression of male supremacism and the worship of phallic power (*The Politics of Reality: Essays in Feminist Theory* [Trumansburg, N.Y.: Crossing Press, 1983]). For a balanced and insightful critique of this strand in lesbian feminism, see Earl Jackson, Jr., *Strategies of Deviance: Studies in Gay Male Representation* (Bloomington: Indiana University Press, 1995), 7–13, 267n. 1. Brooten's own tendency to represent my disagreements with her about the correct interpretation of the ancient sources as symptoms of my supposed resistance to feminism continues this regrettable tradition. And she doesn't help matters when she insists that I look at female homoeroticism "through the phallocentric lens of male pederasty," that I employ "a male model," that I am every bit as much "steeped in the Greek pederastic model" as the Roman authors I study (see Brooten, "Lesbian Historiography before the Name? Response," 616). These characterizations of my approach to the history of sexuality, which read like personal slurs, are beside the point: my account of the hierarchical model used to represent female same-sex sexual relations in antiquity is not a blind projection of my own phallocentric obsessions onto the ancient texts, as Brooten seems to suggest, but a scrupulous description of the salient features of the male-authored ancient sexual discourses themselves. My aim in interpreting such discourses is to reconstruct their terms as accurately as possible and to reproduce their characteristic point of view, whether or not it happens to coincide with my own: after all,

being "steeped" in such ancient discourses is what classical scholars are ideally supposed to be. It says much about the modern social and political context of Brooten's critique that this scholarly immersion in the ancient literature can itself be made to constitute, in the case of an openly gay male scholar, a personal and intellectual disqualification.

47. By this of course I mean specifically *not* to imply that Aristotle in this passage pathologizes all same-sex sexual behavior without distinction, as some have concluded: for convincing arguments that Aristotle's disapproval is limited to certain stigmatized instances of homosexual behavior and does not extend to homosexuality as such, see K. J. Dover, *Greek Homosexuality* (Cambridge, Mass.: Harvard University Press, 1978), 168–69; Winkler, *Constraints,* 69n.

48. For example, Brooten is not, as she claims (*Love between Women,* 3), the first scholar to examine astrological texts in order to document the existence of sexual categories in antiquity: cf. Maud W. Gleason, "The Semiotics of Gender: Physiognomy and Self-Fashioning in the Second Century C.E.," in *Before Sexuality: The Construction of Erotic Experience in the Ancient Greek World,* ed. David M. Halperin, John J. Winkler, and Froma I. Zeitlin (Princeton, N.J.: Princeton University Press, 1990), 389–415 (cited favorably by Brooten, *Love between Women,* 56n, 158n, but not in connection with astrology), and *Making Men: Sophists and Self-Presentation in Ancient Rome* (Princeton, N.J.: Princeton University Press, 1995).

49. Williams, *Roman Homosexuality,* 181.

50. See Halperin, *One Hundred Years of Homosexuality,* 22–24.

51. Brennan (n. 16, above) makes a number of additional and quite cogent criticisms of Brooten's reading of Caelius Aurelianus. See, also, Williams, *Roman Homosexuality,* 353–54, n. 298, whose refutation of Brooten's interpretation of Caelius I have largely followed here. Williams concludes, "In fact, by Caelius' standards, a situation in which a master penetrated his male slave who derived no pleasure from the act but who was merely doing what he was told would be entirely 'disease-free.' "

52. See Halperin, *One Hundred Years of Homosexuality,* 29–33.

53. Brooten herself now prefers a more cautious formulation: "We do not know if the *tribas*'s partner counted as disease-free; we can only say that the text does not focus on her" ("Lesbian Historiography before the Name? Response," 630n. 29). This seems to me grudging but unobjectionable.

54. In "Lesbian Historiography before the Name? Response," 616, 621, Brooten wonders why in my critique of her work I restrict myself to pagan texts. She objects to my division of the ancient sources into pagan and Christian categories, protests against the "artificiality" of the distinction, and wonders about its motivation. Such rebukes are bizarre, coming from her, since that very distinction structures her entire book, separating it into its two major "parts" divided according to this very opposition between the Roman context of Christianity (27–186) and early Christian attitudes (187–357). And for good reason: as Brooten shows (and this is one of the important achievements of her book as a work of history), there are significant differences between pagan and Christian perspectives on same-sex sexual relations: it is only in Christian sources, for example, that male and female homoeroticisms are routinely categorized together and treated analogously. Thus, as she remarks, "early Christians, who generally classified both female and male homoerotic activity as sinful, probably played a crucial role in the development of the concept of homosexuality" (9). All the more reason, then, to treat the Christian sources separately.

55. See Cameron, "Love (and Marriage) between Women," 149n. 37.

56. Brooten herself, of course, strenuously repudiates the categories of "butch" and "femme" as they apply to "ancient lesbians" and accuses me in turn of imposing modern categories on the ancient evidence ("Lesbian Historiography before the Name? Response," 620). She cites a number of excellent historical considerations as reasons against applying, "even tongue in cheek," these modern subcultural terms to the ancient material. But of course my own usage is meant, among other things, not to convey accurately the ancient categories but rather the modern mindset that seems to inform, no doubt inadvertently, Brooten's own approach to the ancient evidence—in particular, her tendency to imply that she is speaking about all women, or all forms of homoeroticism among women, when she is in fact speaking about only one female sexual or social role. It is, I believe, her unreflective adherence to this modern habit of according more lesbian specificity to the butch than to the femme that explains her otherwise uncharacteristic practice of reproducing the prejudices of the ancient sources by problematizing only the active, aggressive, gender-deviant, or sexually deviant partner in female homoerotic relations.

57. See Richlin, "Not before Homosexuality," whose entire argument that sexual relations in the ancient Roman world were "not before homosexuality" rests on the unshakable (if unvoiced and unexamined) presumption that passive males were the real homosexuals of antiquity and that ancient discourses of male passivity were therefore really discourses of homosexuality. The sexually insertive male partners of Richlin's *cinaedi,* who are not comparably vilified by our sources, somehow don't seem to enter into her thinking on the subject or to qualify for inclusion in her concept of homosexuality.

58. For a brilliant critique of such presumptions, see Biddy Martin, "Sexualities without Genders and Other Queer Utopias," *diacritics* 24, nos. 2–3 (summer/fall 1994): 104–21, reprinted in Biddy Martin, *Femininity Played Straight: The Significance of Being Lesbian* (New York: Routledge, 1996), 71–94; more generally, Teresa de Lauretis, "Sexual Indifference and Lesbian Representation," *Theatre Journal* 40 (1988): 155–77, reprinted in *The Lesbian and Gay Studies Reader,* ed. Abelove, Barale, and Halperin, 141–58 (cited approvingly by Brooten, *Love between Women,* 6n).

59. See, for an example of a text that refers to the partner of a tribade as a tribade, Seneca the Elder, *Controversiae* 1.2.23 (discussed by Brooten, *Love between Women,* 43–44, 45). For further discussion, see Brooten, "Lesbian Historiography before the Name? Response," 616–21.

60. Brennan (n. 16 above), too, makes a similar complaint on philological grounds about Brooten's despecification of the term "tribade" and her tendency to understand it as if it were a generic designation for a woman possessed of a lifelong homoerotic orientation.

61. Gayle Rubin, "The Traffic in Women: Notes on the 'Political Economy' of Sex," in *Toward an Anthropology of Women,* ed. Rayna R. Reiter (New York: Monthly Review Press, 1975), 157–210 (quotation on 160).

62. On women's inability to deny men sexual access to themselves, see Marilyn Frye, "Some Reflections on Separatism and Power" (1977), in *The Lesbian and Gay Studies Reader,* ed. Abelove, Barale, and Halperin, 91–98.

63. Traub, "The Renaissance of Lesbianism in Early Modern England" (n. 10 above), 258. For her earlier, classic formulation of this point, see Valerie Traub, "The (In)Significance of 'Lesbian' Desire in Early Modern England," in *Erotic Politics: Desire on the Renaissance Stage,* ed. Susan Zimmerman (New York: Routledge, 1992), 150–69.

64. See Catharine A. MacKinnon, "Does Sexuality Have a History?" in *Discourses of Sexuality: From Aristotle to AIDS,* ed. Domna C. Stanton (Ann Arbor: University of Michigan Press, 1992), 117–27; see, also, Catharine A. MacKinnon, *Toward a Feminist Theory of the State* (Cambridge Mass.: Harvard University Press, 1989), esp. 126–54. See Pierre Bourdieu, *La domination masculine* (Paris: Seuil, 1998), who aligns himself in a general way with MacKinnon, without, however, taking proper account of her work, or Rubin's, or the theoretical differences between them. For a similar critique of MacKinnon's neglect of cultural difference in her account of large-scale social structures of male dominance, see Lori L. Heise, "Violence, Sexuality, and Women's Lives," in *The Gender/Sexuality Reader: Culture, History, Political Economy,* ed. Roger N. Lancaster and Micaela di Leonardo (New York: Routledge, 1997), 411–33.

65. See the polemical but important arguments of Terry Castle, *The Apparitional Lesbian: Female Homosexuality and Modern Culture* (New York: Columbia University Press, 1993).

66. I wish to thank Carolyn Dinshaw for drawing this radical implication from my argument and emphasizing it to me.

67. See, for example, Susan S. Lanser, "Befriending the Body: Female Intimacies as Class Acts," *Eighteenth-Century Studies* 32, no. 2 (1998–99): 179–98; Traub, "The Renaissance of Lesbianism in Early Modern England," and her forthcoming book of the same title (Cambridge: Cambridge University Press, 2002).

CHAPTER THREE

This paper was originally written to be delivered on Valentine's Day, 1991, at a conference on "The Constructed Body" sponsored by the Institute for the Humanities at the University of Michigan in Ann Arbor. The version published here is very much the product of that occasion.

Other versions of this paper were presented at the University of Pennsylvania, the University of Chicago, Duke University, the University of Wisconsin, Pomona College, Cornell University, and the Universities of California at Berkeley, Santa Cruz, Los Angeles, and San Diego. Its first publication was in *Discourses of Sexuality: From Aristotle to AIDS,* ed. Domna C. Stanton (Ann Arbor: University of Michigan Press, 1992), 236–61; a different paper, incorporating a good deal of the same material, appeared in *Foucault and the Writing of History,* ed. Jan Goldstein (Oxford: Basil Blackwell, 1994), 19–34, 255–61. The present version combines elements of both published papers. It has benefited substantially from the discussion it received at each stage of its development. I wish to thank, in particular, David Blank, Peter Burian, Arnold Davidson, Whitney Davis, David N. Dobrin, Page duBois, Jan Goldstein, John Kleiner, Tom Laqueur, Paul Morrison, Ann Pellegrini, Ruth Perry, Joe Powers, Henry Rubin, Eve Kosofsky Sedgwick, Domna C. Stanton, and Tom Vogler for their helpful observations, which unfortunately I have not always known how to exploit to best advantage.

1. The sole exception known to me is the formidable Rebecca Kaplan, who happened to be my student in the fall of 1990, and who came independently to the same conclusion.

2. Doug Sadownick, "Groening against the Grain: Maverick Cartoonist Matt Groening Draws in Readers with Gay Characters Akbar and Jeff," *The Advocate* 571 (26 February 1991): 30–35.

3. Donna Haraway, "The Biopolitics of Postmodern Bodies: Determinations of Self in Immune System Discourse," *differences* 1, no. 1 (winter 1989): 3–43, esp. 10–12,

recast as "The Biopolitics of Postmodern Bodies: Constitutions of Self in Immune System Discourse," in her *Simians, Cyborgs, and Women: The Reinvention of Nature* (New York: Routledge, 1991), 203–30, 251–54, pls. 2–11, esp. 208–9.

4. Michel Foucault, *The History of Sexuality,* vol. 1, *An Introduction,* trans. Robert Hurley (New York: Vintage, 1980), 152; cf. Michel Foucault, *La volonté de savoir,* vol. 1 of *Histoire de la sexualité* (1976; reprinted, Paris: Gallimard, 1984), 200. (I quote, whenever possible, from the published English translation; all unattributed translations are my own.) For other efforts to historicize the body, see, esp., Barbara Duden, *Geschichte unter der Haut* (Stuttgart: Klett-Cotta, 1987); and Michel Feher, ed., *Fragments for a History of the Human Body,* 3 vols., Zone 3–5 (New York: Urzone, 1989).

5. Michel Foucault, *L'usage des plaisirs,* vol. 2 of *Histoire de la sexualité* (Paris: Gallimard, 1984), 11.

6. Rupert Swyer's translation is published as "The Discourse on Language" and reprinted as an app. to Michel Foucault, *The Archaeology of Knowledge,* trans. A. M. Sheridan Smith (New York: Pantheon, 1972), 215–37.

7. Northrop Frye, *Anatomy of Criticism: Four Essays* (Princeton, N.J.: Princeton University Press, 1957), 13: "Most critical efforts to handle such generic terms as 'epic' and 'novel' are chiefly interesting as examples of the psychology of rumor."

8. Julia Kristeva, quoted by L. Jenny in *French Literary Theory Today,* ed. Tzvetan Todorov (Cambridge: Cambridge University Press, 1981), 39.

9. See Gilles Deleuze, "What Is a *Dispositif?*" in *Michel Foucault: Philosopher,* ed. and trans. Timothy J. Armstrong (New York: Routledge, 1992), 159–68.

10. Foucault, *History of Sexuality,* 1:69.

11. Foucault's contention about the modern bourgeois nature of our current conception of sexuality can be found in *La volonté de savoir,* 161–68 and in *History of Sexuality,* 1:122–27. The long quotation is from *History of Sexuality,* 1:105–6 (*La volonté de savoir,* 139).

12. Foucault, *L'usage des plaisirs,* 10.

13. See, generally, Hubert L. Dreyfus and Paul Rabinow, *Michel Foucault: Beyond Structuralism and Hermeneutics,* 2d ed. (Chicago: University of Chicago Press, 1983); Thomas R. Flynn, "Truth and Subjectivation in the Later Foucault," *Journal of Philosophy* 82 (1985): 531–40; and Arnold I. Davidson, "Ethics as Ascetics: Foucault, the History of Ethics, and Ancient Thought," in *Foucault and the Writing of History,* ed. Jan Goldstein (Oxford: Basil Blackwell, 1994), 63–80, 266–71.

14. "The *mise en discours* of sex": Foucault, *La volonté de savoir,* 20–21. "Regulating sex through useful and public discourses": Foucault, *History of Sexuality,* 1:25 (*La volonté de savoir,* 35).

15. The first quotation is from Foucault, *History of Sexuality,* 1:157 (translation slightly adapted; cf. *La volonté de savoir,* 207). The second quotation appears in Foucault, *La volonté de savoir,* 203. See, generally, Foucault, *History of Sexuality,* 1:152–57 (*La volonté de savoir,* 200–208); see, also, Foucault's remarks on this point in *Power/Knowledge: Selected Interviews and Other Writings, 1972–77,* ed. Colin Gordon, trans. Colin Gordon, Leo Marshall, John Mepham, and Kate Soper (Brighton, Sussex: Harvester Press, 1980), 190, 210–11.

16. M. D. Macleod, trans., *Lucian VIII,* Loeb Classical Library (Cambridge, Mass.: Harvard University Press, 1967), 147. Félix Buffière, *Eros adolescent: La pédérastie dans la Grèce antique* (Paris: Belles Lettres, 1980), 481, prefers a date in the second century A.D.

17. A notable example of a Latin dissertation on the *Erôtes* is Robert Bloch, *De pseudo-Luciani Amoribus* (Strasburg: Truebner, 1907). Michel Foucault, *Le Souci de soi,* vol. 3 of *Histoire de la sexualité* (Paris: Gallimard, 1984), 243–61.

18. On this point, see Foucault, *Le souci de soi,* 261. See, esp., *Erôtes* 23–24, 35, 48–49, 51, 53 (where Diotima's "steps" of love in Plato's *Symposium* [211C3] are impertinently transformed into a "ladder of pleasure"), and 54.

19. For example, Plutarch, *Moralia* 751A, 752A; Lucian, *Dialogues of the Courtesans* 10; Alciphron, 4.7; Athenaeus, 13.572B.

20. Plutarch, *Moralia* 748F—771E, and Achilles Tatius, 2.33–38: commentary by Friedrich Wilhelm, "Zu Achilles Tatius," *Rheinisches Museum für Philologie* 57 (1902): 55–75. The literary remains of classical antiquity contain numerous briefer and more glancing comparisons of women to boys as male sexual objects: among Roman sources, see Lucilius, 1186; Plautus, *Truc.* 149 ff.; Propertius, 2.4; Ovid, *Ars Amatoria* 2.683–84; Juvenal, 6.33–37 (cited by Craig Arthur Williams, "Homosexuality and the Roman Man: A Study in the Cultural Construction of Sexuality" [Ph.D. diss., Yale University, 1992], chap. 1, n. 40).

21. On the "Debate between Ganymede and Helen," and other such texts, see John Boswell, *Christianity, Social Tolerance, and Homosexuality: Gay People in Western Europe from the Beginning of the Christian Era to the Fourteenth Century* (Chicago: University of Chicago Press, 1980), 255–65.

Similarly, al-Samau'al ibn Yahyâ, a Jewish convert to Islam who died in 1180, composed a treatise entitled *Book of Conversations with Friends on the Intimate Relations between Lovers in the Domain of the Science of Sexuality,* which is largely given over to "a long and highly technical comparison between the anal sphincter and the muscles of the uterus"; the author, who includes in his discussion a striking account of sexual relations between women, invokes the authority of the Prophet to establish the superiority of women as sexual partners for men: see Danielle Jacquart and Claude Thomasset, *Sexuality and Medicine in the Middle Ages,* trans. Matthew Adamson (Princeton, N.J.: Princeton University Press, 1988), 124–25. A more classical instance—"The Man's Dispute with the Learned Woman concerning the Relative Excellence of Male and Female"— can be found in the 419th Night of *The Book of the Thousand Nights and a Night,* trans. Richard F. Burton (London, c. 1886), 5:154–63 (I wish to thank Joe Boone, of the University of Southern California, for helping me verify this reference); this corresponds to tales 390–93 in the J. C. Mardrus and E. Powys Mathers version of *The Book of the Thousand Nights and One Night* (New York: St. Martin's, 1972), 2:409–15: Boswell, 257n.

Examples of late imperial Chinese literature include *Bian er chai* (Wearing a haircap but also hairpins), dated to the first half of the seventeenth century, with discussion by Keith McMahon, *Causality and Containment in Seventeenth-Century Chinese Fiction,* T'oung-pao Monograph, 15 (Leiden: E. J. Brill, 1988); cf. Charlotte Furth, "Androgynous Males and Deficient Females: Biology and Gender Boundaries in Sixteenth- and Seventeenth-Century China," *Late Imperial China* 9, no. 2 (December 1988): 1–31. See, also, the first chapter of *Pinhua baojian* (Precious mirror for judging flowers), published in 1849 by Chen Sen: commentary by Bret Hinsch, *Passions of the Cut Sleeve: The Male Homosexual Tradition in China* (Berkeley: University of California Press, 1990), 156–61. (I wish to thank Maram Epstein, of the University of Michigan, and Gregory M. Pflugfelder, of Stanford University, for kindly supplying me with these references.)

On the *danjo yûretsu ron*—which is a modern Japanese designation for the largely seventeenth-century genre of erotic debate over the relative merits of women and boys as sexual partners for adult men—see the translator's introduction to Ihara Saikaku, *The Great Mirror of Male Love,* trans. Paul Gordon Schalow (Stanford, Calif.: Stanford University Press, 1990), 7.

22. David M. Halperin, *One Hundred Years of Homosexuality and Other Essays on Greek Love* (New York: Routledge, 1990), 34. I use "boy" here, when speaking about Greek sexual practices, in something of a technical sense: the term "boy" translates the Greek word *pais,* which refers by convention in Greek sexual discourse to the junior partner in a paederastic relationship or to one who plays that role, regardless of his actual age; youths are customarily supposed to be desirable between the onset of puberty and the arrival of the beard: see K. J. Dover, *Greek Homosexuality* (Cambridge, Mass.: Harvard University Press, 1978), 16, 85–87; Buffière, *Eros adolescent,* 605–14. "Boy" refers, then, not to male children categorically but to adolescents or teenagers or to young men more generally in their capacity as objects of male erotic desire.

23. All translations of the *Erôtes* included in this essay follow closely the text and translation of Macleod, though I have freely altered the translation where necessary. The vehemence of Charicles and Callicratidas, the participants in the discussion about the relative sexual merits of women and boys that occupies the body of the text, is balanced by the disengagement of Lycinus and Theomnestus, the speakers in the framing dialogue, who are either indifferent to both women and boys (in the case of Lycinus: 4) or equally attracted to each (in the case of Theomnestus: 3, 4). See Foucault, *Le souci de soi,* 243.

24. Despite what Macleod, 147, claims in the phrase quoted.

25. For an example of the inability to conceive sexual preference in terms other than those of sexual orientation, and of the abuse to which such a rigid approach subjects the Kinsey scale (which Kinsey himself designed specifically in order to categorize sexual behavior without reference to the concepts of hetero- and homosexual identity), see John Boswell, "Categories, Experience and Sexuality," in *Forms of Desire: Sexual Orientation and the Social Constructionist Controversy,* ed. Edward Stein, Garland Gay and Lesbian Studies, 1 (New York: Garland, 1990), 133–73; the abridged version of this essay, which appears in *differences,* 2, no. 1 (spring 1990): 67–87, under the title, "Concepts, Experience, and Sexuality," omits any mention of the Kinsey scale. For some current meditations on the use and abuse of the Kinsey scale, see David P. McWhirter, Stephanie A. Sanders, and June Machover Reinisch, eds., *Homosexuality/Heterosexuality: Concepts of Sexual Orientation,* Kinsey Institute Series (New York: Oxford University Press, 1990).

26. For a critique of such a procedure, emphasizing how historicizing accounts of past sexual formations normally have the effect of homogenizing contemporary sexual discourses, flattening out their crucial incoherences and contradictions, see Eve Kosofsky Sedgwick, *Epistemology of the Closet* (Berkeley: University of California Press, 1990), 44–48.

27. See, for example, Biddy Martin, "Lesbian Identity and Autobiographical Difference[s]," in *Life/Lines: Theorizing Women's Autobiography,* ed. Bella Brodzki and Celeste Schenck (Ithaca, N.Y.: Cornell University Press, 1988), 77–103; Judith Butler, "Imitation and Gender Insubordination," in *Inside/Out: Lesbian Theories, Gay Theories,* ed. Diana Fuss (New York: Routledge, 1991), 13–31.

28. On this genre of argument, see John J. Winkler, "Unnatural Acts: Erotic Protocols in Artemidoros' *Dream Analysis,*" in *The Constraints of Desire: The Anthropol-*

ogy of Sex and Gender in Ancient Greece (New York: Routledge, 1990), 17–44, esp. 18–23.

29. See the brilliant reflections of Marjorie Garber, "Spare Parts: The Surgical Construction of Gender," *differences* 1, no. 3 (fall 1989), 137–59.

30. See Plutarch, *Moralia* 750C—E, and the *Greek Anthology,* 12.245, for similar arguments.

31. See Judith P. Hallett, "Female Homoeroticism and the Denial of Roman Reality in Latin Literature," *Yale Journal of Criticism* 3, no. 1 (fall 1989): 209–27; and cf. George Chauncey, Jr., "From Sexual Inversion to Homosexuality: The Changing Medical Conceptualization of Female Deviance," in *Passion and Power: Sexuality in History,* ed. Kathy Peiss and Christina Simmons (Philadelphia: Temple University Press, 1989), 87–117, esp. 99 and 113 n. 50. Further references to compilations of ancient evidence for the "tribad" can be found in Halperin, *One Hundred Years of Homosexuality,* 166 n. 83; 180 n. 2; and in Bernadette J. Brooten, *Love between Women: Early Christian Responses to Female Homoeroticism* (Chicago: University of Chicago Press, 1996), who understands the term *tribas* rather differently from the way I do.

32. The point seems to be that for a man to keep a boyfriend who is approaching the age of manhood is to cast doubt on his own masculinity—that is, on his identity as sexually "active," or insertive, as opposed to sexually "passive," or receptive; for what else would such a strapping fellow be good for except to get fucked by? For a similar reproach, cf. Dio Cassius, 62.6.4.

33. Compare Saikaku, *The Great Mirror,* 1.4 (p. 69): "It is said that, 'Cherry blossoms forever bloom the same, but people change with every passing year.' This is especially true of a boy in the bloom of youth. . . . When at last he comes of age, his blossom of youth falls cruelly to the ground. All told, loving a boy can be likened to a dream that we are not even given time to have."

34. The phrase "a woman's soul in a man's body" translates *anima muliebris virili corpore inclusa,* the notorious self-description of Karl Heinrich Ulrichs, the mid-nineteenth-century founder of the German movement for homosexual emancipation: see Hubert C. Kennedy, "The 'Third Sex' Theory of Karl Heinrich Ulrichs," *Journal of Homosexuality* (Special issue: "Historical Perspectives on Homosexuality," ed. Salvatore J. Licata and Robert P. Petersen), 6, nos. 1–2 (1980/81): 103–11, and *Ulrichs: The Life and Works of Karl Heinrich Ulrichs, Pioneer of the Modern Gay Movement* (Boston: Alyson, 1988), 43–53. The phrase "sexual intermediate" refers to the theories of Magnus Hirschfeld and Edward Carpenter, two early writers and activists: Hirschfeld's journal (which began publication at the turn of the century) was entitled *Jahrbuch für sexuelle Zwischenstufen;* cf. Carpenter, *The Intermediate Sex: A Study of Some Transitional Types of Men and Women,* 2d ed. (London: S. Sonnenschein, 1909). For the best general account of the inversion model, see Chauncey, "From Sexual Inversion to Homosexuality"; for the classic literary representation of male inversion, see Marcel Proust, *Remembrance of Things Past,* trans. C. K. Scott-Moncrieff and Terence Kilmartin (New York: Random House, 1981), 2:623–56 (pt. 1 of *Cities of the Plain*).

35. This is what Eve Kosofsky Sedgwick, *Epistemology of the Closet,* 87–90, terms the "gender separatist" model—which, as she notes, is still with us today and which coexists with the inversion model.

36. See, for example, *Homeric Hymn to Aphrodite* lines 225–36; Dio Chrysostom, 7.117; Pausanias, 7.23.1–2; Lucian, *Dialogues of the Courtesans* 7.2–3.

37. For cosmetic adornment as a feminine practice, see Dio Cassius, 62.6.3, who

makes Boudicca, the female leader of the Britons, remark that "Nero is a man in name but he is a woman in deed" (the implication being that he plays a "feminine" or "passive" role in sexual relations), whereof one "sign" (*sêmeion*) is his use of cosmetics (*kallôpizetai*). (I owe this citation to a paper by Amy Richlin, "Barbarian Queens," delivered at the 1992 meeting of the Philological Association of the Pacific Coast, San Diego, Calif., November.) Plutarch, *Pericles* 12, similarly associates cosmetics (*kallôpizein*) with women.

See also Chariton, *Chaereas and Callirhoe* 1.4, where a man who wishes to be mistaken for an adulterer makes a similarly lavish use of cosmetics: "His hair was gleaming and heavily scented; his eyes were made up; he had a soft cloak and fine shoes; heavy rings gleamed on his fingers" (trans. B. P. Reardon, in *Collected Ancient Greek Novels,* ed. B. P. Reardon [Berkeley: University of California Press, 1989], 27). Similarly, Artemidorus observes that men who dream of wearing facial make-up, jewelry, or unguents will be disgraced (for example, by being exposed as adulterers), implying that the practice is regarded by most men as shameful: see pp. 81.15–17, 106.16–107.2, and 269.11–13 Pack, cited and discussed by Suzanne MacAlister, "Gender as Sign and Symbolism in Artemidoros' *Oneirokritika*: Social Aspirations and Anxieties," *Helios* 19, nos. 1–2 (1992): 140–60, esp. 149–50. Compare the representations of Agathon in Old Comedy: commentary by Froma I. Zeitlin, "Travesties of Gender and Genre in Aristophanes' *Thesmophorizusae*," in *Playing the Other: Gender and Society in Classical Greek Literature* (Chicago: University of Chicago Press, 1996), 375–416; Frances Muecke, "A Portrait of the Artist as a Young Woman," *Classical Quarterly* 32 (1982): 41–55.

38. See, for example, Rosemary Daniell, *Sleeping with Soldiers: In Search of the Macho Man* (New York: Holt, Rinehart, & Winston, 1984), 71. The passage is quoted, and the point considerably elaborated, in the final essay in this volume, "How to Do the History of Male Homosexuality."

39. Foucault, *History of Sexuality,* 1:43.

40. See, for example, Achilles Tatius, 2.38.2; generally, Bernard Grillet, *Les femmes et les fards dans l'antiquité grecque* (Lyon: Centre national de la recherche scientifique, 1975).

41. Could this phrase, *hôs hêdys ho gelôs,* be the source of Rilke's "Sonst . . . im leisen Drehen / der Lenden könnte nicht ein Lächeln gehen / zu jener Mitte, die die Zeugung trug," in his famous sonnet (in the second part of the *Neue Gedichte*) on an "Archaic Torso of Apollo"?

42. Discussion by David Freedberg, *The Power of Images: Studies in the History and Theory of Response* (Chicago: University of Chicago Press, 1989), 331–32, with notes.

43. I wish to thank the late Kevin Lee, formerly professor of Greek at the University of Sydney, for this attractive interpretation of the comparative force of the Greek adverb *paidikôteron.*

44. A reply to the argument about the relative durability of women and boys as objects of male sexual enjoyment is provided by a character in Achilles Tatius, 2.36: "Kleitophon, you don't know the principal fact about pleasure: to be unsatisfied is always a desirable state. Constant recourse to anything makes satisfaction shrivel into satiation. What can only be snatched is always fresh and blooming—its pleasure never grows old. And as much as beauty's span is diminished in time, so is it intensified in desire. The rose for this reason is lovelier than other plants: its beauty soon is gone" (trans. John J. Winkler, in *Collected Ancient Greek Novels,* ed. Reardon, 205–6).

45. W. H. Auden, *Collected Poems,* ed. Edward Mendelson (New York: Random House, 1976), 129.

46. See Foucault, *Le souci de soi,* 246–59, for a detailed elaboration of this point. Compare Saikaku, *The Great Mirror,* 5.2, in which a boy is held back momentarily from having sex with a beautiful girl who offers herself to him—not by his own lack of desire for her but by his personal commitments, specifically by his hitherto unswerving devotion to the way of boy-love (200–201).

47. "Julian and Maddalo," vv. 39–42.

48. Saikaku, *The Great Mirror,* 53, 56. Paul Gordon Schalow, the translator, explains in his introduction that

> in the first case, Saikaku is describing the age when boys and girls first become aware of themselves sexually. The girl fusses over her outward appearance in a mirror, whereas the boy is concerned about the less noticeable but in some ways more important cleanliness of his teeth. The preference implicit here is for the boy's more innocent and perhaps less calculating concern with hygiene than with superficial appearances. In the second case, neither situation with courtesan or actor allows sexual intercourse for the paying patron, but the "intimate conversation" possible with the kabuki boy provides a recompense of sorts, suggesting a nonsexual satisfaction found in having an affair with an actor that is lacking with a courtesan. The third example juxtaposes two financially draining situations, supporting a sick wife versus supporting a spendthrift boy. Again the implication is that the sick wife represents a hopeless situation, whereas the boy, in spite of his spending habits, offers some pleasurable compensations.
>
> (12)

I wonder if a similarly earnest account could be given of the fourth example. For further arguments, see my review of Schalow's translation in the *Journal of Japanese Studies* 17 (1991): 398–403.

In the *Erôtes,* similarly, Callicratidas juxtaposes the image of a girl with a mirror and a comb to that of a boy with a book and a lyre (44).

49. For fuller documentation, see Dover, *Greek Homosexuality;* Winkler, *Constraints of Desire;* Halperin, *One Hundred Years of Homosexuality;* David M. Halperin, John J. Winkler, and Froma I. Zeitlin, eds., *Before Sexuality: The Construction of Erotic Experience in the Ancient Greek World* (Princeton, N.J.: Princeton University Press, 1990); and the various studies cited in those works.

50. Compare Paul Gordon Schalow, "Male Love in Early Modern Japan: A Literary Depiction of the 'Youth,'" in *Hidden from History: Reclaiming the Gay and Lesbian Past,* ed. Martin Bauml Duberman, Martha Vicinus, and George Chauncey, Jr. (New York: New American Library, 1989), 118–28, 506–9, esp. 120: "Those who pursued sexual relations exclusively with women or exclusively with youths were in a minority and were considered mildly eccentric for limiting their pleasurable options."

51. Compare Jacques Derrida, *The Truth in Painting,* trans. Geoff Bennington and Ian McLeod (Chicago: University of Chicago Press, 1987), esp. 332–35, 373–79, on the strange relations or irrelations among and within the terms "two," "the pair," "parity,"

"the couple," "the double," "fetishism," "homosexuality," "heterosexuality," "bisexuality." In a similar vein, it may be worth noting the various relations of resemblance, doubling, and difference that U.S. Postal Service Poster 669 (fig. 1) constructs by juxtaposing the philatelic series of four stamps to the quilt that presumably inspired their design. Like the mirror-opposite figures of the lovebirds on the stamp, each stamp in the series of repeated stamps resembles its counterparts exactly: they are all identical replicas of one another and, as such, indicate indexically the process of mechanical engraving or imaging, and the technology of industrial mass production, that created them. The quilt, by contrast, is a unique, handmade, labor-intensive, and originally non-commodified artifact emanating from an indigenous folk tradition. The stamp is intended to glorify that tradition as a precious part of the national heritage of the United States. It does so by supposedly appropriating elements of the quilt's design and reproducing them in a new medium, thereby claiming for the products of impersonal mechanized industrial labor the aura of the artifactual and the homely. In that sense, the two opposites on the poster are not the paired lovebirds but the implicit couple constituted by the two featured modes of inscription or representation: quilting and engraving (or computer graphics).

52. For more elaborate philosophical arguments to this effect, see my essays, "Platonic Erôs and What Men Call Love," *Ancient Philosophy* 5 (1985): 161–204, esp. 182–87, and "Plato and the Metaphysics of Desire," in *Proceedings of the Boston Area Colloquium in Ancient Philosophy*, vol. 5, *1989*, ed. John J. Cleary and Daniel C. Shartin (Lanham, Md.: University Press of America, 1991), 27–52, esp. 29–36.

53. D. A. Miller, "The Late Jane Austen," *Raritan* 10, no. 1 (summer 1990): 55–79 (quotation on 57; my emphasis). Much of the remainder of Miller's essay is taken up with adumbrating that fundamental insight. More recently, Miller's point has been made with aphoristic economy by Regina Kunzel, "Situating Sex: The Problem of Prison Sexual Culture in the Mid-Twentieth-Century U.S.," *GLQ: A Journal of Lesbian and Gay Studies* 8, no. 3 (2002): 253–70, esp. 265: "naturalization does not happen naturally; it requires cultural work."

CHAPTER FOUR

The title of my essay pays tribute to the work of Arnold I. Davidson, which has consistently, enduringly, and powerfully shaped my own: see, esp., his essays "How to Do the History of Psychoanalysis: A Reading of Freud's *Three Essays on the Theory of Sexuality*," *Critical Inquiry* 13, no. 2 (1987): 252–77, "Sex and the Emergence of Sexuality," *Critical Inquiry* 14, no. 1 (1987): 16–48, and "Closing Up the Corpses: Diseases of Sexuality and the Emergence of the Psychiatric Style of Reasoning," in *Meaning and Method: Essays in Honor of Hilary Putnam,* ed. George Boolos (Cambridge: Cambridge University Press, 1990), 295–325. In my recent work on the history of sexuality, particularly in this essay and in "Forgetting Foucault" (in this volume), I have returned to a set of issues that Davidson's work first opened up for me and that I have pondered for well over a decade now.

Many people have discussed with me the ideas touched on in this essay; I cannot list all their names here, as I would like to do. But I must thank Patricia Crawford and Hilary Fraser, who invited me to participate in their Australian Academy of the Social Sciences Workshop "Gender, Sexualities, and Historical Change," University of Western Australia, 31 July—1 August 1998. Discussions among members of that workshop provided the immediate stimulus for this essay. I owe a particular debt in this regard to Judith M. Bennett.

This essay was written for delivery at the conference "Sex and Conflict: Gay and Lesbian Studies in the Humanities and Social Sciences," Lund University, 9–10 October 1998. I wish to thank Eva Österberg and Johanna Esseveld for giving me that opportunity to present my work and Martha Vicinus and Lillian Faderman, my fellow participants, for encouraging me to persevere with it.

Finally, I would like to thank George E. Haggerty, whose work and conversation originally prompted me to broach some of these ideas. See his *Men in Love: Masculinity and Sexuality in the Eighteenth Century* (New York: Columbia University Press, 1999), which offers a refreshingly different solution from the one proposed here to a similar question about how to do the history of male homosexuality.

Some of the material and the argumentation presented here also appear in my entry "Sex, Sexuality, Sexual Classification," in *Critical Terms for Gender Studies,* ed. Catharine Stimpson and Gilbert Herdt (Chicago: University of Chicago Press, 2003), in press.

1. See, for example, Jacqueline Murray, "Twice Marginal and Twice Invisible: Lesbians in the Middle Ages," in *Handbook of Medieval Sexuality*, ed. Vern L. Bullough and James A. Brundage (London: Garland, 1996), 191–222; or the otherwise excellent article by Anna Clark, "Anne Lister's Construction of Lesbian Identity," *Journal of the History of Sexuality* 7 (1996): 23–50.

2. Or so I argue in "Historicizing the Subject of Desire" and in "Forgetting Foucault." For a quite different but powerful and persuasive argument for the importance of emphasizing continuities in women's history, see Judith M. Bennett, "Confronting Continuity," *Journal of Women's History* 9, no. 3 (1997): 73–94.

3. The demonstration of the existence of such an irreducible definitional uncertainty is the central, invaluable accomplishment of Eve Kosofsky Sedgwick, *Epistemology of the Closet* (Berkeley: University of California Press, 1990). As will become evident, I have taken on board her critique (45–48) of my earlier work, *One Hundred Years of Homosexuality and Other Essays on Greek Love* (New York: Routledge, 1990), applying her lesson about the irresolvable contradictions in what we are too quick to call "homosexuality as we understand it today." At the same time, however, I will continue to insist on documenting the existence of what she terms, sarcastically, "a Great Paradigm Shift" in the history of homosexuality—namely, the emergence of the discourses of homosexuality themselves in the modern period. Far from seeing a conflict between a historical inquiry into the construction of homosexuality and a discursive analysis of the contradictions in the modern notion of homosexuality, I see such a historical inquiry as helping account for the ineradicable incoherence of the modern notion. Sedgwick's own work, in fact, has enabled me to bring the historical and discursive critiques of homosexuality into closer and more systematic alignment.

4. Martin Bauml Duberman, Martha Vicinus, and George Chauncey, Jr., eds., *Hidden from History: Reclaiming the Gay and Lesbian Past* (New York: New American Library, 1989), 8.

5. Dipesh Chakrabarty, *Provincializing Europe: Postcolonial Thought and Historical Difference* (Princeton, N.J.: Princeton University Press, 2000), 107.

6. See Randolph Trumbach, "London's Sodomites: Homosexual Behavior and Western Culture in the Eighteenth Century," *Journal of Social History* 11 (1977): 1–33; Barry

D. Adam, "Age, Structure, and Sexuality: Reflections on the Anthropological Evidence on Homosexual Relations," in *Anthropology and Homosexual Behavior,* ed. Evelyn Blackwood (New York: Haworth, 1986), 19–33, and "Structural Foundations of the Gay World," *Comparative Studies in Society and History* 27 (1985): 658–71, reprinted in *Queer Theory/Sociology,* ed. Steven Seidman (Oxford: Blackwell, 1996), 111–26; Gilbert Herdt, "Homosexuality," in *Encyclopedia of Religion,* ed. Mircea Eliade, 10 vols. (New York: Macmillan, 1987), 6:445–52, and *Same Sex, Different Cultures* (Boulder, Colo.: Westview, 1997); and David F. Greenberg, *The Construction of Homosexuality* (Chicago: University of Chicago Press, 1988), 25. Not all of these authors employ a fourfold taxonomy, and they use different names for their categories. Greenberg speaks of "transgenderal," "transgenerational," and "egalitarian" types (the last two terms are, in my view, misleading).

Finally, in a series of articles and books beginning in the 1970s, Stephen O. Murray has been defining and refining the sociological or typological models according to which forms of male same-sex behavior around the world have been elaborated and institutionalized: for his most recent and comprehensive treatment of the topic, see Stephen O. Murray, *Homosexualities* (Chicago: University of Chicago Press, 2000), esp. 1–21, where he differentiates among "age-stratified," "gender-stratified," and "egalitarian" (gay or lesbian) organizations of homosexuality. Murray makes the important and fundamental point that "there is diversity [in homosexual behavior and classification], but there are only a few recurring patterns. Relatively few of the imaginable structurings of same-sex sex recur in the panorama of known societies. . . . There are not hundreds or even dozens of different social organizations of same-sex sexual relations in human societies. . . . Only a few categorization systems recur across space and time" (1–2). For earlier soundings of this note in Murray's previous work, see his *Social Theory, Homosexual Realities* (New York: Gay Academic Union, 1984), 46, "Homosexual Acts and Selves in Early Modern Europe," in *The Pursuit of Sodomy: Male Homosexuality in Renaissance and Enlightenment Europe,* ed. Kent Gerard and Gert Hekma (New York: Harrington Park Press, 1989), originally published as *Journal of Homosexuality,* vol. 16, nos. 1–2 (1988), with Murray's article at 457–77, but see esp. 469, and "Homosexual Categorization in Cross-Cultural Perspective," in *Latin American Male Homosexualities* (Albuquerque: University of New Mexico Press, 1995), 3–31, esp. 4. In the latter essay, Murray had proposed a fourfold typology, including a category called "profession-defined organization of homosexuality"; in his recent book, *Homosexualities,* that category has been collapsed into "gender-stratified" homosexuality (5).

7. Sedgwick, *Epistemology of the Closet,* 47.

8. The quoted material is from ibid., 85, 47.

9. I respond in greater detail to Sedgwick's critique of constructionist history in the introduction to this volume.

10. Michel Foucault, *The History of Sexuality,* vol. 1, *An Introduction,* trans. Robert Hurley (New York: Vintage, 1980), 101.

11. Rosemary Daniell, *Sleeping with Soldiers: In Search of the Macho Man* (New York: Holt, Rinehart, & Winston, 1984), 71.

12. Pseudo-Lucian, *Erôtes* 9, trans. M. D. Macleod, in *Lucian VIII* (Cambridge, Mass.: Harvard University Press, 1967). See, generally, "Historicizing the Subject of Desire," in this volume.

13. Chariton, *Chaereas and Callirhoe* 1.4, trans. B. P. Reardon, in *Collected Ancient Greek Novels,* ed. B. P. Reardon (Berkeley: University of California Press, 1989), 27.

Similarly, Artemidorus observes that men who dream that they wear facial makeup, jewelry, or unguents will suffer disgrace (i.e., will be exposed) as adulterers: see 81.15–17, 106.16–107.2, and 269.11–13 Pack, cited with discussion by Suzanne MacAlister, "Gender as Sign and Symbolism in Artemidoros' *Oneirokritika*: Social Aspirations and Anxieties," *Helios* 19 (1992): 140–60, esp. 149–50. Compare the representations of Agathon in Old Comedy: commentary by Froma I. Zeitlin, "Travesties of Gender and Genre in Aristophanes' *Thesmophorizusae*," in *Playing the Other: Gender and Society in Classical Greek Literature* (Chicago: University of Chicago Press, 1996), 375–416; Frances Muecke, "A Portrait of the Artist as a Young Woman," *Classical Quarterly* 32 (1982): 41–55.

14. See Nicole Loraux, "Herakles: The Super-Male and the Feminine," trans. Robert Lamberton, in *Before Sexuality: The Construction of Erotic Experience in the Ancient Greek World,* ed. David M. Halperin, John J. Winkler, and Froma I. Zeitlin (Princeton, N.J.: Princeton University Press, 1990), 21–52.

15. See Stephen Orgel, *Impersonations: The Performance of Gender in Shake-speare's England* (Cambridge: Cambridge University Press, 1996), 25–26. I wish to thank Vernon Rosario for suggesting the humoral gloss on this passage. See also Joseph Cady, "The 'Masculine Love' of the 'Princes of Sodom' 'Practising the Art of Ganymede' at Henri III's Court: The Homosexuality of Henri III and His Mignons in Pierre de L'Estoile's *Mémoires-Journaux*," in *Desire and Discipline: Sex and Sexuality in the Premodern West,* ed. Jacqueline Murray and Konrad Eisenbichler (Toronto: University of Toronto Press, 1996), 123–54, esp. 132–33: "However, in the Renaissance the word 'effeminate,' when applied to a man, did not automatically connote homosexuality, but instead had a diversity of meaning it lacks today. For instance, the term sometimes designated a kind of hyper or helpless male heterosexuality, a usage that, of course, no longer exists. Donne's remark that he is called 'effeminat' because he 'love[s] womens joyes,' in his epigram 'The Jughler' (1587?—1596?), belongs to this Renaissance tradition." For further details Cady refers the reader to his earlier essay "Renaissance Awareness and Language for Heterosexuality: 'Love' and 'Feminine Love,' " in *Renaissance Discourses of Desire,* ed. Claude J. Summers and Ted-Larry Pebworth (Columbia: University of Missouri Press, 1993), 143–58.

16. Individual cultural systems of social and sexual hierarchy tend to collapse the distinctions among these different categories or orders of subordination, treating boys as feminine, or women as minors, or passive sexual partners (of whatever sex) as feminine, or feminized partners as junior: hence, Alan Sinfield speaks of "a *conflation of subor-dinations*" and foregrounds the element of unequal power that consistently structures erotic life, noting that "the elaborate social structures of modernity offer equally potent hierarchies of class and race, and they too may be conflated with subordinations of age and gender" (*Gay and After* [London: Serpent's Tail, 1998], 66). See also, by Sinfield, "The Production of Gay and the Return of Power," in *De-Centring Sexualities: Politics and Representations beyond the Metropolis,* ed. Richard Phillips, Diane Watt, and David Shuttleton (London: Routledge, 2000), 21–36, esp. 30. Sinfield develops the point further in "Lesbian and Gay Taxonomies," forthcoming. While I welcome the political emphasis on power inequities that Sinfield brings to his account of eroticism, I wish to keep the different categories or orders of subordination separate, both analytically and empirically, so as to be able to describe, in any particular social situation, the exact nature of the hierarchy at issue. Not *all* systems of hierarchy conflate *all* subordinations, nor do they do so in the same way. Moreover, in any particular social context, important distinctions among types of subordinate identities may be made: that is, boys may

be viewed as junior but not necessarily as feminine; women may be seen as subordinate but not necessarily as minors; passive sexual partners may be seen as dominated but not necessarily as feminized. It is important to preserve the possibility of attending to these differences, which may figure significantly in the minds of individual social actors as well as in the sexual codes of social groups.

17. Quoted by Davidson, "Closing Up the Corpses," 315 (cited in full in my headnote to this chap.).

18. On the aristocratic types mentioned, see Randolph Trumbach, "The Birth of the Queen: Sodomy and the Emergence of Gender Equality in Modern Culture, 1660–1750," in *Hidden from History,* ed. Duberman, Vicinus, and Chauncey, 129–40, 509–11.

19. I follow here the arguments of Davidson, "Closing Up the Corpses"; and George Chauncey, Jr., "From Sexual Inversion to Homosexuality: Medicine and the Changing Conceptualization of Female Deviance," in *Passion and Power: Sexuality in History,* ed. Kathy Peiss and Christina Simmons, with Robert A. Padgug (Philadelphia: Temple University Press, 1989), 87–117.

20. See, for some recent examples, Thorkil Vanggaard, *Phallos: A Symbol and Its History in the Male World,* trans. from the Danish by Thorkil Vanggaard (New York: International Universities Press, 1972), 17 and passim; Lionel Ovesey, *Homosexuality and Pseudohomosexuality* (New York: Science House, 1969); and Richard A. Posner, *Sex and Reason* (Cambridge, Mass.: Harvard University Press, 1992), esp. 105–7, 152, 296.

For a genealogy of this distinction between situational homosexuality and true homosexuality, see the trenchant analysis by Regina Kunzel, "Situating Sex: The Problem of Prison Sexual Culture in the Mid-Twentieth-Century U.S.," *GLQ: A Journal of Lesbian and Gay Studies* 8, no. 3 (2002): 253–70, who also notes the continuities between so-called situational homosexuality and earlier sexual formations, such as paederasty/sodomy and inversion (my terms, not hers).

21. For example, Gary W. Dowsett, *Practicing Desire: Homosexual Sex in the Era of AIDS* (Stanford, Calif.: Stanford University Press, 1996).

22. For Bronze Age Crete, see Robert B. Koehl, "The Chieftain Cup and a Minoan Rite of Passage," *Journal of Hellenic Studies* 106 (1986): 99–110, and "Ephoros and Ritualized Homosexuality in Bronze Age Crete," in *Queer Representations: Reading Lives, Reading Cultures,* ed. Martin Duberman (New York: New York University Press, 1997), 7–13.

23. For some modern instances, see George Chauncey, Jr., "Christian Brotherhood or Sexual Perversion? Homosexual Identities and the Construction of Sexual Boundaries in the World War One Era," *Journal of Social History* 19 (1985/86): 189–211, reprinted in *Hidden from History,* ed. Duberman, Vicinus, and Chauncey, 294–317, 541–46; John Marshall, "Pansies, Perverts and Macho Men: Changing Conceptions of Male Homosexuality," in *The Making of the Modern Homosexual,* ed. Kenneth Plummer (London: Hutchinson, 1981), 133–54, esp. 149–52; Albert J. Reiss, Jr., "The Social Integration of Queers and Peers," *Social Problems* 9 (1961/62): 102–20, reprinted in *Social Perspectives in Lesbian and Gay Studies: A Reader,* ed. Peter M. Nardi (New York: Routledge, 1998), 12–28; John H. Gagnon and William Simon, *Sexual Conduct: The Social Sources of Human Sexuality* (Chicago: Aldine, 1973), 240–51.

Alan Sinfield, "Lesbian and Gay Taxonomies," protests that "the age model" of homosexual relations still flourishes in Western post-industrial cultures today and, in fact, "figures in many of the most influential books of our time," such as Alan Hollinghurst's

The Swimming-Pool Library (London: Vintage, 1989) or Neil Bartlett's *Ready to Catch Him Should He Fall* (New York: Dutton, 1991). Similarly, Stephen Murray claims that "pederastic relationships continue to exist even today in cities with generally recognized gay neighborhoods and institutions" (*Homosexualities,* 12). But the pattern I am describing here is not defined simply by a difference in age or in generation between the two male partners but by (among other things) a largely lopsided or non-reciprocal pattern of desire and pleasure, which is hardly a prominent element in the two novels cited by Sinfield or, I should think, in the contemporary relationships to which Murray refers. "Paederasty/sodomy" is a much more specific pattern than what Sinfield intends by "the age model" which, for him, is really a subcategory of homosexuality.

24. Michael Rocke, *Forbidden Friendships: Homosexuality and Male Culture in Renaissance Florence* (New York: Oxford University Press, 1996), 4, 96–97. Rocke's statistics have come in for some criticism, however, from Samuel K. Cohen, Jr., in his review of the book in *Speculum* 74, no. 2 (April 1999): 481–83.

25. Thus, for example, the fourteenth- and fifteenth-century Florentine definitions of "sodomy" and "sodomite" refer to the "active" or insertive partner in anal intercourse only (Rocke, *Forbidden Friendships,* 14, 110).

26. See Halperin, *One Hundred Years of Homosexuality,* 163n. 53, for an admittedly incomplete list of ancient Greek and Roman texts documenting a conscious erotic preference on the part of men for sexual intercourse with members of one sex rather than the other.

27. For more detailed references, see "Historicizing the Subject of Desire," in this volume, esp. 180–81, nn. 20–21; also Everett K. Rowson, "The Categorization of Gender and Sexual Irregularity in Medieval Arabic Vice Lists," in *Body Guards: The Cultural Politics of Gender Ambiguity,* ed. Julia Epstein and Kristina Straub (New York: Routledge, 1991), 50–79; and J. W. Wright and Everett K. Rowson, eds., *Homoeroticism in Classical Arabic Literature* (New York: Columbia University Press, 1997).

28. See Cynthia B. Herrup, *A House in Gross Disorder: Sex, Law, and the Second Earl of Castlehaven* (New York: Oxford University Press, 1999), 33: "The prosecutions for sodomy about which we have information before the late seventeenth century rarely condemned defendants for effeminate behavior; conversely, reproaches for effeminacy rarely included sexual examples."

29. John Boswell, *Christianity, Social Tolerance, and Homosexuality: Gay People in Western Europe from the Beginning of the Christian Era to the Fourteenth Century* (Chicago: University of Chicago Press, 1980), 44.

30. For an attempt to document several instances of same-sex sexual object-choice, and even of conscious erotic preferences for persons of the same sex as oneself, that nonetheless do not satisfy the criteria for homosexuality, see "Historicizing the Subject of Desire," in this volume.

31. See, for more on James and his male courtiers, Alan Bray and Michel Rey, "The Body of the Friend: Continuity and Change in Masculine Friendship in the Seventeenth Century," in *English Masculinities 1660–1800,* ed. Tim Hitchcock and Michèle Cohen (London: Addison Wesley Longman, 1999), 65–84. More generally, on the patterns of asymmetry in male friendships, see Halperin, "Heroes and Their Pals," in *One Hundred Years of Homosexuality,* 75–87, 176–79.

32. See Alan Bray, "Homosexuality and the Signs of Male Friendship in Elizabethan England," in *Queering the Renaissance,* ed. Jonathan Goldberg (Durham, N.C.: Duke University Press, 1994), 40–61. I interpret Bray to provide evidence for this claim, al-

though he does not quite make it himself. See also Herrup, *A House in Gross Disorder,* 33: "Whether or not actually pederastic, the sodomitical relationships described in the legal records invariably paired authority and dependency—men and boys, masters and servants, teachers and pupils, patrons and clients."

33. Alan Sinfield emphasizes what he seems to regard as the intrinsic sexiness of power (as opposed to its contingent sexiness within specific historical and cultural contexts, as I would prefer) in "The Production of Gay and the Return of Power," 27 ("Power is sexy"). By contrast, Bray and Rey, "The Body of the Friend," emphasize quite properly that virtuous friendship between men unequal in rank was worlds apart from what counted as "sodomy" in England before the later seventeenth century.

34. See, again, Bray and Rey, "The Body of the Friend," for a brief but panoramic survey of the patron-client model of friendship in England from the middle ages until the later seventeenth century.

35. *The Complete Essays of Montaigne,* trans. Donald M. Frame (Stanford, Calif.: Stanford University Press, 1958), 139.

36. Ibid., 139–40.

37. I owe this citation to Haggerty, *Men in Love,* 25 (cited in full in the headnote to this chap.), who interprets it eloquently but almost exactly contrary to the way I do. For a contrasting approach to this topic, see C. Stephen Jaeger, *Ennobling Love: In Search of a Lost Sensibility* (Philadelphia: University of Pennsylvania Press, 1999).

38. See Marc D. Schachter, " 'That Friendship Which Possesses the Soul': Montaigne Loves La Boétie," *Journal of Homosexuality* 41, nos. 3–4 (2001): 5–21, for a detailed study of this tension in Montaigne.

39. I overstate for the sake of emphasis. For a more nuanced and complex account of the interrelations of sexuality and gender in transgenderism, see Don Kulick, *Travesti: Sex, Gender, and Culture among Brazilian Transgendered Prostitutes* (Chicago: University of Chicago Press, 1998), and, esp., "Problematic Childhood Sexuality," paper presented at the annual meeting of the American Anthropological Association, Philadelphia, 2–6 December 1999.

40. See Sedgwick, *Epistemology of the Closet,* esp. 1, 9, 85–86, whence I derive the distinction between "universalizing" and "minoritizing" constructions of sexual identity.

41. For a more detailed contrast between the invert and the sodomite as discursive types see Halperin, "Forgetting Foucault," in this volume.

42. Cited and translated by Maud W. Gleason, *Making Men: Sophists and Self-Presentation in Ancient Rome* (Princeton, N.J.: Princeton University Press, 1995), 68.

43. Quintilian, *Institutes* 5.9.14, cited and translated by Amy Richlin, "Not before Homosexuality: The Materiality of *Cinaedus* and the Roman Law against Love between Men," *Journal of the History of Sexuality* 3, no. 4 (April 1993): 523–73, esp. 542.

44. This is a composite passage by ancient physiognomic writers, assembled by Gleason, *Making Men,* 63.

45. Another composite passage, ibid., 78.

46. Aulus Gellius, 6.12.5, cited and translated by Craig A. Williams, *Roman Homosexuality: Ideologies of Masculinity in Classical Antiquity* (New York: Oxford University Press, 1999), 23. A measure of the distance between inversion or passivity and male love can be gauged from the fact that Scipio was quite willing to identify himself publicly as bound to his friend Laelius by a "bond of love," according to the Roman historian Valerius Maximus (8.8.1). (I wish to thank Tom Hillard of Macquarie University for

this observation and citation.) There would not necessarily have been any inconsistency or hypocrisy in Scipio's attitude.

47. *Historia ecclesiastica* 8.10, cited and translated by Glenn W. Olsen, "St. Anselm and Homosexuality," *Anselm Studies: An Occasional Journal* (Special issue: "Proceedings of the Fifth International Saint Anselm Conference: St. Anselm and St. Augustine—Episcopi ad Saecula," ed. Joseph C. Schnaubelt et al.), vol. 2 (1988), 93–141, esp. 110.

48. Cited and translated (with slight alterations here) by Cady, " 'Masculine Love' of the 'Princes of Sodom,' " 133. Cady, of course, draws a different conclusion about the existence of homosexuality in the Renaissance from this and other comments by Pierre de L'Estoile.

49. The two passages are cited and quoted by Alan Bray, *Homosexuality in Renaissance England* (London: Gay Men's Press, 1982), 81, 87.

50. Quoted and discussed by Lisa L. Moore, *Dangerous Intimacies: Toward a Sapphic History of the British Novel* (Durham, N.C.: Duke University Press, 1997), 72–74.

51. C. Westphal, "Die conträre Sexualempfindung, Symptom eines neuropathischen (psychopathischen) Zustandes," *Archiv für Psychiatrie und Nervenkrankheiten* 2 (1870): 73–108.

52. Arrigo Tamassia, "Sull' inversione dell' istinto sessuale," *Rivista sperimentale di freniatria e di medicina legale* 4 (1878): 97–117.

53. Of course, the molly himself is a complex figure, already verging on the homosexual, as Trumbach and others have shown. For one thing, mollies clearly have sex with other mollies. I do not mean to skip over the vexed interpretative issues; I merely wish to make the point that the figure of the molly—however forward-looking he may be in other respects—retains many of the features traditionally ascribed to male inverts or passives.

54. The basic study is Hubert Kennedy, *Ulrichs: The Life and Works of Karl Heinrich Ulrichs, Pioneer of the Modern Gay Movement* (Boston: Alyson, 1988). Westphal cites Ulrichs, under his pseudonym Numa Numantius, in "Die conträre Sexualempfindung," 92 ff.

55. See Chauncey, "From Sexual Inversion to Homosexuality."

56. My account derives from Chauncey, ibid. Long before Krafft-Ebing, Westphal, in "Die conträre Sexualempfindung," 108, emphasized that not all cases of "unnatural lewdness" (the conduct criminalized by article 143 of the Prussian criminal law code, soon to become the infamous article 175 of the imperial German law code) proceed from pathological causes: just as it is possible to identify some thefts as the result of pathological compulsion without implying that most thefts are motivated by mental illness, so ordinary human viciousness, not psychological disturbance, is to blame for many cases of "unnatural lewdness."

57. Westphal, "Die conträre Sexualempfindung," 107n: "Dass es sich nicht immer gleichzeitig um den Geschlechtstrieb als solchen handle" (emphasis shown in text is mine).

58. Ibid., 98, accepts the subject's claims about his sexual normality both on the basis of his own testimony and on the basis of the independent fact that at the time of his arrest he was found to be suffering from gonorrhea (which Westphal, like Karl Maria Kertbeny in this respect, evidently believes could not be transmitted by homosexual sex). Far from being an embarrassment or an obstacle to the diagnosis, the subject's heterosexual desire is underscored in Westphal's account.

59. Ibid., 82–91, 97–100. I have been aided by Robert Grimm, "The Dawn of Contrary Sexual Sensitivity" (unpublished manuscript, University of Washington), who cites, translates, and discusses a number of the passages quoted here.

60. Alfred C. Kinsey, Wardell B. Pomeroy, and Clyde E. Martin, *Sexual Behavior in the Human Male* (Philadelphia: Saunders, 1948), 615. For a detailed elaboration of the distinction between homosexuality and inversion, see C. A. Tripp, *The Homosexual Matrix* (New York: McGraw-Hill, 1975), 22–35.

61. In this one respect, at least, Kinsey proves a more reliable historian than Foucault. In *The History of Sexuality* Foucault dated the birth of homosexuality (as a discursive category) to Westphal's article:

> We must not forget that the psychological, psychiatric, medical category of homosexuality was constituted from the moment it was characterized—Westphal's famous article of 1870 on "contrary sexual sensations" can stand as its date of birth—less by a type of sexual relations than by a certain quality of sexual sensibility, a certain way of inverting the masculine and the feminine in oneself. Homosexuality appeared as one of the forms of sexuality when it was transposed from the practice of sodomy onto a kind of interior androgyny, a hermaphrodism of the soul. The sodomite had been a temporary aberration; the homosexual was now a species.
>
> (43)

I believe Foucault was right to see in Westphal the emergence of a modern psychiatric notion of erotic orientation, which brought with it a specification of deviant individuals and a shift from a juridical discourse of prohibited acts to a normalizing discourse of perverted psychology. But I also believe Foucault was wrong to identify Westphal's category of "contrary sexual feeling" with homosexuality. In *Epistemology of the Closet* Sedgwick ingeniously argued that my "reading of 'homosexuality' as 'we currently understand it' . . . is virtually the opposite of Foucault's," insofar as Foucault has a "gender transitive" understanding of homosexuality, whereas I have a "gender intransitive" one (46). That may well explain why Foucault did not take what I regard as the historically necessary step of systematically differentiating "sexual inversion" from "homosexuality." Still, the ultimate issue here may not be a difference of opinion about what homosexuality is so much as an uncertainty about whether it is possible to draw a meaningful distinction in the history of modern European discourses between an "orientation" and a "sexuality."

62. Kinsey, Pomeroy, and Martin, *Sexual Behavior,* 616, 623.

63. The aptly chosen word *fades* here derives from Adam, who writes that in homosexuality "sex-role definitions fade from interpersonal bonding" ("Structural Foundations," 111). This paragraph and much of what follows have been inspired by Adam.

64. Quoted by Dan Savage, *Savage Love: Straight Answers from America's Most Popular Sex Columnist* (New York: Plume, 1998), 189–90.

65. See, in addition to Kinsey, Pomeroy, and Martin, *Sexual Behavior,* the following: Chauncey, "Christian Brotherhood or Sexual Perversion?" 294–317, 541–46; and Michael Bartos, John McLeod, and Phil Nott, *Meanings of Sex between Men: A Study Conducted by the Australian Federation of AIDS Organisations for the Commonwealth*

Department of Human Services and Health, 1993 (Canberra: Australian Government Publishing Service, 1994).

66. See Barry D. Adam, "Age Preferences among Gay and Bisexual Men," *GLQ: A Journal of Lesbian and Gay Studies* 6, no. 3 (2000): 413–34. See, also, the data on gay men in London and Cardiff collected by Anthony P. M. Coxon, *Between the Sheets: Sexual Diaries and Gay Men's Sex in the Era of AIDS* (London: Cassell, 1996), esp. 94–96: although he notes that "if a man engages in a particular sexual practice it is more likely that he will do so in both active and passive modalities (even over a period of a month) than restrict himself to only one of them," he also points out some "interesting contrary trends," including exceptional "role rigidity" in the case of anal intercourse, in which "those who were either exclusively active or exclusively passive now equal or exceed those who are both." Even Coxon, however, concludes that his "results do not support the idea that, even over a one-month period, gay men tend to be exclusively active or passive during anal intercourse," and he cites a Dutch study that suggests that the percentage of gay men who switch roles may be significantly larger in Amsterdam. Similarly, role swapping appears to be the norm today in gay male relations in Australia, according to Dowsett, *Practicing Desire*, 81: "Although there was a decided preference among some gay men [in the group sampled] in their assessment of sexual 'enjoyment' for the insertive or the receptive *mode* in anal intercourse, in practice such activity is commonly reciprocal, men moving from insertive to receptive modes at will." Dowsett's conclusions have been massively confirmed by a recent review of the empirical literature on anal intercourse around the world by Gary Smith, "Heterosexual and Homosexual Anal Intercourse: An International Perspective," *Venereology* 14, no. 1 (2001): 28–37, who finds that "among gay-identified predominantly homosexually active men who engage in anal intercourse, most are both insertive and receptive," noting that this finding remained constant in studies of societies belonging to the so-called post-industrial West undertaken "from the mid-1960s to the late 1990s."

It is possible that such results have been overstated, or their significance exaggerated, perhaps owing to the distaste with which supposedly "liberated" gay men view rigid role playing. Moreover, Gary Smith cautions me (in an e-mail message, 7 August 2001) that the quantitative data on anal intercourse among gay men should not be taken to indicate equal preference for the insertive and receptive role, since no allowance is made in that data for frequency or predilection (in other words, there may still be many more tops and bottoms out there than are reflected in the quantitative data on sexual practice). Dr. Sasho Lambevski, a researcher at the National Centre in HIV Social Research at the University of New South Wales in Sydney, writes to me (e-mail message, 13 April 2000) as follows: "I gather from my own empirical research and my colleagues' research that the claims of reciprocity in sexual/gender roles in gay relationships are grossly exaggerated. In the interviews we have done with gay couples, the lip service that the interviewed men pay to the lofty ideals of gay liberation (reciprocity, versatility, etc.) serves as a rhetorical strategy to cover the real tensions between partners caused by various forms of power (mostly gender) imbalances." He refers to Gary Smith and Susan Kippax, "Anal Intercourse and Power in Sex between Men," *Sexualities* 4, no. 4 (2001): 413–34, who argue, however, not that reciprocity has been overreported but that its mere existence does not erase the significance of hierarchies in practices of anal intercourse in gay male relationships, noting that "in Western cultures there remains a conceptual distinction between the insertive and receptive partners that marks the receptive person as feminine and insertive as masculine." Sinfield, "The Production of Gay and the Return of

Power," 27, sees the persistence of social hierarchies in gay relationships as undermining the supposed triumph of the "egalitarian" model of "modern" homosexuality.

67. See, once again, Adam, "Structural Foundations."

68. See Michel Foucault, *Discipline and Punish: The Birth of the Prison,* trans. Alan Sheridan (New York: Vintage, 1979), 182–84:

> In short, under a regime of disciplinary power, the art of punishing . . . brings five quite distinct operations into play: it refers individual acts, performances, and conducts to a group ensemble that is at once a field of comparison, a space of differentiation, and a source of the rule to be followed. It differentiates individuals in relation to one another and in terms of that group rule, whether the rule be made to function as a minimal threshold, as an average to be looked to, or as an optimum to be approximated. It measures in quantitative terms and hierarchizes in terms of value the abilities, the level of attainment, and the "nature" of individuals. It imposes, through this "valorizing" measurement, the constraint of a conformity to be achieved. Lastly, it traces the limit that will define difference in relation to all other differences, the external frontier of the abnormal. . . . [To recapitulate, it] compares, differentiates, hierarchizes, homogenizes, excludes. In a word, it normalizes. . . . Like surveillance and together with it, normalization becomes one of the great instruments of power at the end of the classical age. The marks that once indicated status, privilege, and group membership come to be replaced, or at least to be supplemented, by a whole range of degrees of normality: these are signs of membership in a homogeneous social body, but they also play a part themselves in classification, in hierarchization, and in the distribution of ranks. In one sense, the power of normalization enforces homogeneity; but it individualizes by making it possible to measure deviations, to set levels, to define specialties, and to render differences useful by calibrating them one to another. The power of the norm functions easily within a system of formal equality, since within a homogeneity that is the rule, the norm introduces, as a useful imperative and as the result of measurement, all the gradations of individual differences.

(The translation has been extensively modified.)

69. For recent historical discussions of the incident Bartlett alludes to here, see William A. Cohen, *Sex Scandal: The Private Parts of Victorian Fiction* (Durham, N.C.: Duke University Press, 1996), 73–129; Morris B. Kaplan, "Who's Afraid of John Saul? Urban Culture and the Politics of Desire in Late Victorian London," *GLQ: A Journal of Lesbian and Gay Studies* 5, no. 3 (1999): 267–314.

70. Neil Bartlett, *Who Was That Man? A Present for Mr Oscar Wilde* (London: Serpent's Tail, 1988), 223.

APPENDIX

1. The three papers referred to here were originally delivered as a panel titled "Homosexual Behavior in the Ancient Mediterranean World" at the conference "At the

Frontier: Homosexuality and the Social Sciences." The conference was organized by the Center for Lesbian and Gay Studies of the City University of New York, and it took place in December 1993. I served as commentator. The three papers, and an earlier version of my commentary, have since been published in pt. 1 ("Ancient Genealogies") of *Queer Representations: Reading Lives, Reading Cultures,* ed. Martin Duberman (New York: New York University Press, 1997), 7–54: Robert B. Koehl, "Ephoros and Ritualized Homosexuality in Bronze Age Crete" (7–13), Keith DeVries, "The 'Frigid Eromenoi' and their Wooers Revisited: A Closer Look at Greek Homosexuality in Vase Painting" (14–24), and Craig A. Williams, "*Pudicitia* and *Pueri*: Roman Concepts of Male Sexual Experience" (25–38).

2. See Barry D. Adam, "Structural Foundations of the Gay World," *Comparative Studies in Society and History* 27 (1985): 658–71; reprinted in *Queer Theory/Sociology,* ed. Steven Seidman (Oxford: Blackwell, 1996), 111–26.

3. Indeed, role swapping appears to be the norm in gay male relations today, according to Gary W. Dowsett, *Practicing Desire: Homosexual Sex in the Era of AIDS* (Stanford, Calif.: Stanford University Press, 1996), 81: "Although there was a decided preference among some gay men [in the group sampled] in their assessment of sexual 'enjoyment' for the insertive or the receptive *mode* in anal intercourse, in practice such activity is commonly reciprocal, men moving from insertive to receptive modes at will." Dowsett's conclusions, which apply to contemporary gay male life in New South Wales, Australia, have been massively confirmed by a review of the empirical literature on anal intercourse around the world by Gary Smith, "Heterosexual and Homosexual Anal Intercourse: An International Perspective," *Venereology* 14, no. 1 (2001): 28–37, who finds that "among gay-identified predominantly homosexually active men who engage in anal intercourse, most are both insertive and receptive," noting that this finding remained constant in studies of societies belonging to the so-called post-industrial West undertaken "from the mid-1960s to the late 1990s."

However, Smith cautions me that the quantitative data on anal intercourse among gay men should not be taken to indicate equal preference for the insertive and receptive role, since no allowance is made in that data for frequency or predilection (e-mail message, 7 August 2001). See, also, the data on gay men in London and Cardiff collected by Anthony P. M. Coxon, *Between the Sheets: Sexual Diaries and Gay Men's Sex in the Era of AIDS* (London: Cassell, 1996), esp. 94–96: although he notes that "if a man engages in a particular sexual practice it is more likely that he will do so in both active and passive modalities (even over a period of a month) than restrict himself to only one of them," he also points out some "interesting contrary trends," including exceptional "role rigidity" in the case of anal intercourse, in which "those who were either exclusively active or exclusively passive now equal or exceed those who are both." Even so, Coxon concludes that his "results do not support the idea that, even over a one-month period, gay men tend to be exclusively active or passive during anal intercourse," but he does cite a Dutch study that suggests that the percentage of gay men who switch roles may be significantly smaller in London and Cardiff than in Amsterdam. Clearly, all generalizations about gay men's sexual behavior need to take local cultural conditions and practices into account.

4. For a more detailed argument to this effect, see David M. Halperin, *One Hundred Years of Homosexuality and Other Essays on Greek Love* (New York: Routledge, 1990), 58.

5. For a survey and a critique of this trend in recent classical scholarship, see ibid., 54–61. A new, powerful effort to rehabilitate this approach has now been made by Craig

A. Williams, "Ritual Patterns in Ancient Greek Pederasty," in *The Trouble with Boys: Comparative Studies in Age-Structured Homoerotic Relations in History and Anthropology,* ed. Gilbert Herdt (Chicago: University of Chicago Press, forthcoming).

6. See K. J. Dover, "Greek Homosexuality and Initiation," in *The Greeks and Their Legacy: Collected Papers,* vol. 2, *Prose Literature, History, Society, Transmission, Influence* (Oxford: Oxford University Press, 1988), 115–34; Halperin, *One Hundred Years of Homosexuality,* 56–61, and my entry on "homosexuality" in the *Oxford Classical Dictionary,* 3d ed., 720–23.

7. My own observations on the subject can be found in *One Hundred Years of Homosexuality,* 183, n. 31.

8. Michel Foucault, "Des caresses d'hommes considérées comme un art," *Libération,* 1 June 1982, 27; reprinted in Foucault, *Dits et écrits, 1954–1988,* ed. Daniel Defert and François Ewald (Paris: Gallimard, 1994), 4:315–17, esp. 315: "C'est que les Grecs, à l'âge classique, en ont montré plus qu'ils n'en ont dit: les peintures de vase sont infiniment plus explicites que les textes qui nous restent—fussent-ils de comédie. Mais en retour, beaucoup de scènes peintes seraient muettes (et le sont restées jusqu'ici) sans le recours au text qui en dit la valeur amoureuse. Un jeune homme donne un lièvre à un garçon? Cadeau d'amour. Il lui caresse le menton? Proposition."

9. Ibid.: "Le coeur de l'analyse de Dover est là: retrouver ce que disaient ces gestes du sexe et du plaisir, gestes que nous croyons universels (quoi de plus commun finalement que le gestuaire de l'amour) et qui, analysés dans leur spécificité historique, tiennent un discours bien singulier."

10. Eva C. Keuls, *The Reign of the Phallus: Sexual Politics in Ancient Athens* (New York: Harper & Row, 1985), 277–85, esp. 277: "In some cases the youth is shown with what may be termed a 'puerile erection'; evidently the vase painters wanted to show that the passive partner does derive some pleasure from the contact, even without active participation." Of particular interest in this regard are two vases discussed by Keuls: London W 39 (*ABV,* p. 297, #16) = Keuls, 281, pls. 249 and 250, and W. Berlin F 2279 (*ARV,* p. 115, #2) = Keuls, 222, pls. 196 and 197, both illustrated also by Dover (who, after considering the evidence, interprets it differently [95–97]) as B250 and R196.

On the apparent impassivity of the boys, see Mark Golden, "Slavery and Homosexuality at Athens," *Phoenix* 38 (1984): 308–24.

11. See my essay entitled, "Plato and Erotic Reciprocity," *Classical Antiquity* 5 (1986): 60–80, esp. 70–71, and 64–66, with nn. 10, 13, and 14.

12. I pointed all this out fifteen years ago in ibid.; see also *One Hundred Years of Homosexuality,* 130–37. None of the new and interesting evidence that DeVries has unearthed requires me to "retract" my previous claims about the significance of asymmetry and inequality in ancient Greek same-sex sexual relations between males, despite the extravagant assertion of John Boswell, *Same-Sex Unions in Premodern Europe* (New York: Villard Books, 1994), 58n. 20.

13. For the fuller version of this argument, see once again Halperin, "Plato and Erotic Reciprocity."

14. See K. J. Dover, *Greek Homosexuality* (Cambridge, Mass.: Harvard University Press, 1978), 52, to whose list of citations should be added the following: Euripides, *Rhesus* 184; Plutarch, *Moralia* 760B, and *Lycurgus* 18.4; Athenaeus, 540E.

15. So Claude Calame, "Eros inventore e organizzatore della società greca antica," in *L'Amore in Grecia,* ed. Claude Calame, 3d ed. (Rome: Laterza, 1984), ix–xl, esp. xii–xiii; Halperin, "Plato and Erotic Reciprocity," 66n. 14.

16. See Anne [Carson] Giacomelli, "The Justice of Aphrodite in Sappho Fr. 1," *Transactions of the American Philological Association* 110 (1980): 135–42; John J. Winkler, *The Constraints of Desire: The Anthropology of Sex and Gender in Ancient Greece* (New York: Routledge, 1990), 71–98.

17. Pat Barker, *The Regeneration Trilogy* (London: Penguin Books, 1995), 531. The passage is aptly cited in this connection by Gary Smith and Susan Kippax, "Anal Intercourse and Power in Sex between Men," *Sexualities* 4, no. 4 (2001): 413–34 (quotation on 425).

18. Foucault, "Des caresses d'hommes considérées comme un art": "Bien sûr, on trouvera encore des esprits aimables pour penser qu'en somme l'homosexualité a toujours existé. . . . A de tels naïfs, Dover donne une bonne leçon de nominalisme historique. Le rapport entre deux individus du même sexe est une chose. Mais aimer le même sexe que soi, prendre avec lui un plaisir, c'est autre chose, c'est toute une expérience, avec ses objets et leurs valeurs, avec la manière d'être du sujet et la conscience qu'il a de lui-même. Cette expérience est complexe, elle est diverse, elle change de formes" (315–16).

Index

References to figures are printed in italic.